LIFELONG LEARNING ON THE INFC
SERIES EDITOR: JUDITH M. ROB



# Classrooms with a Difference

## Facilitating Learning on the Information Highway

**SECOND EDITION**

ELIZABETH J.
**Burge**

JUDITH M.
**Roberts**

**Chenelière/McGraw-Hill**
MONTRÉAL • TORONTO

**Classrooms with a Difference**
Facilitating Learning on the Information Highway (2nd ed.)

Elizabeth J. Burge, Judith M. Roberts



*Project coordinator:* Gertrude D'Urso
*Copy editor:* Jane Pavanel
*Proofreader:* Geraldine Kikuta
*Typesetting:* Julie Leclerc
*Cover:* Opus House and Norman Lavoie
*Illustrations:* Norman Lavoie



**Canadian Cataloguing in Publication Data**

Burge, Elizabeth J

Classrooms with a difference: facilitating learning on the information highway

(Lifelong learning on the information highway)

Includes bibliographical references.

ISBN 2-89461-160-9

1. Educational innovations. 2. Educational technology. 3. Distance education. 4. Information superhighway in education. I. Roberts, Judy. II. Title. III. Series.

LB1028.3.B88 1998 371.33 C97-941494-6

**Chenelière/McGraw-Hill**
7001 Saint-Laurent Blvd.
Montréal (Québec)
Canada H2S 3E3
Telephone: (514) 273-1066
Fax: (514) 276-0324
chene@dlcmcgrawhill.ca



**ISBN 2-89461-160-9**

Legal deposit: 1st quarter 1998
Bibliothèque nationale du Québec
National Library of Canada

Printed in Canada by AGMV Marquis Imprimeur inc.
1 2 3 4 5 02 01 00 99 98

# TABLE OF CONTENTS

ACKNOWLEDGMENTS v

PREFACE vii

**PART 1**
WHAT ARE THE KEY ISSUES IN THE LEARNING ENVIRONMENT? 1

**Chapter 1**
How Do We See Classrooms Changing?

Introduction 3
What social and educational changes are affecting classrooms? 3
What four technologies are included in this book? 5
What are our values? 6
Conclusion 7
References 7

**Chapter 2**
What Do Learners Bring to Learning?

Introduction 8
What are the key characteristics of adult learners? 8
What are the ergonomic needs of adult learners? 14
What do learners say they need? 16
Conclusion 16
References 17

**Chapter 3**
What Is Adult Learning All About?

Introduction 18
What is important about learning principles? 18
How do learning strategies work? 22
Why does collaborative learning pay off? 25
Conclusion 27
References 28

**Chapter 4**
How May Instructors Best Respond?

Introduction 29
How do models of teaching differ? 29
Which of the five appeal to you? 30
What is an efficient way to set learning objectives? 31
How do I actually plan my response? 37
Conclusion 43
References 44

**Chapter 5**
What Does the Real Action Look Like?

Introduction 45
What is a learner's manual? 45
What is in a learner's manual? 46
How do I produce the best possible manual? 52
Conclusion 54
References 54

**PART 2**
WHAT ARE THE KEY ISSUES IN USING THE TECHNOLOGIES? 55

**Chapter 6**
How Do We See the Information Highway?

Introduction 57
What does the Information Highway mean for instructors? 57
What opportunities does the Information Highway offer in the classroom? 60
How do I choose appropriate technology? 64
Conclusion 68
References 69

**Chapter 7**
Audio and Audiographic Learning: Why Are They the Cornerstone of the Information Highway?

Introduction 71
How do Audio and Audiographic Learning work? 71
What are AL and AGL's strengths? What are some key issues? 74
How do I use AL and AGL appropriately? 76
Who is using AL and AGL successfully? 82
Conclusion 87
References 88

**Chapter 8**
Networked Learning: How Do We Facilitate Learning on the Internet?

Introduction 89
How does Networked Learning work? 89
What are Networked Learning's strengths? What are some key issues? 92
How do I use Networked Learning appropriately? 97
Who is using Networked Learning successfully? 102
Conclusion 105
References 105

**Chapter 9**
Compressed Video Learning: How Do We Create Active Learners?

Introduction 106
How does Compressed Video Learning work? 106
What are Compressed Video Learning's strengths? What are some key issues? 109
How do I use Compressed Video Learning appropriately? 116
Who is using Compressed Video Learning effectively? 122
Conclusion 126
References 126

**Chapter 10**
What Does It Look Like When We Bring It All Together?

Introduction 127
How can I integrate all the elements? 127
What are our top ten learnings? 129
What should I do when Murphy's Law hits? 130
Conclusion 131
References 131

FURTHER READINGS 132

GLOSSARY 138

CONTACT NAMES FOR THE SUCCESS STORIES 142

# Acknowledgments

We are deeply indebted to many people who assisted us in writing this book: to colleagues who agreed to be quoted; to Lisa Kay, senior secretary in the Department of Adult and Vocational Education at the University of New Brunswick, who rescued Liz on several occasions; to Joan Howard, JLH Educational Services in Toronto, who provided valuable editorial and research assistance; and to Jamie Rossiter and Scott Duncan, Knowledge Connection Corporation in Toronto, who willingly shared the Series load when its editor needed to become an author. To all, our thanks.

Liz Burge
Judy Roberts

# PREFACE

This second edition of *Classrooms with a Difference* is a foundational part of the *Lifelong Learning on the Information Highway*™ Series.

## GOALS

This Series is designed for professionals who want to use learning technologies in ways that facilitate the interdependent functions of learning and communication. More specifically, the Series will enable you to:

- know why learning professionals are using these technologies
- master the basic details you need to know to use the equipment appropriately
- learn from the successes of a range of public and private sector organizations throughout the world
- design, deliver and evaluate presentations that use the technologies effectively

You should feel comfortable with the idea of facilitating learning and communication by the time you have finished reading each book in the Series. They have been designed as a starting point, however, and not as a final destination. To that end, each book contains Further Readings for you to pursue if you are interested.

## APPROACH

The Series reflects practitioners' experiences and relies heavily on original, unpublished material that reflects current practice in the public and private sectors. Many personal communications from practitioners and researchers have been gathered and appear in quotation marks throughout the book but have not been referenced by date. An informal style is used to describe these practitioners, so that the reader knows their full name, title and organizational affiliation. Where the authors know the practitioners personally, first names are often used after the first use of their full names.

Published quotes are cited by date in the text and are fully referenced in the References section at the end of each chapter. Contact information is provided for all practitioners whose stories are included in the book so that you may get in touch with them by mail, telephone, fax or e-mail to learn more about their work.

The Series shows how each technology can be used separately; it also integrates the technologies and prepares you, as the classroom instructor, for their convergence. Particularly pertinent suggestions are displayed in the margin.

## CONTENT

The Series addresses the issue of how to facilitate learning in a classroom equipped with one or more of compressed video, computer and/or audio or audiographic learning technologies. It consists of four titles.

- *Classrooms with a Difference: Facilitating Learning on the Information Highway* (2nd Edition) integrates three key aspects of the new classroom: learners, models of course or workshop design and their application to interactive, distributed technologies. It emphasizes the first two elements and provides an introduction to each of the three technologies that are the subject of separate books in the Series.
- *Audio and Audiographic Learning: The Cornerstone of the Information Highway* reminds us of the potential offered by audio and audiographic technologies, both in their own right and as basic skills for other approaches.
- *Networked Learning: The Pedagogy of the Internet* introduces the basic tools and strategies you need to create learning opportunities through computer networks.
- *Compressed Video Learning: Creating Active Learners* describes instructional techniques that produce interactive learners in classrooms or at desktops.

## FORMAT

The Series integrates multi-mode materials chosen to suit the needs of each book.

Modularized print is the foundation of the Series, since we believe it is still the most widely available learning technology. This book, *Classrooms with a Difference*, is divided into two parts, each of which contains chapters designed to answer common questions about the book's topic. Each part and each chapter is as self-contained as possible so that you can read them in whatever order responds to your needs and learning style. For example, your first priority may be to find out who is active in the field, or you may want to know about adult learning principles or see what the various technologies look like. We encourage you to proceed through the book in an order that makes sense to you; don't feel constrained by our structure.

The Series also contains an appropriate blend of resources other than print and uses technology to teach technology: for example, a videotape illustrates the manual on Compressed Video Learning and a computer disk supplements the guide to Networked Learning. The print Resource Kit that accompanies this book contains valuable material that supplements and extends the book's content. We refer to it wherever appropriate in the text and encourage you to explore it independently as you deem necessary.

## THE READER

This Series was developed as an introductory tool for instructors in the public and private sectors who have practical experience in teaching but who are novice users of technology. Designed primarily for a broad audience of instructors beyond the traditional distance learning community, each book covers practice, theories and research that administrators, learning designers and evaluation specialists will find helpful.

Readers from both the public and private sectors are addressed in this Series because many applications involve partnerships between schools, colleges, universities, government and business—partnerships that often transcend national boundaries. We hope to enhance such collaborations within and across the public and private education and training sectors by providing a common platform for understanding the learning and training potential of the Information Highway. Additional specialized resources are referenced so that readers in each sector can pursue its unique interests in more detail.

## TERMINOLOGY

We believe that the term *Information Highway* refers to all information and communications technologies, not just the Internet. We therefore include several types of technologies in this Series and refer often to other learning technologies not dealt with to date as separate titles in the Series.

Jargon-free language is used in a conversational writing style throughout all the books in the Series. Inclusive language is used wherever possible. The term *instructor*, for example, is employed as we find that it is less directly associated with a given sector than *teacher* or *professor*. We use instructor to mean a person who facilitates active learning in a variety of ways, not someone who is a conveyer of content through lectures. The terms *learner* and *participant* are used for a similar reason. Exceptions occur when quoting specific examples where the word *professor* or *student* is appropriate to the case study being described. Sometimes, the instructor's role is so clearly that of a moderator or facilitator that those terms may be employed.

Where technical terms are unavoidable, they are used and included in a Glossary at the end of the book.

## WORKSHOPS

The *Lifelong Learning on the Information Highway*™ team is available to assist you in designing workshops and other types of learning activities based on the Series. The team will customize workshops to meet your specific needs or act as resource people in sessions that you design. In addition to the books and multi-mode learning materials described in this Preface, a set of "workbooks for workshops" is available based on the Series.

## LEARNER'S GUIDE

A Learner's Guide is also available as part of the Series. Like *Classrooms with a Difference*, it contains a chapter on each of Networked, Audio, Audiographic and Compressed Video Learning. Nineteen learners were interviewed as the Guide was written; their stories and advice to other learners are the Guide's key resource.

# PART 1

## WHAT ARE THE KEY ISSUES IN THE LEARNING ENVIRONMENT?

The first five chapters of this book set the learning context for the appropriate use of interactive technologies. If you already know some of this material, the chapters may serve as a review that's useful because of the explicit experience-theory links. If the ideas are new to you, we hope they provide useful leads to new strategies.

In Chapter 1 we introduce you to some key changes in education and training. In Chapter 2 we outline what we know about what learners bring to learning. Chapter 3 deals with the most important principles and strategies needed for the design of effective learning, while Chapter 4 describes the kinds of responses that instructors and workshop leaders may best apply to meet the needs of adult learners in technological settings. In Chapter 5 we offer ideas and practical suggestions that focus on the learner's manual, a tool that will enable you to integrate the various decisions you make in the real world of training and educational settings.

# Chapter 1

# How Do We See Classrooms Changing?

*New ideas arise daily. We have learned that almost anything is possible and that education and business are not so different after all. But, most important of all, the opportunities for our students have grown immensely. A key factor in that growth is the rapid development of learning applications for the Information Highway.*

CATHERINE HENDERSON,
CENTENNIAL COLLEGE, SCARBOROUGH, ONTARIO

## INTRODUCTION

This chapter describes two changes in education and training, presents our rationale for selecting the four technologies of this book, and explains the values that guided our writing. The changes deal with approaches to teaching people and the physical qualities of the new classrooms. The technologies focus on audio, audiographic, compressed video and computer-based conferencing. The values look at our own professional behavior and how we believe technology may be best integrated with teaching and learning.

## WHAT SOCIAL AND EDUCATIONAL CHANGES ARE AFFECTING CLASSROOMS?

The first change relates to the macro context of societal thinking about education and training. The term *paradigm* is applied to show the scope of that change, for example, a shift in a whole world view. People tend to talk about paradigms when old ways of doing things aren't getting the same results, and they are struggling to find new ways of doing things.

In the higher education sector, there is extensive discussion surrounding two learning paradigms, or ways of approaching how people learn. Is the major goal of educators to transfer information, or to guide learners to generate knowledge? Robert Barr (1995), the director of institutional planning at Palomar College in California, and John Tagg, an associate professor also at Palomar, describe the two approaches as choosing between an Instruction Paradigm and a Learning Paradigm. They present a convincing set of differences between the two paradigms regarding purpose, course content, criteria for success, features of the learning environment, processes of learning, role of the instructor and several other features. We acknowledge a preference for the Learning Paradigm, where learners are helped to acquire the skills of information literacy, critical and independent thinking, active participation in collaborative activities, and self-assessment of learning outcomes. We discuss in Chapter 3 some of the implications of the Learning Paradigm for instructors.

In the business sector in North America, discussions are well under way about how organizations can promote learning to their benefit, and how the role of the trainer is changing in companies. No longer, it is argued, should trainers spend all their time planning how to "stand and deliver" programs in special classrooms without paying sufficient attention to long-term measurable changes in productivity. Bob Mager (1996) recently used his decades of experience in the United States and internationally as a writer and trainer to explain to his colleagues that they face a number of serious challenges to their survival. "Morphing into a 21st century trainer," as he puts it, requires a new set of skills and orientations, including mastery of training technologies and the ability to think in terms of solving problems, not just resorting to other training programs. The new trainers will have to spend much more time than before in researching with staff workplace productivity and human performance problems to jointly figure out solutions and specific outcomes over the short and long term. And then some, as Marc Hequet (1995) says in a hard-hitting editor's review of these changes in *Training* magazine: "... don't only think of yourself as a performance troubleshooter who is also in the communications-infrastructure racket. Think of yourself as being in the same business as the organization for which you work ... [Trainers] have to learn to speak business" (p. 26).

So the key areas of change here are that the trainer has to learn more about the company's activities and performance problems, and ensure that training and multiple-level evaluation take into account the broader company goals. The Learning Paradigm looks at the bottom line, too; it defines productivity in terms of "cost per unit of learning per student," whereas the Instruction Paradigm defines productivity in terms of "cost per hour of instruction per student" (Barr & Tagg, 1995, p. 17).

While thinking of business settings, we want to note here another change that reflects the holistic nature of the Learning Paradigm. The Conference Board of Canada has listed three sets of skills in its Employability Skills Profile (1993), which indicate that employers want to see that their employees can perform beyond specific job skills. Employees now need two additional sets of skills—in self-management and in teamwork. The Conference Board and employers have issued a real challenge to trainers in the workplace, as well as educators in universities and colleges, because those latter sets of skills often don't get recognition in settings where training dollars are scarce—even for training in job-related skills.

The second change relates to the micro context of the classroom and to its characteristics. Many of today's classrooms differ markedly from the traditional "face-to-face" walled room. Learners now can be scattered over a wide geographical area and still be connected as a group. They can meet their own demanding time schedules and still stay in regular contact with their instructor and "classmates." They may never see their instructor in person, but may feel as if they know that person quite well. They can use a combination of the technologies in this book to acquire and discuss the very latest information before testing it out. Moreover, even when learners and instructors do meet in person, the walls are becoming permeable. Any of these technologies can be used to supplement in-person resources with ones outside the walls. The old "classroom" gains new meaning.

Marc Rosenberg from AT&T notes: "... the opportunities are there to create fabulous new information streams to replace training" (Geber, 1995, p. 68). As these alternative approaches are critically examined, and terms such as open learning and distance education are used in everyday language, then conferencing technologies may encourage greater use of the Learning Paradigm, as opposed to simply perpetuating the more traditional Instruction Paradigm. The traditional distinction between classroom and distance learning is, we believe, fading. In other words, instructors have the opportunity to develop new methods, not just speed up old methods.

## WHAT FOUR TECHNOLOGIES ARE INCLUDED IN THIS BOOK?

The interactive features of audio, audiographic, compressed video and networked "classrooms" continue to create excitement. Sometimes that excitement becomes hyperbole (hype); grand statements are made about revolutions in ways of learning because of the awesome power of the Information Highway to move massive amounts of data at very high speeds or to enable the fast indexing of millions of pages of text in the Internet. But we believe, on the basis of our research and experience, that the underlying dynamics of human learning have not changed. Learners still have to acquire information and process it into meaningful mental frameworks and practical applications. Learners are still involved with the interpersonal dynamics of learning and still need to use their time with peers, instructors, librarians and others, productively. We agree with the argument made by Neil Postman (1992), an education and media researcher in New York, who has stated for a number of years now that technology brings both strengths and weaknesses, so we have to "negotiate" with technology, because "technology giveth and it also taketh away" (p. 5).

The challenge for instructors, therefore, regardless of where they work, is to accommodate the conferencing technologies to learning without creating a division between the techno-rich (the technological "haves") and the techno-poor (the technological "have-nots").

The four interactive technologies we examine in this book enable us to construct networks of classrooms that are symmetrical in two ways:

1. Each node, or site, has exactly the same technical opportunities for the creation and the reception of intensive interactions in real- or delayed-time.
2. In many ways, learners can talk across the class space to one another and expect a response, just as they can in a traditional classroom.

The technologies are treated as a group because they are the most cost-effective and accessible technologies to provide such symmetry and emulation. They differ, therefore, from other media used in training and education such as one-way video with two-way audioconferencing, audiocassettes and multimedia.

We assume that any of these technologies will be integrated with print, audio-visual packaged materials. Such packages can deliver most of the content of a workshop or course, especially if the goal is to memorize facts such as health and safety regulations. The technologies enable real- or delayed-time person-to-person dialogue to occur that uses both public information and the comparatively personal, practical knowledge that is learned as part of life. In the health and safety example, the discussion might focus on how to apply regulations and could result in creative new solutions to old problems.

Applications of each technology need to promote interaction among and between learners and a whole range of relevant resources: instructor, external experts, workplace colleagues, library and Internet-based materials and mentors. Furthermore, the skillful use of the technologies will encourage creative interaction among the learners themselves, without the controlling presence of the instructor. Such dialogue is key to learning if you value the development of responsible learners who have reasonable levels of all three sets of employability skills.

## WHAT ARE OUR VALUES?

Since no training or education is value-neutral, we must identify our values about professional behavior and about the integration of technology with teaching and learning. Declaring our values allows us to be somewhat prescriptive. Drawing upon the lessons we have learned from our own experience and that of others "in the trenches," we make a number of recommendations throughout the book. You are free to accept, reject or modify our guidelines. You may, of course, disagree with anything we say; after all, your own values and experiences are different from ours, and we respect that.

Our first value is our bias toward the Learning Paradigm. This belief means that we want the learner to develop a broad repertoire of learning skills, including the ability to think critically and creatively. It also means that we try to plan for mutually respectful, collaborative and productive relationships between learners and teacher, and among learners. We acknowledge that this is not easy for either learner or instructor; in any significant learning, learners often feel some stress. And instructors who have few choices in how they run their course may not have the time to think more about learning development.

Our second value lies in being congruent, in other words, in practicing what we preach, even though that may cause difficulties. For example, we still advocate the value of print as a cost-effective and learner-friendly medium, while some of our colleagues are eager to digitize as many resources for learners as possible so they can be presented on a computer screen. We have therefore written this book to convey information, and we invite you to find ways to discuss the content.

Our third value is that learning is an integrated, holistic process involving all the dimensions of being human and living in today's world. We have realized, for example, the importance of knowing that factors in a learner's private life or covert dynamics in the workplace can have profound effects on learning, not all of which are positive. So this book identifies strategies for learning and teaching that focus not just on the intellectual elements of learning but also on its social, physiological and emotional elements. Some people think that such a focus is a waste of time, when simply finding training hours can be a difficult task. But we believe that front-end time spent in helping learners prepare themselves for productive learning and measurable outcomes can pay off in spades as the course or workshop proceeds.

Our fourth value relates to how we assess our educational skills. The skills should center on effectively helping to establish and maintain all the conditions of learning and teaching, rather than on being able to use specific technologies and software. As Erin Keough, director of the Open Learning and Information Network in St. John's, Newfoundland, says with some flourish: "Let the techies figure out how to do it; I have to worry about what to do and why." This book, therefore, focuses on issues in learning and teaching before it focuses on the technologies. We believe that any technology is only as good as the people who design and use it. So we identify people-centered strategies to inform decision making and to keep technology transparent—easy to use, reliable and serving the interests of learners first.

## CONCLUSION

In this chapter we highlighted key changes in how we think about education and training in the new kinds of "classrooms" created by communications technologies. We introduced the four technologies that are the focus of this book and defined our values about the roles of technology and the nature of professional behavior. Now it is time to look more closely at learners to see what they bring to these changed learning environments. Chapter 2 identifies their key needs and characteristics.

# References

Barr, R. B., & Tagg, J. (1995). From teaching to learning: A new paradigm for undergraduate education. *Change, 27*(6), 12-25.

(The) Conference Board of Canada. (1993). *Employability Skills Profile: What are employers looking for?* Ottawa, ON: Author.Geber, B. (1995). A rabble-rousing roundtable. *Training, 32*(6), 61-68.

Hequet, M. (1995). The new trainer. *Training, 32*(12), 23-29.

Mager, R. (1996). Morphing into a 21st century trainer. *Training, 33*(6), 47-54.

Postman, N. (1992). *Technopoly: The surrender of culture to technology.* New York, NY: Knopf.

# Chapter 2

## What Do Learners Bring to Learning?

*In my experience, learners have two goals when engaging in a formal learning opportunity: achieving a desired level of academic skill and experiencing a social connectedness. The significance of each goal depends on the learner's past experiences, level of self-confidence, and motivation for taking the course.*

KERRY ROBINSON,
AURORA COLLEGE, FORT SMITH,
NORTHWEST TERRITORIES

### INTRODUCTION

By the time you have read this chapter, you will be able to identify five key learner characteristics and three types of ergonomic needs that affect education and training in all learning environments. Learners bring to a class or workshop a bundle of characteristics and needs: some they may talk about, others not. In fact, they may not even be able to express their needs and preferences for effective learning. A perceptive instructor who takes a learner-centered approach will look for these needs and choose the technology with care.

### WHAT ARE THE KEY CHARACTERISTICS OF ADULT LEARNERS?

Adults have their own varied ways of learning how to live and work. As instructors, we try to ensure that the education and training environment we create does not hinder these current capacities. We shall highlight five learner characteristics in this section:

1. motivational drives to action
2. developmental stages (thinking and group process)
3. gender influences
4. cultural differences
5. learning style differences

We cannot of course cover all the topics to the extent required; for example, the 10 percent of Canadians who learn successfully despite one or more learning disabilities. Refer to the Further Readings for leads to current material on this topic (Learning Disabilities Association of Canada, Office of Learning Technologies, etc.).

#### Motivational Drives to Action

Adults have two key motivators that drive their actions: (1) the need to feel competent—to feel a sense of mastery in acting independently and successfully in the world; and (2) the need to feel connected and to belong in supportive relationships. These motivators are internal to each of us; they cannot be forced to operate by any outside person. So when you hear talk such as "How can I motivate my employees?" the problem usually lies either in what the instructor is doing or in other conditions that negatively affect the learners' drive to feel competent and connected. The instructor, for example, may be ignoring the practical knowledge that the adult learners bring to the class or may be imposing activities that the learners think are a waste of time. A realistic strategy is to determine how you can help adult learners tap into their inherent drives or motivators with help from relevant and timely resources, role modeling and guidance. Avoid setting up demotivating conditions that work against these drives, such as allowing for very little chance for ongoing contact with helpful colleagues after a workshop or course has finished.

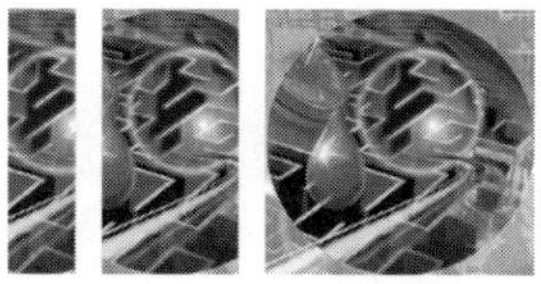

THINK ABOUT WHICH CONDITIONS IN LEARNING HELP MAKE YOU FEEL COMPETENT AND CONNECTED, AND WHAT AN INSTRUCTOR COULD DO TO MAKE YOU FEEL RELEVANT TO THE ACTION. YOU-AS-LEARNER WILL BE A USEFUL ADVISER FOR YOU-AS-INSTRUCTOR.

## Stages in Thinking and Group Development

Given the right conditions, adults can progress through developmental stages of thinking and also through interaction styles when part of a group. Their ways of thinking, for example, may develop from (1) rather "black and white" thinking, where they look for the "right" answers from the "authorities," to (2) an acceptance of multiple sources of authority, including their own personal experience, to (3) developing an informed and personal set of beliefs about knowledge and how it is created. Learners may or may not work their way through these stages. It depends on whether the instructor can set up the right conditions for learning, and on whether the learners can cope with the difficulties of changing from their earlier style of passively absorbing, without question, the knowledge of experts. William Perry's (1981) research, which identified these thinking stages, is still considered by many people to have merit today. Howard MacLachlan of New Brunswick told us that it has been quite an experience for him to change his attitudes toward how he thinks about learning. Now retired from being a gunnery instructor in the Canadian armed forces, and taking university courses, he is changing how he participates in the courses. He no longer simply accepts what others tell him; he now takes a more active part in gathering his own information and critically assessing its usefulness. He sees this change as equivalent in scope to going from "using the British longbow to using multiple-launch rockets."

A group of American researchers studied how women come to "know," and they discovered five broad ways. Their book, *Women's Ways of Knowing* (Belenky, Clinchy, Goldberger, & Tarule, 1986), has become a classic since it was first published, and it spurred a new book equally as important, *Knowledge, Difference and Power* (Goldberger, Tarule, Clinchy, & Belenky, 1996). It is relevant for us to consider because in any class, an alert instructor will recognize some of the characteristics of each way of "knowing." They are not stages in the sense that progression is automatic and sequential. Each way of knowing has very distinct features. A woman who "knows" only by uncritically receiving knowledge from others is a different person from one who knows by using analytical thinking and deliberate attempts to stay in control of events. The most integrated way of knowing, the "constructed" way, is related to the fifth, most sophisticated way: the woman uses her own and other's knowledge, integrates head, heart and hand in learning, and does not accept any theory as necessarily the "truth." Such an independent thinker will need different help from an instructor than the "received knower."

Growth stages are often easy to perceive in small group interactions. Two American social science researchers, Bruce Tuckman and Mary Jensen (1977), wrote a now classic report that showed how a group can experience four sequenced stages of growth:

1. forming (the first meeting, in which there are no conflicts)
2. storming (with uncertainties, conflicts arise about group goals and process)
3. norming (setting up ground rules for productive and comfortable work)
4. performing (getting the job done)

These stages cannot be short-circuited if the group is to develop past its initial innocence. Some groups may experience the "storms" quite quickly, resulting in members complaining aloud or just sitting there feeling frustrated. An instructor cannot ignore these feelings, because they may build up to cause negative emotions in others or even unhelpful public behavior. Technological settings demand more attention to these stages because the instructor and learners have fewer body-language clues to help them interpret how people are feeling or thinking.

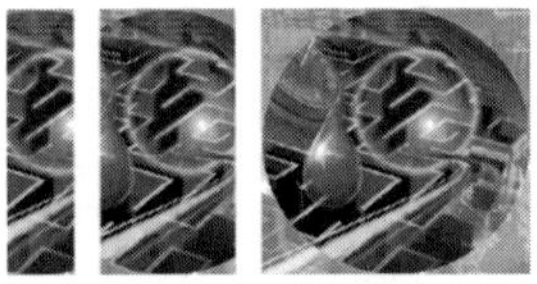

EXPECT AND DON'T BE ALARMED BY CONFLICT IN GROUPS. OUTLINE THE STAGES AS EXPECTED CONDITIONS, AND HELP PARTICIPANTS IDENTIFY PROBLEMS.

Groups need skillful guidance, not benevolent rescuing, as they figure out how to operate. Sometimes a smart instructor only needs to tell the group that it's quite usual for these stages to happen; to name the problem is halfway to solving it. For example, once a group of learners in an Audio Learning series, or a project-based team using Networked Learning, works through the forming, storming and norming stages, it can achieve more than a facilitator or instructor might imagine. We have seen groups take off after what were shaky starts, and we know now to watch carefully in the early stages of a course for signs of arguments about who does what, when and how. Wise instructors will take time early in a course to discuss and watch for these dynamics, because they know that time spent here may mean time and energy saved later.

## Gender Influences

Gender-sensitive education and training has attracted a lot of attention over the past decade. It has emerged as a particularly relevant factor in the use of technologies in learning. For example, many women regard computers differently than do men. Dale Spender (1996), an internationally known feminist researcher and teacher based in Australia, summarizes the results of much research: "... the consensus is that women use them, whereas men fall in love with them" (p. 188).

The word *gender* refers to the behavioral expectations and value norms that society places on women and men because of their sex. Many men and women are socialized at very early ages to conform to various social rules, attitudes and expectations, which often incorporate patterns of dominance for one sex and reduced power for the other. We believe that certain gender-related patterns of behavior significantly influence how many men and women behave in learning contexts and see themselves as learners. Women-friendly teaching (WFT), therefore, is not just good adult education in its emphasis on the learner; WFT pays attention to the origins and impacts of gender-related difficulties in society and to the value of a holistic approach to understanding how the self operates in the world. A holistic approach does not see as mutually exclusive such things as head and heart, action and reflection, personal and public knowledge.

Women's learning has been extensively researched in terms of what is learned, how it is learned, and with what results. One of the big discoveries has been that many, but not all, women learners prefer to use relational styles of learning behavior, and that many, but not all, men prefer to use more independent styles. Dorothy MacKeracher (1996), an adult educator based in Fredericton, New Brunswick, in her book *Making Sense of Adult Learning*, describes how we can recognize each style and offers many practical tips on how to create gender-sensitive learning environments.

Gender-based differences are often evident in how people communicate. You may have read one of Deborah Tannen's books (1990, 1994) on how our use of language reflects the power structures that are based in gender socialization. She explains for example, how many men use a "report" style of speech, while many

BE FEARLESS IF CONFRONTED BY DENIALS OF MALE DOMINANCE, BUT BE TACTFUL IN SHOWING HOW GENDER-EXCLUSION CAN OCCUR. HELP PEOPLE TALK WITH, NOT PAST OR DOWN TO, EACH OTHER. WHEREVER POSSIBLE, HAVE A MAN TALK TO OTHER MEN ABOUT GENDER-RELATED ISSUES.

**TABLE 2.1:** WOMEN-FRIENDLY TEACHING GUIDELINES

| A. TEACHER BEHAVIOR | B. COURSE CONTENT | C. LEARNING ACTIVITIES |
|---|---|---|
| • Acknowledge that any group of women will show many individual differences based on age, class, race and other factors; in other words, don't expect homogeneity based on gender.<br>• Watch for examples of self-denigration during class discussions.<br>• Watch for gender-based differences in communication styles and women's expectations to be heard by others in class.<br>• Be sensitive to the emotions that often arise as women begin to be aware of experiences in which they have felt disadvantaged because they are women.<br>• Help them develop their own strategies for dealing with forms of power differences.<br>• Avoid language that is gender-biased or gender-exclusive.<br>• Ensure that women students get equal attention and respect.<br>• Promote talking, which gives voice literally *and* metaphorically. | • Use women-based analyses to examine the lived experience of women, including their early socialization and schooling.<br>• Value the contributions made by women to their production of knowledge.<br>• Examine assumptions and values that underline accepted "truths."<br>• Use the personal common sense and practical knowledge held by women. | • Use cooperative and collaborative processes, as distinct from competitive and hierarchial ones.<br>• Establish a climate safe enough to encourage open questions, appropriate personal disclosures and making mistakes.<br>• Pay attention to factors outside the classroom that may be impeding studies such as spousal difficulties, child-care problems or the double burdens of paid and unpaid work on the job and at home.<br>• Use the experience and knowledge of women in your learning resources and tasks. Avoid at all costs the "add women and stir" approach.<br>• Watch for women setting unreasonably high expectations for themselves. |

women use a "rapport" style. Report refers to a style designed to maintain personal status and independence and to display one's own knowledge as a first priority of communication. Rapport refers to a style designed to create and maintain collaborative relationships while attending to the other's knowledge and feelings. These two styles can be felt acutely in technological settings using audio or computer conferencing, for example, where learners cannot see or hear each other to better interpret what is being said. The widespread insistence now on gender-inclusive, non-sexist language continues to be supported by the increase in numbers of reference books for writers, speakers and researchers. Table 2.1 shows a basic set of strategies for women-friendly teaching.

Assess how some of the techniques suggested in Chapters 7 to 9 build on the rapport, not the report, style of communication.

## Cultural Differences

Cultural backgrounds influence what learners bring to learning. To illustrate the complexity of this, we focus on aboriginal peoples as they are now gaining the respectful attention of educators in places such as Canada, Australia and the Nordic countries. Aboriginal learners in Canada include First Nations peoples, Métis and the Inuit.

A recent personal experience by Liz Burge has made her more aware of how the norms in one culture may inhibit a learner from another culture. When an aboriginal student in her adult education class had to prepare a first assignment that focused only on the problems faced by learning-disabled students, the student submitted a paper that dealt with how to solve those problems. She could not accept that she was supposed to delay the solution, and instead, treat the topic in an analytical and abstract way, not in the holistic and caring way her culture demanded. Do you have a similar example from a different cultural setting?

In this section, we summarize five key cultural principles important to aboriginals, and then we apply them to learning. The first theme is cultural disruption. Barbara Spronk, a Canadian anthropologist and distance educator at the International Extension College in England, explains how difficult it is for members of a dominant European culture to understand fully how aboriginal societies governed by their own rules of conduct and sense of history have been invaded by a society bent on being dominant (Roberts & Keough, 1995). The second theme is living life holistically, which means paying attention to physical, mental, emotional and spiritual needs. The third theme is responsibility: to one's inner self as an aboriginal, to one's family and extended family as a caregiver and to one's community as a role model. Response to a community crisis or family need takes precedence over anything else. The fourth theme is tradition and history. Debra Alivisatos, an aboriginal adult educator and consultant in New Brunswick, sums it up: "Moving into the future means understanding who and where we've been in the past." Such connectedness through cultural validation to ancestors and achievements helps twentieth-century aboriginals reclaim their identity and experience a renewed self-respect.

To apply these five principles, an effective teacher will be

- known personally by her or his learners
- willing to evaluate and manage learning using aboriginal needs
- co-present, as apposed to being a dominating presence
- flexible
- supportive of learners who want to watch before experimenting and who want to go at their own pace
- encouraging toward learners who want to incorporate aboriginal culture into their learning
- a person who uses communications technologies not to enhance her or his own voice, but rather the learners' voices

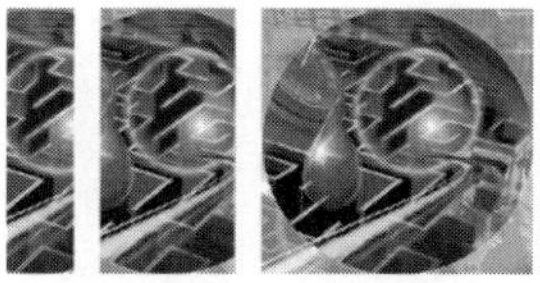

USE THE FIRST 10 MINUTES OF A THREE-HOUR AUDIO-CONFERENCING SESSION FOR LEARNERS TO RECOGNIZE EACH OTHER AS INDIVIDUALS WITH MANY ROLES.

## Learning Styles

Before you read any further, look at the five questions below and jot down fast answers.

1. What is the first thing you do when you start learning something?
2. What can others do to help you in your learning?
3. What can others do to create problems or difficulties with your learning?
4. What types of learning resources do you look for?
5. What is it about being evaluated that concerns you the most?

How did you feel about being asked to stop reading and think about yourself? Did you feel quite comfortable? Did you secretly think the request was a silly interruption? Did you think: "Well, most people would give the same answers anyway, so why bother?"

This section introduces the topic of differences in learning styles. This topic has engendered arguments as well as research, but we know intuitively that no one person acquires information or processes it in exactly the same way as another person, regardless of what an instructor does. The popular way of thinking about style differences is to say such things as: "I'm a morning person," or "Don't tell me, show me," or "I get mad when the teacher won't let me try it out first and think later."

When James Keefe (1987) was the director of research for the U.S. National Association of Secondary School Principals, he gave us one of the classic definitions of learning styles: "They are the cognitive, affective, and physiological traits that serve as relatively stable indicators of how learners perceive, interact with, and respond to the learning environment" (p. 5).

There are many ways to think about individual differences in learning styles, and we mention just a few here. The first way concerns what is called "experiential learning." David Kolb (1985, 1984), an American researcher in education, designed what is now a widely used tool called the *Learning Style Inventory*, which is available for purchase from McBer & Company, Training Resources Group, in Boston, Massachusetts. It shows the four styles of learning mapped out as quadrants in a circle. Take a pen and draw a circle. Mark the letters CE at the 12 o'clock position, RO at the 3 o'clock position, AC at the 6 o'clock position and AE at the 9 o'clock position. Each quadrant relates to a style of getting and processing information. The vertical axis (from CE to AC) relates to the gathering of information using various styles, from the use of concrete experience (the CE point) to the use of abstract knowledge acquired from books or other sources (the AC point). The horizontal axis (from AE to RO) relates to the processing of information using various styles, from an active way (AE) to a reflective way (RO). Now look at each quadrant. The quadrant between the CE and the RO represents a "Diverger" learning style. The quadrant between the RO and the AC represents an "Assimilator" style. The quadrant between the AC and the AE represents a "Converger" style. The quadrant between the AE and the CE represents an "Accommodator" style.

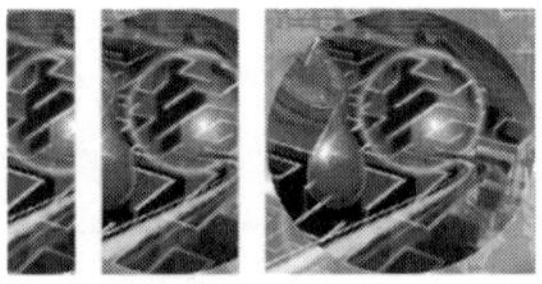

VARY THE WAYS IN WHICH YOU ASK LEARNERS TO ACQUIRE AND PROCESS INFORMATION. BEGIN A WORKSHOP, FOR EXAMPLE, WITH A DIRECT EXPERIENCE (CE), THEN HAVE THE PARTICIPANTS REFLECT ON AND ANALYZE IT (RO), DRAW CONCLUSIONS AND COMPARE THEIR NEW KNOWLEDGE WITH EXPERT KNOWLEDGE (AC). PREPARE WAYS TO APPLY THAT LEARNING (AE), THEN ACTUALLY TAKE THE NEW ACTION (CE). THIS IS THE CYCLE, AND THE MORE LEARNERS WORK AROUND IT, THE MORE SKILLED THEY BECOME.

Instructors who are aware will see the differences related to each style. For example, an accommodator will get comfortably involved in task completion and taking real-world risks and be impatient with too much theoretical talk; an assimilator, on the other hand, will be happy linking a wide variety of ideas in order to build models or theories. Working together, these two may make a great team—once they accept their different ways of getting and processing information.

If you always use the lecture or presentation method (AC), you will deny your learners the chance to experience a new situation or skill (CE) and to figure things out (RO and AC).

We refer you to James Keefe's (1987) outline, or Bob Filipczak's summary in *Training* magazine of March 1995. Bob is a training industry writer, and he makes the point that if "you want your training to transfer, you'd better reach trainees where they live" (p. 43). This means you must try to gain some idea of how your learners think they learn best, and use enough variety in learning activities so that, at any given time in a workshop or class, a fair proportion of your learners feel okay about how they are acquiring and processing information. Liz, for example, knows that she prefers to move around the classroom while thinking and dislikes having an instructor lean over the keyboard and use the software with a triumphant flourish (leaving her still quite ignorant!). She is a highly intuitive thinker (and often cannot immediately explain a correct conclusion in analytical terms), is rather visual (has to create diagrams of ideas), tends to be a global thinker (has to see the big picture before the details), gets impatient with too much structure and likes being very divergent in thinking up new ideas.

Question: Which of the four technologies in Part 2 do you think Liz feels most comfortable with, and why?

## WHAT ARE THE ERGONOMIC NEEDS OF ADULT LEARNERS?

Ergonomics is the study of how humans interact with various machines and environments. We believe that a basic knowledge of ergonomics is essential for educators and learners. Many people now spend comparatively large amounts of time sitting at computers or participating in video conferences, both of which involve reduced movement and working in conditions of artificial light.

They may not be aware, however, of which physical conditions are essential for their productivity. If you know enough to be able to judge whether the colors, furniture and lighting in a room meet acceptable standards of ergonomics, you'll go a long way toward reducing employee health problems and building an effective environment for learning. We refer to (1) equipment such as computers, workstations, chairs and tables, (2) noise level, air quality and air temperature, and (3) color and light.

A useful *Office Ergonomics Safety Guide* has been prepared by the Canadian Centre for Occupational Health and Safety (1996) and is excerpted in the Resource Kit.

## Equipment

Look at how you and people around you use furniture and space to carry out the tasks of learning. Assess the fit between body, furniture and machinery. How much space do people need to move around and spread out their papers? Do they have to look up at a screen and bend their necks? Chairs are key to ergonomic health: at minimum they should be height adjustable, rotational, have five (not four) support struts at their base, be on casters, and supply firm support for the lower back.

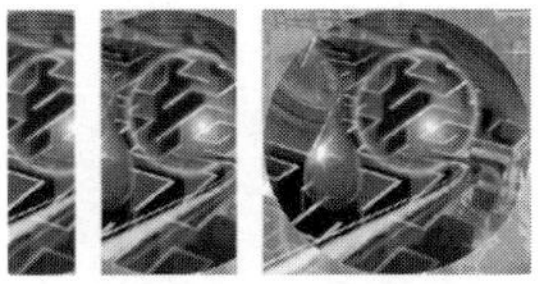

TAKE A CLOSE LOOK AT THE FURNITURE YOU PROVIDE YOUR LEARNERS. WOULD YOU LIKE TO USE IT FOR EIGHT HOURS STRAIGHT?

## Noise Level, Air Quality and Air Temperature

Noise level, air quality and air temperature are key elements in the learning environment. Unwanted noise will aggravate many learners and create extra information for everyone to process. Place noisy equipment away from designated quiet areas. A photocopier or fax machine should not be close to the learners or their microphones during an audio or video learning session. Air humidity levels should be between 30 and 60 percent, and the room temperature should stay between 20 and 24 degrees Celsius. Air-conditioning ducts may need cleaning to reduce the amount of airborne pollutants; ventilation generally is a key issue in closed buildings.

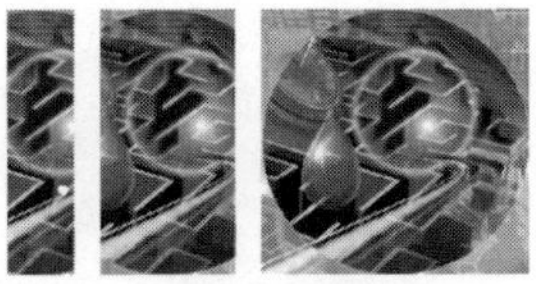

TRY THESE RECOMMENDATIONS FROM ROBLYNN:

1. IF YOU HAVE TO USE STANDARD-ISSUE PALE GRAY FURNITURE FOR A DISCUSSION ROOM, MAKE THE CEILING BRIGHT WHITE (RENEWAL), THE WALLS PALE YELLOW OR LIGHT CORAL (STIMULATION), AND THE FLOOR RUST OR HUNTER GREEN (RELAXATION).
2. IF YOU HAVE A ROOM FULL OF BEIGE-TOPPED AND CHROME-LEGGED COMPUTER STATIONS, MAKE THE CEILING LIGHT BLUE, THE WALLS AQUA, PEACH, YELLOW OR PALE GREEN, AND THE FLOOR HUNTER GREEN, NAVY BLUE, OR TURQUOISE OR A COMBINATION IN A FLECKED CARPET.

## Color and Light

Have you noticed how people rely on "safe" colors (beige, gray, bone) in offices and seminar rooms? Roblynn Harris, a graduate of The New York Design School who is now based in Fredericton, New Brunswick, gets frustrated with seeing too many environments that could be made more user-friendly just with a change of paint color: "One of my biggest headaches with trainers and office managers is to overcome their 'pale gray is safe' idea!" Responses to color are physiological as well as psychological. Colors enable or disable the processes of relaxation, stimulation and focus. By relaxation, we mean feeling de-stressed enough to be re-energized and creative; by stimulation we mean activating brain functions and physical posture and energy; and by focus we mean attention to the tasks at hand. The absence of certain colors, and the predominant use of beiges and grays, can cause sensory deprivation and visual monotony, with consequent loss of productivity.

While the use of color is important in all classrooms, it is particularly pertinent to video and audiographic learning, which we discuss in Part 2.

## WHAT DO LEARNERS SAY THEY NEED?

It's time to let some learners speak. They know what they need to learn effectively and can often explain very well the "real action" of their learning. Here is one example of how learners see themselves operating in lively classrooms that use one or more of the technologies described in this book.

A group of 15 adult learners were asked to choose one or more words that best described the term *interactivity*. This is a big buzz word in education and training circles. Table 2.2 below lists their choices. We believe they reflect the dynamics and unpredictability in significant learning. Use the list as a set of criteria for your activities design.

**TABLE 2.2:** WHAT IT MEANS TO BE INTERACTIVE

| TO BE INTERACTIVE IS TO BE |
|---|
| ☞ spontaneous ☞ intellectually explanatory ☞ competitive |
| ☞ reciprocal ☞ aware of having some control ☞ cognitively challenged |
| ☞ emotionally supportive of others ☞ able to take risks ☞ challenged |
| ☞ regulated by the protocols of productive conversation ☞ able to disagree |
| ☞ unpredictable ☞ capable of giving feedback to maintain a dynamic equilibrium |
| ☞ capable of giving feedforward to input the correct ingredients ☞ engaging |
| ☞ included ☞ confirmed ☞ able to let go of old assumptions |

## CONCLUSION

You now have some basic organizing ideas about five key learner characteristics—motivating drives to action, stages in development of thinking and group interaction, gender and cultural impacts on learning and individual differences in learning style. We introduced three types of ergonomic needs—equipment; noise level, air quality and air temperature; and light and color—that learners bring to learning settings. Finally, we heard from a group of learners about their needs for interaction. This introductory trip over a complex and interesting landscape will lead, we hope, to further explorations when you are able to follow up with some of the readings. In the meantime, it's time to take a look at what learners do once they have entered a learning setting. In Chapter 3 we examine what we regard as core learning principles and practical strategies to guide you in applying the technologies described in Part 2.

# References

Belenky, M. F., Clinchy, B. M., Goldberger, N. R., & Tarule, J. M. (1986). *Women's ways of knowing: The development of self, voice, and mind.* New York, NY: Basic Books.

Canadian Centre for Occupational Health and Safety. (1996). *Office Ergonomics Safety Guide*. Hamilton, ON: Author.

Filipczak, B. (1995). Different strokes: Learning styles in the classroom. *Training, 32*(3), 43-48.

Goldberger, N., Tarule, J., Clinchy, B., & Belenky, M. (1996). *Knowledge, difference and power*. New York, NY: Basic Books.

Keefe, J. W. (1987). *Learning style: Theory and practice*. Reston, VA: National Association of Secondary School Principals.

Kolb, D. A. (1985). *Learning Style Inventory*. Boston, MA: McBer & Company.

———. (1984). *Experiential learning: Experience as the source of learning and development.* Englewood Cliffs, NJ: Prentice-Hall.

MacKeracher, D. (1996). *Making sense of adult learning*. Toronto, ON: Culture Concepts.

Perry, W. G. (1981). Cognitive and ethical growth: The making of meaning. In A. W. Chickering (Ed.), *The modern American college* (pp. 76-116). San Francisco, CA: Jossey-Bass.

Roberts, J. M., & Keough, E. M. (Eds.). (1995). *Why the Information Highway? Lessons from open and distance learning*. Toronto, ON: Trifolium Books Inc.

Spender, D. (1996). *Nattering on the Net*. Toronto, ON: Garamond Press.

Spronk, B. J. (1995). Appropriating learning technologies: Aboriginal learners, needs, and practices. In J. M. Roberts & E. M. Keough (Eds.), *Why the information highway? Lessons from open and distance learning* (pp. 77-101). Toronto, ON: Trifolium Books Inc.

Tannen, D. (1994). *Talking from 9 to 5: How women's and men's conversational styles affect who gets heard, who gets credit, and what gets done at work*. New York, NY: Morrow.

———. (1990). *You just don't understand: Women and men in conversation*. New York, NY: Morrow.

Tuckman, B., & Jensen, M. (1977). Stages of small group development revisited. *Group and Organization Studies*, *2*(4), 419-426.

# Chapter 3

## What Is Adult Learning All About?

*Adult learning is about making meanings from what we experience in life, using those meanings to think, decide, or solve problems and then to act in ways to help us get feedback that either confirms (or disconfirms) those meanings.*

DOROTHY MACKERACHER,
FACULTY OF EDUCATION,
UNIVERSITY OF NEW BRUNSWICK,
FREDERICTON, NEW BRUNSWICK

### INTRODUCTION

This chapter provides a summary of adult learning principles and strategies to guide you in designing effective learning opportunities and using technologies appropriately. When you have finished reading the chapter, you will feel comfortable with one overarching set of principles and two sets of practical strategies.

We believe that these principles and strategies model a holistic approach to understanding the dynamics of learning. These dynamics involve the head, heart, soul and body. The importance of seeing people as integrated wholes can, in our view, be summarized by the question posed by Virginia Griffin (1993), an adult educator who is now retired from the University of Toronto: "Would you play a one-string guitar?" The dynamics of learning operate in all sorts of ways, often making irrelevant all those prescriptions for rational, linear and evenly modulated sequences in learning.

The principles themselves are closely interrelated. They are also inextricably linked to the characteristics and needs of learners that we outlined in Chapter 2 and the educational changes outlined in Chapter 1.

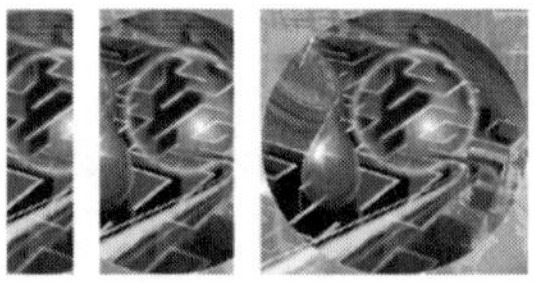

IS THIS A GOOD TIME FOR YOU TO BE READING THIS CHAPTER? DO LEARNING PRINCIPLES SOUND TOO ABSTRACT RIGHT NOW? IF SO, DON'T HESITATE TO SKIP OVER THIS CHAPTER AND BROWSE THROUGH CHAPTER 5, FOR EXAMPLE, WHICH EXPLAINS HOW TO TURN THEORY INTO ACTION.

### WHAT IS IMPORTANT ABOUT LEARNING PRINCIPLES?

One of the key principles is timeliness. Ron Zemke and Susan Zemke (1995), who work in the United States as consultants in training for corporations, make the point quite colorfully: "There is a window of opportunity during which adults are most receptive to learning—and a time after which they cannot be enticed with a chateaubriand or a baseball bat" (p. 32).

A second principle is the proper organization of information. People can easily feel overloaded (especially in computer conferences) if they get a torrent of information when all they needed was a glassful. Effective instructors help learners separate complex materials into manageable pieces so that they can better organize it and assess its relevance. Because this principle is so important, we "walk our talk" and use the acronym CARE to organize what we know about adult learning principles. Table 3.1 shows how the acronym categorizes the principles.

# Chapter 3

**TABLE 3.1:** LEARNING PRINCIPLES

| | |
|---|---|
| C | **Construction and Confusion** |
| A | **Achievement, Affiliation and Acknowledgment** |
| R | **Relevance, Responsibility and Relationships** |
| E | **Expression** |

## Construction and Confusion

Construction refers to how adults create their own framework of knowledge. They are best able to do this when they are encouraged to be mentally and physically active, and when they have to develop for themselves their own constructions of knowledge, as distinct from accepting without question someone else's constructions. This latter feature recognizes that our brains are "wired" to actively try to make sense out of information that is presented. This process of meaning-making happens most effectively when learners are asked to confront real-world puzzles, challenges or problems, and then talk through their ideas as they develop. Meaning-making happens least effectively when learners are restricted to listening and repeating exactly what they have heard (sometimes called the "load and dump" or "drill and fill" model). We are exaggerating a little to make the point that, while there are some training situations where you have to insist that learners know certain facts, a passive mental treatment of them will not help long-term memorization.

The predisposition of people for constructing their own meanings is recognized as key for designing effective learning in all settings, including workplace settings. In the October 1993 issue of *Training and Development*, the authors use terms such as "action research" and "learning by doing" to name the sometimes messy and unpredictable but always rewarding process of meaning-making. Educators in formal settings use terms such as "constructivist learning." We abbreviate the term slightly in this book to construction. Here is how one team of educators based at Penn State University describe learners in such environments:

> ... [learners] are actively engaged in perceiving different perspectives and organizing and representing their own interpretations... This is not "active" in the sense that learners actively listen and then mirror the one correct view of reality, but rather active in the sense that learners must participate and interact with the surrounding environment.
>
> *(Jonassen, Myers, & McKillop, 1996, pp. 95-96)*

Using a constructive approach does not imply that learning standards go downhill, or that memorization is not important in some circumstances, or that the instructor becomes unnecessary. Learners work hard to analyze the complexities of real-world contexts, to figure out solutions to messy problems or to apply new skills. Instructors guide and challenge, rather than serve only

**TABLE 3.2:** IMPLICATIONS OF APPLYING CONSTRUCTIVE APPROACHES

| LEARNING RESOURCES SHOULD HAVE SOME OR ALL OF THESE CHARACTERISTICS | A CONSTRUCTIVE LEARNER | A CONSTRUCTIVE INSTRUCTOR |
|---|---|---|
| 1. Relevance to learner and to real-world problems and contexts<br>2. A variety of problems and contexts (breadth of information)<br>3. Controversial or complex problems (depth of information)<br>4. Conflicting ideas and attitudes in a context<br>5. Personal practical knowledge held by the learner | 1. Challenges her or his own knowledge and values<br>2. Uses many types of thinking, such as metaphorical, intuitive, creative and logical/analytical<br>3. Looks to discover and analyze all the elements in a complex situation<br>4. Generates alternative solutions or procedures<br>5. Reality-checks a proposed solution or new procedure<br>6. Uses errors as part of learning<br>7. Talks in order to think<br>8. Revisits new learning to develop ideas in more depth and across new situations<br>9. Accepts the ambiguities in how the real world operates | 1. Encourages learners to produce, not reproduce, ideas<br>2. Helps learners revisit information for greater depth of analysis<br>3. Lets learners struggle a bit to figure things out<br>4. Offers learners the opportunity to watch an expert in action<br>5. Asks for proof of learning, for example: "Show us how you do that" (new skill); or "How did you reach that conclusion?" (new idea)<br>6. Confirms, corrects and challenges learners<br>7. Helps learners use different perspectives to look at a problem<br>8. Knows when to get out of the learners' space<br>9. Ensures access to adequate resources |

a transmission function. You will see how in Chapter 4. Table 3.2 lists some implications of applying constructive approaches to education and training.

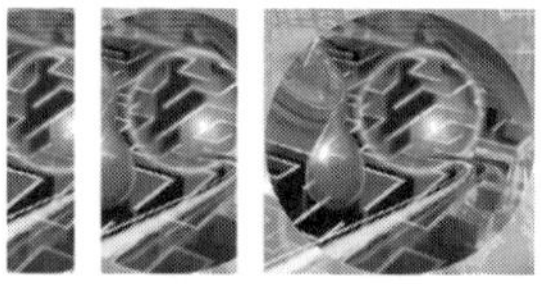

TELL YOUR LEARNERS THAT SIGNIFICANT LEARNING CAN BE A CONFUSING, MESSY AND UNPREDICTABLE PROCESS. NAMING THE PROBLEM IS HALFWAY TO KEEPING IT A TEMPORARY, NOT A PERMANENT, STATE OF AFFAIRS.

Confusion is an expected stage in all kinds of learning, especially when learners try to organize a mass of incoming information in a hurry. Instructors need to resist their desire to rescue learners from their confusion, as they need to work through their confusion to develop better learning skills. A careful instructor will assess whether learners can be left alone for a while to handle the confusion and will decide when assistance should be offered, first by class peers, and then by the instructor. These choices demand good judgment that is based on the instructor's knowledge of the learners. Confusion may act as a positive stress in learning, as is often the case with provocative or puzzling statements, deadlines to complete papers and small-group project research.

## Achievement, Affiliation and Acknowledgment

Achievement and affiliation are different words for the two motivators we discussed in Chapter 2, that is, feeling competent and being connected to others. You cannot go wrong if you use these motivators as your chief guiding principles. Think about how good it feels to know you are getting value for the money and time spent on a workshop or course, and you will understand how the two drives operate. Then consider that your learners will make the same kinds of judgments in your workshop or course. Finally, explore how you could arrange the elements of audio, computer or video conferencing to help learners activate their drives toward competence and connectedness.

Acknowledging what learners bring to learning is essential. To take into account learner characteristics, needs, prior life experiences and differences in learning style (Chapter 2) may sound a little like "parenthood and apple pie," but in our experience the way they are interrelated is often not fully understood. In her practical book for trainers and educators, Dorothy MacKeracher (1996), one of Canada's many experienced and skillful instructors of adults, explains just how powerfully interrelationships operate in a learner's life. It is sometimes easy to forget, in the stress of covering the prescribed course content or "getting the message out," that prior knowledge, skills and attitudes shape how people perceive and interpret the content or message. Adult learners are not empty buckets into which we can pour information without causing a ripple. A wise instructor will not think of "pouring"; rather, she or he will find out how much the learners know already about a topic and be prepared to adjust the objectives and activities accordingly. This instructor will also ensure that the learners respect each other's individuality and life experience and use them as information resources. But sometimes it takes a while to figure out and adjust to differences in thinking and in styles of expression.

Acknowledging the value of mistakes is another principle of learning. Mistakes are part of building knowledge, and peers can help each other learn from errors they make while practicing new skills. When the same mistakes are repeated, however, the instructor has a signal that something is wrong. The learner may have an undiagnosed learning disability, cannot critically reflect on her or his actions, or lacks enough time or freedom from stress to learn in a productive way.

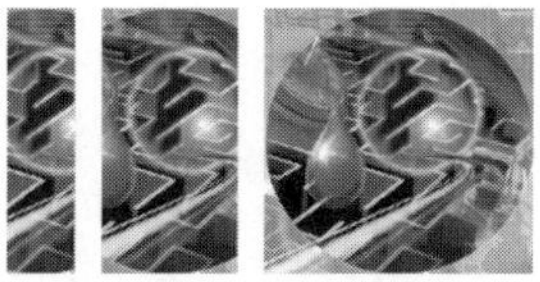

YOUR OWN LIFE EXPERIENCE AND PSYCHOLOGICAL NEEDS IN LEARNING CONTEXTS ARE USUALLY GOOD GUIDES FOR THINKING ABOUT ADULT LEARNING. TAKE TIME TO REFLECT ON WHAT HELPS AND HINDERS YOUR LEARNING.

## Relevance, Responsibility and Relationships

Life experience and personal knowledge are relevant to learners and may be useful resources for learning. But personal experience and existing knowledge also act as filters for incoming information, so a sensitive instructor will try to create opportunities that enable learners to identify which knowledge is helpful and which is not. For situations in which learners talk about personal experiences or use new knowledge to think critically about new applications, it is essential to ensure conditions of confidentiality. Otherwise, unauthorized "leaks" of information may occur that inhibit open and critical discussion. In technologically mediated settings such as audioconferencing, this issue is particularly important. Relevance also applies to new information—learners want to know how and why the course or workshop they are taking will be relevant to their immediate needs. This may sound obvious, but some instructors don't find out until it is too late what it is that their learners think they need to know.

Responsibility is a key principle because it is interrelated with connectedness and competence. Some learners, especially those who are accustomed to sitting safely in the back row or who resist getting involved, may assume that it is the instructor's responsibility alone to ensure that they learn. A savvy instructor will help learners figure out that the responsibility is divided. The learner is responsible for her or his own learning (no one can learn for anyone else), and the instructor is responsible for setting up and managing whatever conditions it takes to help the learners reach their performance goals. Liz has seen students initially look quite shocked when all this is explained. Only later, as they grow in competence and connectedness as learners, does the idea of their being responsible for their own learning take root. Howard MacLachlan, the retired gunnery instructor, describes his change in thinking about responsibility in this way: "How do I know I'm working differently? The lack of flexibility in traditional courses is starting to frustrate me; I now dislike "spoon-feeding"; and I tend to ponder over course issues during my leisure time."

Relationships are evident everywhere in learning. To a major degree, they are affected by the kind of teaching model chosen by the instructor (see Chapter 4). Collaborative rather than competitive relationships create a climate that allows for talking in order to think, making mistakes, letting go of old ideas or attitudes and being open to anything new. An effective instructor builds as many links as possible between the learners' existing knowledge and the new ideas or skills to be learned (anchors for new knowledge), between all the people in the course or workshop (a larger pool of resources) and between all the course components and technologies (no waste of resources). One way to build effective learning relationships is to use as learning resources people who have direct experience of a topic and who can relate to novices without being too abstract or unconsciously condescending. Another way is to use the collaborative learning strategies we outline here. Finally, involve learners in continuous adjustments to the program as it proceeds.

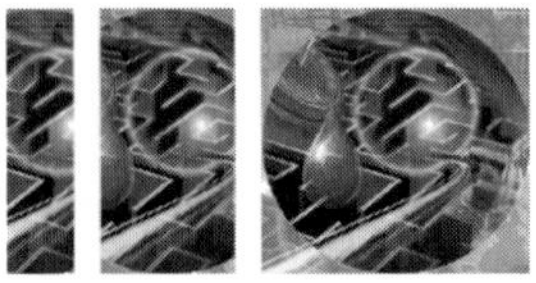

CONNECT, CONNECT, CONNECT...

### Expression

Being able to express skill, knowledge or changes in attitude enables learners to see themselves perform, hear themselves think, compare their thoughts and skills to those of their peers, and open their minds to feedback. Decisions about the kinds and amount of expression learners are allowed in discussions are influenced by the choice of teaching model, the combination of communications technologies and the impact of gender-based differences in communication styles. Instructors who spend much of their time listening carefully to learners talking in order to think gain a more accurate sense of how to help them progress to the next stage, either by not interfering or by giving specific guidance. We know of some colleagues who think that if they talk for more than 30 percent of the class time, they are not doing their job properly.

## HOW DO LEARNING STRATEGIES WORK?

Strategies for acquiring and processing information differ from learning principles and learning styles, although they are interconnected. Principles are abstract statements about learning. They reflect a certain set of values, and they give general guidance to instructors. Learning strategies is a term used to cover the specific thinking, feeling and acting processes that show the principles in

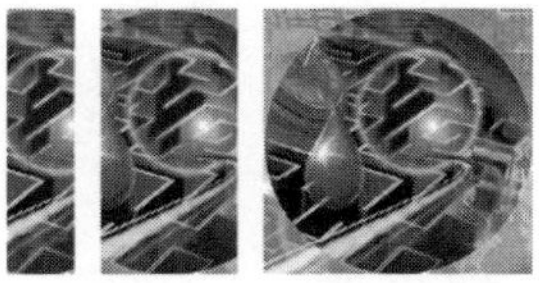

EXPRESSING WHAT IS BEING LEARNED IS AN ONGOING PROCESS IN A COURSE OR WORKSHOP, NOT SOMETHING THAT SHOULD BE SAVED FOR THE LAST CLASS OR SESSION.

operation. Learning styles (discussed in Chapter 2) refer to our individual, habitual and preferred ways of using learning strategies.

Various approaches are used to categorize the large number of learning strategies available to learners. We present two approaches that we like because they show a holistic orientation, which means that head, heart and body are inescapably interconnected in learning.

## Learning-to-Learn Strategies

The first approach is a Canadian one. It was developed as a set of learning-to-learn strategies in Alberta by a group of basic education teachers and adult students and was written up by David Collett (1990). The Albertans devised seven categories that we think are relevant for any training or educational environment. The categories cover three contexts of learning: the self, the external environment, and internal strategies for constructive information processing and skill learning. Table 3.3 shows how the broad levels of strategies are grouped. Collett provides more detail in his writing.

How can you use these seven key strategies? When you plan a learning event, and especially one that uses one or more of the four technologies discussed in Part 2 of this book, consider first which are the most relevant strategies for the

**TABLE 3.3:** LEARNING-TO-LEARN STRATEGIES

| | |
|---|---|
| **1. UNDERSTAND SELF AS STUDENT** | |
| • Develop confidence in one's ability to learn<br>• Develop insight into own learning style | • Establish short-term and long-term goals<br>• Accept responsibility |
| **2. MANAGE SELF AS STUDENT** | |
| • Maintain health of mind and body | • Manage time |
| **3. UNDERSTAND THE LEARNING ENVIRONMENT** | |
| • Use the complete services and resources | • Create a conducive home environment |
| **4. USE VARIOUS METHODS** | |
| • Learn on own, in group, by doing and by self-direction | |
| **5. THINK PRACTICALLY** | |
| • Apply six types of thinking: creative, lateral/divergent, convergent, critical, analytical and logical reasoning | |
| **6. RECALL AND APPLY DATA TO NEW SITUATIONS** | |
| • Use recall techniques | • Apply knowledge |
| **7. APPLY PROBLEM-SOLVING TECHNIQUES FOR RATIONAL DECISIONS** | |
| • Identify problem<br>• Establish decision parameters<br>• Evaluate alternatives | • Collect information<br>• Generate alternatives<br>• Make decisions and evaluate results |

desired learning outcomes. Then, once you have a list of, say, 12 strategies taken from different paragraphs, think about how each strategy would be applied in individual and group activities.

Here is an example. The strategy of "practical thinking" (Table 3.3, item 5) lists six types of thinking: creative, lateral/divergent, convergent, critical, analytical and logical reasoning. Draw up a chart with those six types along the left vertical axis. Alongside, for each type, jot down one or two activities that would enable your learners to apply that strategy. We supply the beginning; you fill in the rest.

**TABLE 3.4:** Six Types of Thinking and Related Learner Activities

| | |
|---|---|
| 1. Creative thinking | |
| 2. Lateral/divergent thinking | Brainstorming |
| 3. Convergent thinking | |
| 4. Critical thinking | |
| 5. Analytical thinking | Identify origins and impacts of a problem |
| 6. Logical reasoning | |

**TABLE 3.5:** Learning Strategies Developed by Tessmer and Jonassen

1. Information processing strategies help learners recall, integrate, organize and elaborate on information. Learners use these strategies when they separate incoming information into manageable "bites" by paraphrasing, finding examples, categorizing into logical or meaningful frameworks or generating implications about new information.
2. Active study strategies help learners interact with learning resources. Learners actively study when they highlight text, scan a document and make personal notes.
3. Meta-learning strategies help learners monitor how the first and second categories operate. Learners plan goals, focus their attention and assess what is required by the instructor.
4. Preparatory and executive strategies help learners create optimum psychological conditions. They manage their time, energy and concentration levels, try to be relaxed and keep their expected confusions and anxieties to tolerable levels.

## Managing Learning Strategies

The second approach to categorizing learning strategies comes from cognitive psychologists. They focus on cognitive and self-management strategies needed for individual learning. Martin Tessmer and David Jonassen (1988), educational technologists based at the University of South Alabama and Penn State University respectively, represent this group. They use four broad categories to organize their summary of learning strategies, as displayed in Table 3.5.

How can you use these four strategies? Let's again walk our talk about differences in learning styles. Here we give you an opportunity to leave our abstract ideas for the moment and think in practical ways. Imagine that you are enrolled in a rather expensive graduate program to enhance your professional development. You will have to participate in audio and computer-based small-group and whole-class discussions. What things would have to happen to allow you to use all of those four strategies consistently throughout the program?

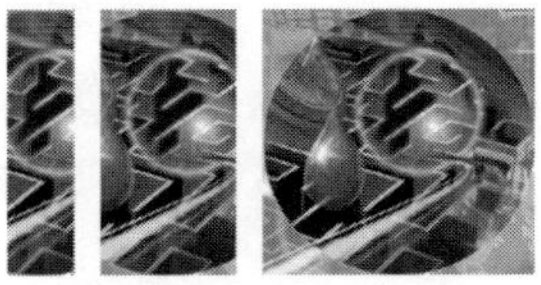

FOR ANY LEARNING SITUATION, THINK LEARNING STRATEGIES FIRST, THEN HOW YOU CAN HELP LEARNERS APPLY THEM IN ACTIVITIES AT HOME OR IN THE CLASSROOM. THINK TECHNOLOGY APPLICATIONS AFTERWARDS.

## WHY DOES COLLABORATIVE LEARNING PAY OFF?

This book is designed to integrate the world of learning with the interactive opportunities provided by four technologies, and to do so with a learner-centered focus. We decided, therefore, that this would be a good place to introduce some detailed guidelines about collaborative learning.

In our experience, some instructors are wary about using collaborative learning methods. They fear that they will waste time, or create classrooms where no rigorous academic work is completed. They wonder whether the learners will think the teacher is "opting out," or that the teacher's role will be diminished. Learners can have fears too—people talking with each other may highlight differences in learning abilities, or expose polarities in opinion that are difficult to accept. These perceptions are natural and should be acknowledged at the beginning of the course in a discussion about the process and outcomes of collaborative learning.

Instructors need to understand that collaborative learning requires preparation and management; it does not come naturally to many teachers or students, especially if they are accustomed to instructor-dependent styles of teaching, or "report," not "rapport," styles of communication. But when learners are helped to learn with and from each other, the result as a whole can be greater than the sum of its parts. This section, therefore, focuses on the functions of and conditions for productive and sociable learning discussions.

According to Ron McBeath, an experienced education technology consultant based in the United States, discussions generally fall into one of three types, each having its own goals. They are outlined in Table 3.6 (McBeath, 1992, p. 71).

**TABLE 3.6:** DISCUSSION TYPES AND GOALS DEVELOPED BY MCBEATH

| 1. INSTRUCTOR-DIRECTED DISCUSSION | 2. GROUP-CENTERED DISCUSSION | 3. COLLABORATIVE DISCUSSION |
|---|---|---|
| • Motivate participation<br>• Provide for interaction<br>• Recognize contributions<br>• Define terms<br>• Clarify content<br>• Identify assumptions | • Build on experience<br>• Strengthen relationships<br>• Raise questions<br>• Explore hypotheses<br>• Formulate ideas<br>• Examine assumptions | • Involve in problem solving<br>• Share responsibilities<br>• Compare alternatives<br>• Test hypotheses<br>• Base action on criteria<br>• Modify assumptions |

David Johnson and Roger Johnson (1992, 1991), experienced teachers and writers in Minnesota, have explained in detail in their popular books how collaborative group discussions help people gather information and draw meaning from it. Here is a summary of the key points (summarized from Johnson & Johnson, 1992, pp. 123-125).

- Group discussions allow learners to
  - summarize
  - explain
  - elaborate on information, which helps encode into long-term memory
  - seek feedback
  - strengthen what is known
- Learners develop creative and divergent thinking styles as they adjust to different styles of thinking and expression.
- Learners temporarily suspend the expression of their own opinions while listening to other points of view.
- Learners monitor and regulate each other's thinking as it is held up for critical review and exploration.
- Peer expectations can increase motivation to come to class prepared.
- Peers can give and get process feedback (ongoing), as well as terminal feedback at the end of the course.

If you want collaborative learning to work successfully, monitor its task and social elements, and remember the participants' basic motivating drives toward competence and connectedness. Our guidelines below apply to whole-class discussions and in structured small-group activities.

1. In the first session, ask the learners to share responsibility for productive discussions. You as the instructor don't have to carry the "albatross" of total responsibility for everything that happens in the class. Learners have to understand that collaborative learning demands self-discipline and respectful attention to peers; it is not a license for self-indulgence. Negotiate the ground rules for acceptable behavior early in such a way that the learners "own" the rules; in other words, don't present them as a *fait accompli.*
2. Encourage each person to participate. Restrict the "talkers," as their need to talk a lot may create problems for the others. Avoid giving implicit permission for continual silence from those students who always "just listen because I'm thinking." Too much silence from a participant may damage a feeling of joint responsibility for the success of the session. And, just to make matters more complicated, remember that you can "never judge a learner by her or his blank look," as Liz's students so aptly put it recently; behind that peaceful face could be a very active mind!
3. Use short, clear questions when setting a task for a small group. Avoid questions that begin with "Why..." (too threatening), or questions that are too vague or too obviously lead toward the answer you are seeking.

4. Ensure that the small-group discussion tasks are clearly understood and are manageable in the time allotted. Also, be sure to allow enough time for a general discussion of the results of the small-group work. If participants think that their work may not be given adequate time for reporting and analysis by the large group, they will adjust their commitment accordingly.
5. Avoid hovering over or eavesdropping on the participants. If you trust them, and if the task is clear and relevant, let them get on with it. Let them know that they have to give a succinct report to their peers and to you.
6. When the small groups reconvene as one large group, be a referee, not a traffic cop. Let each small group report to the whole class, then ask for a critical response from another small group, then have general talk before you cut in. Our experience indicates that participants may need some guidance to assume these responsibilities, but once they feel comfortable, the discussions will be much livelier and more creative than if you tried to work the magic by yourself. We've had participants, for example, come back from their groups with mini role plays, diagrams and sound effects.
7. Be prepared to discuss a change in agenda if it will help people's interest and energy levels. Flexibility is a strength, not a weakness.
8. Provide a summary, or ask one or more of the learners in each class to provide one. It is important to bring closure to discussions and to check understandings before plunging into the next topic.

In short, act as "the guide on the side, not the sage on the stage" (not our words, but we don't know who first coined the phrase). You may feel uncomfortable at first and want to talk to fill up the thinking silences. But don't. Trust yourself, your proactive learners and the collaborative process.

## CONCLUSION

At this point we have given you some new ideas about adult learning principles as summarized using the CARE acronym, and two sets of learning strategies that you could implement in an educational or training program. This knowledge is a tool for facilitating learning—a complex series of seen and unseen activities, feelings and outcomes. Incorporating prior knowledge and experience and the present learning needs are key to helping adults be responsible and productive learners. There is great potential for relationship building to meet the learners' drives for achievement and affiliation; this gives the instructor many opportunities to be creative and collegial. Chapter 4 suggests some hands-on ways to optimize those opportunities.

# References

Collett, D. J. (1990). Learning-to-learn needs for adult basic education. In R. M. Smith & Associates (Eds.), *Learning to learn across the lifespan* (pp. 247-266). San Francisco, CA: Jossey-Bass.

Griffin, V. R. (1993). Holistic learning and teaching: Would you play a one-string guitar? In T. Barer-Stein & J. A. Draper (Eds.), *The craft of teaching adults* (rev. ed.) (pp.105-130). Toronto, ON: Culture Concepts.

Johnson, D. W., & Johnson, R. T. (1992). Encouraging thinking through constructive controversy. In N. Davidson & T. Worsham (Eds.), *Enhancing thinking through cooperative learning* (pp. 120-127). New York, NY: Teachers College Press.

———. (1991). *Joining together: Group theory and group skills* (4th ed.). Englewood Cliffs, NJ: Prentice-Hall.

Jonassen, D. H., Myers, J. M., & McKillop, A. M. (1996). From constructivism to constructionism: Learning with hypermedia/multimedia rather than from it. In B. G. Wilson (Ed.), *Constructivist learning environments: Case studies in instructional design* (pp. 93-106). Englewood Cliffs, NJ: Educational Technology Publications.

MacKeracher, D. (1996). *Making sense of adult learning*. Toronto, ON: Culture Concepts.

McBeath, R. J. (Ed.). (1992). *Instructing and evaluating in higher education: A guidebook for planning learning outcomes.* Englewood Cliffs, NJ: Educational Technology Publications.

Tessmer, M., & Jonassen, D. (1988). Learning strategies: A new instructional technology. *World Yearbook of Education, 1988* (pp. 29-47). London, UK: Kogan Page.

Zemke, R., & Zemke, S. (1995). Adult learners: What do we know for sure? *Training, 32*(6), 31-40.

# Chapter 4

## How May Instructors Best Respond?

*Success is when both teacher and learner no longer notice the delivery mode. The session feels like a "regular" class—lively, highly interactive and real-time. The trick lies in fostering interactivity by proactively building it into the session content.*

SANDRA HODDER,
SHERIDAN COLLEGE, OAKVILLE, ONTARIO

### INTRODUCTION

Having outlined learner needs, the key adult learning principles and specific strategies of learning, we now explore how instructors can respond to learners in ways that use those principles and strategies. When you have finished this chapter, you will know something about choosing a model of teaching, deciding on levels and objectives of learning and addressing 10 planning questions.

### HOW DO MODELS OF TEACHING DIFFER?

Here we outline two approaches to teaching that cover a total of nine models. You will see how the nine are interlinked as we go through each one. But first, why use a model anyway? Here is one answer from an educator at a Canadian university, as quoted by Anne Percival (1994) of the University of Saskatchewan: "The beauty of a model is that, at least if you have a model, you can modify it or change it or throw it away and start with something new. At least you know that you have got something to bounce [your ideas] off" (p. 81).

A model is a generalized and structured way of seeing events and processes in the world, rather than a way of carrying out specific skill-based procedures. A model (or representation) of something helps people clarify their own values and outlooks, see linkages between events, predict likely results, figure out alternative solutions to problems and compare what they can do with what they might do. A model can steer thinking and help define strategies and opportunities. It can also limit an instructor's perceptions of events and analysis of ideas because it may set boundaries around people's field of vision.

Models are important in education and training for two additional reasons: (1) learners will very quickly pick up the values and attitudes toward learning that the instructor holds and will react accordingly; and (2) a model will influence how an instructor chooses technologies, and technologies amplify the good and bad aspects of the teaching behaviors of each model.

The first five models come from Daniel Pratt (1992), an experienced adult educator at the University of British Columbia. Dan supervised extensive research into how people in various countries "see" teaching. He took a comprehensive view, looking at goals, course content, teaching methods, the role of learners and contextual factors. His results show that five models can be drawn out of how people understand teaching:

1. The engineering model focuses on how efficiently the teacher organizes and presents specific packages of information to a "target audience," which is expected to conform to the values and behaviors prescribed by the teacher. Training for the military or for bank employment are two examples.
2. The apprenticeship model focuses on modeling appropriate values and behaviors of "elders" or acknowledged expert practitioners working in specific contexts. Medical internships and professional mentoring are two examples.
3. The developmental model focuses on developing the learner's intellectual skills, especially those used in the critical questioning of existing knowledge. Graduate study and continuing professional education settings are two examples.
4. The nurturing model also refers to the learner, but this time in terms of the two motivating drives we mentioned in Chapter 2—competence and connectedness. The instructor alternates caring behaviors with those designed to challenge and direct as necessary. Programs for adult basic education and self-help agencies are two examples.
5. The social reform model focuses on generally improving a society by the application of ideals based on religion, ethics or politics. The examples are all individual, such as a modern-day Ghandi or a feminist adult educator.

## WHICH OF THE FIVE APPEAL TO YOU?

The next four models come from a 1987 presentation by K. Patricia Cross, a teacher, educational administrator and researcher now based at the University of California at Berkeley. Her models (see Table 4.1) are somewhat similar to Dan Pratt's research results in that they show teacher-centered views and learner-centered views.

No model is inherently better than any other. Deciding on which model to employ depends on how you analyze all the contextual factors, especially learner needs. For training safety engineers, for example, Model 1 would be appropriate; in a course for newly qualified lawyers, Model 3 would be appropriate.

Because you need to consider the unique features of each communications technology, there is more thinking to be done about the appropriateness of your preferred model. If you generally prefer a learner-centered approach and use the apprenticeship model, you will use technologies such as tape recorders and video cameras, which enable learners to gather information from events and people in the real world before engaging in reflective and spontaneous discussions with class peers and yourself using technologies such as audio and computer conferencing. If you generally prefer an instructor-centered approach

**TABLE 4.1:** FOUR TEACHING MODELS

| MODEL 1<br>*I TEACH WHAT I KNOW* | MODEL 2<br>*I TEACH WHAT I AM* | MODEL 3<br>*I DEVELOP MINDS* | MODEL 4<br>*I DEVELOP PEOPLE* |
|---|---|---|---|
| The teacher:<br>• covers the course information systematically and in an orderly way<br>• presents facts and principles<br>• uses short-answer tests for understanding of facts<br>• sees knowledge as an end product, not as a process<br>• spends most of the class time lecturing | The teacher:<br>• models how the educated mind works<br>• shows, via lectures, how a competent mind deals with the knowledge of a discipline<br>• does not try to cover all content<br>• sees learning as a process, not a product<br>• evaluates by asking learners to show mental competence | The teacher:<br>• is concerned about intellectual development<br>• argues that the key student tasks are analysis, synthesis and evaluation of information<br>• uses discussions, case studies and questioning for discovery<br>• evaluates learning by essays or problem solving | The teacher:<br>• is concerned about whole person development (a holistic approach)<br>• has a relatively informal (but not irresponsible) style<br>• knows learners well, on and off campus<br>• diagnoses for development of learning skills |

and use the engineering model, you will look for technologies that enable you to efficiently design and deliver the prescribed course content and assess predetermined learning outcomes. Paper-based text and computer-based training packages are examples of such technologies.

When you think in general terms about your role and rationale as an instructor, you think about how relationships work and whose goals are predominant. In short, you think about models. What comes next are the operational details. A basic component of these details are the levels and objectives of learning.

## WHAT IS AN EFFICIENT WAY TO SET LEARNING OBJECTIVES?

Learning levels and objectives are related but not the same. A learning level refers to the development level of skill or knowledge or attitude. For example, we may "understand" something, but how much we know and how well we have it organized in our heads so that we can effectively transfer our knowledge to other situations is yet to be determined. Specific details on how you can do this are explained below.

A learning objective is a statement that, at minimum, prescribes the required learning outcome in terms that indicate the level of learning, for example: "You will be able to evaluate the usefulness of the Brown statistical model." A precise writer of objectives would go further and specify the conditions under which that outcome must be demonstrated and the criteria for meeting that high level of thinking (evaluating). So now the objective would look like this: "Using your own criteria for assessment, you will be able to evaluate over a three-month period the usefulness of the Brown statistical model as it may apply to forest management." Now that's a high level of learning written as a very clear objective.

CHET MYERS AND THOMAS JONES, TWO PROFESSORS AT METROPOLITAN STATE UNIVERSITY IN THE UNITED STATES, SUMMARIZE WHAT THEY HAVE LEARNED ABOUT SPECIFYING CLEAR OUTCOMES FOR THE LEARNER: "WE ARE CONVINCED THAT IN ALMOST EVERY DISCIPLINE, TEACHERS CAN WINNOW CONTENT DOWN TO THE ESSENTIALS... A GOOD TECHNIQUE IS TO POSE THIS SIMPLE QUESTION: 'WHAT DO I WANT STUDENTS TO *KNOW* AND BE ABLE TO *DO* BY THE END OF THIS CLASS?' (1993, PP. 34-35).

Clearly stated learning levels and objectives are important for three reasons. First, many instructors experience difficulty in defining the learning outcomes for their students. They know what they do in the classroom ("I use demonstrations and discussions a lot."), but they draw a blank or give a vague answer when asked to think in terms of the learners' goals ("They have to know about effective teamwork for our company."). Because the instructors are not quite sure about the specific learning outcomes, they experience difficulties when they have to test or grade learners. After discussions with an instructor, we can usually find a set of fairly specific statements of expected learner performance by the end of the course or workshop ("The participants will be able to explain, with local examples, the six Smith and White strategies for team building in a corporate downsizing context.").

The second reason for having clear levels and objectives of learning relates to how the students manage themselves during the course, and how competent and connected they feel. Myers and Jones (1993) agree: "The clearer students are about what is expected of them, the greater their chances to meet those expectations" (p. 40). The third reason for clarity relates to the present need in society for a highly trained workforce and for competent citizenship. As we mentioned in Chapter 1, today's workplaces demand a range of employability skills rather than just job-specific skills, for example, staff need skills in higher-level thinking and doing, in self-management and in teamwork. We have seen many course objectives and assessment exercises that keep the learners operating at comparatively low levels of thinking and performing; for example, they can explain something but not apply it or critique its theoretical base.

Defining the differences between higher levels of thinking and lower levels of thinking or performance is still mostly based on a set of learning levels and objectives developed over 40 years ago in the United States by a psychologist, Benjamin Bloom, and his associates (1956). They published concise outlines of what they called three domains, or categories, of learning objectives. Each domain works as a hierarchy, or taxonomy, showing a progression of levels from low to high. Norman Gronlund (1991), a professor emeritus, educational psychology, the University of Illinois, developed a set of three tables based on Bloom's taxonomy as practical guidelines. The Cognitive Domain (Table 4.2) is probably the most widely used table by teachers and instructors. It refers to knowledge development and the thinking skills that characterize each level of knowledge acquisition. The higher the level of required knowledge, the more sophisticated are the required thinking skills. The Affective Domain (Table 4.3) is just as important, in our opinion, because of how strongly our attitudes influence our behavior and capacity for change. This domain refers to the development of values, emotions and attitudes, and the outlooks and behaviors that characterize each level of development. The Psychomotor Domain (Table 4.4) refers to operational skills of equipment and the physical movements and controls that characterize each level of skill.

Armed with these handy tools, you can better decide which level of learning your learners need to aim for in each domain. For example, if we had to set up learning objectives for a workshop in team-building skills, we would use first the cognitive and affective domains (Tables 4.2 and 4.3). If we had to design learning objectives for lathe operators, then we would first focus on the psychomotor and cognitive domains (Tables 4.2 and 4.4). Note the use of the word "first" in the preceding sentence. A savvy instructor knows that once you have dealt with your first priorities, you must not omit the other domains. For example, we heard about a training event for parents who were abusive toward their young children. The trainers focused on the cognitive and psychomotor domains and gave lots of readings and skill-based exercises. The affective domain, however, was all but ignored: the parents' existing attitudes toward children were not dealt with—not confronted and assessed. At the end of the course, all the parents passed all the tests of knowledge and skill. But one set of parents then went right back to abusing their children. This couple had not been helped to learn new values about children and new attitudes about parenting that would have anchored their recently acquired knowledge and physical skill development, and thus stopped the child abuse.

Use our tables to figure out and indicate to the learners what exactly (or as far as possible) they will do to prove new learning. If you write an objective like this one: "You will understand the Jones principles of corporate taxation," your learners cannot figure out if you want them to repeat verbatim what you gave them to read about the Jones principles (low level), whether you want them to apply the principles in their actual work setting (medium level) or whether you want them to critique the principles and suggest some amendments (high level). So in addition to deciding on the required level of learning, you should also decide what the learner will actually have to do in order to prove a new competence.

Armed with this knowledge, you can then figure out the objectives for your workshop or course. We recognize that in some training settings you or a standards committee would have already set the objectives so that uniformity of skill and knowledge development would be achieved across all training contexts. For example, we have seen extremely detailed learning objectives for air traffic control training. However, there are other settings in which it is appropriate to engage the learners in a joint setting of objectives. Sometimes you may be surprised at the high levels that learners set for themselves.

Once the required levels of knowledge, skill and attitudes are established, think about how each one might be shown in observable action. Use our ACC rule to write out clear objectives. "A" refers to the actual actions of the learners (do they really build a house frame, or draw the specs for one?). "C" refers to the conditions under which the action is carried out (at actual size on a real building site, or as a model in a highly equipped classroom laboratory?). The last "C" refers to the criteria for the actions under those conditions (under supervision? in so many days? to which official building standards?). Being specific is admittedly easier for some courses than for others, but we believe that many prescribed learning outcomes are almost always capable of being specified with a fair degree of clarity. A training program on corporate teamwork in an electronic performance support system, for example, could specify the completion of team

**TABLE 4.2:** COGNITIVE LEARNING OUTCOMES

| | ◄------ LOWER LEVELS OF LEARNING (SIMPLE) | | ------------------► HIGHER LEVELS OF LEARNING (COMPLEX) | | | | |
|---|---|---|---|---|---|---|---|
| | **Knowledge** | **Comprehension** | **Application** | | **Analysis** | **Synthesis** | **Evaluation** |
| COGNITIVE Thinking | *(recall)* | *(understand in own words)* | *(use in actual contexts)* | | *(break down into components to understand structures)* | *(form new patterns and structures)* | *(judge value using criteria)* |
| | Define | Convert | Apply | Manipulate | Categorize | Combine | Appraise |
| | Describe | Defend | Calculate | Operate | Diagram | Create | Compare |
| | Identify | Distinguish | Compute | Practice | Differentiate | Design | Contrast |
| | Label | Explain | Demonstrate | Prepare | Discriminate | Devise | Conclude |
| | List | Generalize | Draft | Produce | Distinguish | Generate | Critique |
| | Locate | Give examples | Dramatize | Schedule | Illustrate | Organize | Evaluate |
| | Quote | Paraphrase | Draw | Solve | Select | Plan | Judge |
| | Recite | Predict | Estimate | Use | Separate | Reorganize | Recommend |
| | Repeat | Summarize | Manage | | Sort | Revise | |
| | Restate | | | | Subdivide | Write | |
| | Select | | | | | | |
| | *(Repeats another's definition of a principle)* | *(Explains a principle, using examples of its use elsewhere)* | *(Personally applies that principle to procedures in a real situation)* | | *(Can separate a fact from an assumption in that principle)* | *(Combines several principles into a new operating strategy)* | *(Judges the use of that new strategy)* |

Summarized by Liz Burge, using Gronlund, N. E. (1991). *How to write and use instructional objectives* (4th ed.). New York, NY: Macmillan.

**TABLE 4.3:** AFFECTIVE LEARNING OUTCOMES

| ◄------ LOWER LEVELS OF LEARNING (SIMPLE) ------► HIGHER LEVELS OF LEARNING (COMPLEX) | | | | | |
|---|---|---|---|---|---|
| | **Receiving** *(early awareness and selective attention)* | **Responding** *(willing attention and satisfied reaction)* | **Valuing** *(internalized values with consistent supporting behavior)* | **Organizing** *(integrating different values into a coherent whole)* | **Characterizing** *(new behaviors—based on value organization—are consistent and characteristic)* |
| **A** | Ask | Assist | Choose | Accept | Act |
| **F** | Choose | Attempt | Complete | Arrange | Defend |
| **F** | Describe | Comply | Demonstrate | Change | Demonstrate |
| **E** | Follow | Discuss | Describe | Combine | Distinguish |
| **C** | Give | Help | Distinguish | Compare | Influence |
| **T** | Identify | Perform | Explain | Complete | Maintain |
| **I** | Locate | Practice | Follow | Defend | Mediate |
| **V** | Name | Read | Initiate | Explain | Perform |
| **E** | Request | Request | Invite | Generalize | Question |
| | Select | Select | Join | Identify | Revise |
| Feeling & Attitude | Use | Write | Justify | Integrate | Show |
| | Volunteer | Volunteer | Report | Organize | Solve |
| | | | Share | Recognize | Use |
| | | | Suggest | Select | Verify |
| | | | | Synthesize | |
| | *(Listens carefully)* | *(Voluntarily does something)* | *(Actively shows concern about something)* | *(Accepts responsibility for own behavior and personal strengths and limitations)* | *(Shows self-discipline and initiative in a variety of contexts)* |

Summarized by Liz Burge, using Gronlund, N. E. (1991). *How to write and use instructional objectives* (4th ed.). New York, NY: Macmillan.

**TABLE 4.4:** PSYCHOMOTOR LEARNING OUTCOMES

| | ◄------ LOWER LEVELS OF LEARNING (SIMPLE) | | | -------► HIGHER LEVELS OF LEARNING (COMPLEX) | | | |
|---|---|---|---|---|---|---|---|
| **PSYCHOMOTOR** | **Perception** | **Set** | **Guided Response** | **Mechanism** | **Complex Overt Response** | **Adaptation** | **Origination** |
| | *(get cues to guide actions)* | *(readiness to act)* | *(early learnings of skills)* | *(habitual responses and efficient performance for less complex skills)* | *(expert and fast performance of complex skills)* | *(adapts skills as necessary)* | *(creation of new movements)* |
| | Choose<br>Detect<br>Distinguish<br>Identify<br>Isolate<br>Link<br>Select<br>Separate | Display<br>Explain<br>Point to<br>Proceed<br>Show | Adjust<br>Assemble<br>Build/Construct<br>Calibrate<br>Close<br>Dismantle<br>Dissect | Disconnect<br>Draw<br>Duplicate<br>Fasten<br>Grind<br>Heat<br>Load<br>Loosen | Manipulate<br>Mend<br>Open<br>Organize<br>Sort<br>Replace<br>Rotate<br>Select | Adapt<br>Change<br>Modify<br>Rearrange<br>Revise<br>Reorganize | Create<br>Compose<br>Construct<br>Design |
| Doing | *(Sees how a technical procedure is set up)* | *(Shows correct handling of an instrument)* | *(Practices a simple procedure)* | *(Consistently and correctly carries out a simple procedure, without supervision)* | *(Easily and correctly handles more complex tasks)* | *(Adjusts use of instruments according to different contexts)* | *(Creates a new procedure)* |

Summarized by Liz Burge, using Gronlund, N. E. (1991). *How to write and use instructional objectives* (4th ed.). New York, NY: Macmillan.

projects within a certain time frame using certain principles of group development and project management, and using certain standards of software application.

## HOW DO I ACTUALLY PLAN MY RESPONSE?

It is time now to place levels and objectives of learning into the broader context of planning a course or workshop. The whole process is a balancing act. The objectives and dynamics in learning and learner characteristics have to be taken into account. Add to them the impact of the instructor's preferred teaching model and the strengths and weaknesses of each technology, and the balancing act becomes more complex.

One way to meet this challenge is to use a set of planning questions. We don't give you a linear prescription or flowchart for two reasons: (1) each planning context is different, and (2) a good planning process is a series of cycling around and back and forth between all the contextual factors. But we do give you a set of 10 questions and ask that you think of more and consult the Further Readings.

Our questions match fairly closely with most models for program planning in adult education, especially one jointly published in 1989 by Thomas Sork of the University of British Columbia and Rosemary Caffarella of the University of Northern Colorado. A good discussion of their model can be found in Anne Percival's (1994) practical guide to planning, published by the Extension Division of the University of Saskatchewan.

THERE IS ANOTHER BIG ADVANTAGE TO BEING SPECIFIC ABOUT LEARNING OUTCOMES. WHEN YOU ARE ABLE TO WRITE OUT OBJECTIVES LIKE THIS ONE: "YOU WILL BE ABLE TO APPLY, IN A REAL-OFFICE CONTEXT, WITHOUT SUPERVISION, ALL SEVEN PRINCIPLES OF THE JONES THEORY OF CORPORATE TAXATION TO CORRECTLY CALCULATE THE TAX FOR THREE VENTURE CAPITALISTS," YOU HAVE A TEST ITEM ALREADY WRITTEN. JUST DELETE THE FIRST FIVE WORDS OF THE ABOVE SENTENCE. YOU WILL FIND MORE DETAIL IN THE FURTHER READINGS FOR THIS CHAPTER.

**TABLE 4.5:** TOP 10 PLANNING QUESTIONS

1. What are the learning needs?
2. What are the helping and hindering factors in the macro context?
3. Who is expected to participate? What are their characteristics?
4. What kinds of resources are available?
5. How will I get variety in learning activities?
6. Which mix of technologies will best support the learning?
7. How will the learners know what to do?
8. What will I do?
9. What kinds of problems might arise?
10. How will I know if things are working well?

FIRST, "THINK MACRO" ABOUT THE NEEDS AND CONSTRAINTS PRESENTED BY YOUR INSTITUTION AND ITS COMMUNITY. THEN, "THINK MICRO" ABOUT THE TEACHING AND LEARNING ISSUES OF YOUR COURSE OR EVENT.

Let's explore the top 10 questions.

### *QUESTION 1: What are the learning needs?*

Try to balance as much as you can the needs as they may be specified by a company or accreditation agency and the learners' expressions of what they need in order to do something better. The level of the learners' involvement can vary. As we explained in Chapter 2, learners need to be involved in defining their interests, if not their actual needs, for learning. Wallace Hannum (1990), a faculty member in the School of Education, University of North Carolina at Chapel Hill, notes: "Studies have shown that students make good choices about the pace of the instruction, the amount of practice, and whether to see an overview. Students with high levels of prior knowledge of the content make good choices about the instructional strategy; students with low prior knowledge do not..." (p. 8).

Consider, too, how the final decision is made: Will it be a negotiated settlement or a prescription?

*QUESTION 2: What are the helping and hindering factors in the macro context?*

What kinds of things are your company or institutional leaders worried about these days? What kinds of results do they expect from training programs? Do you have to recover all the costs of the program? Is there a technological infrastructure with adequate staff to facilitate your program? Is there a legal requirement to offer certain types of training in order to meet specified performance standards? How flexible is your institution regarding payments and schedules? How are you perceived by your leaders and peers? Are your resources fairly secure?

*QUESTION 3: Who is expected to participate? What are their characteristics?*

Keep in mind the two basic motivating drives to action—competence and connectedness. Think about how you can apply the learning principles we outlined in Chapter 3. Take no prior information for granted. Carry out as thorough a needs assessment as you can. Don't rely on promises of attendance being kept; things happen to keep people away.

*QUESTION 4: What kinds of resources are available?*

We highlight here three types of resources: information, library and teaching support. Information resources exist in human and material forms. Because learners differ markedly in their learning style preferences, you should provide variety in the formats of learning resources. Can the core material for your learners be supplied in written text with some audio-visual forms? Do your learners already have access to printed information or does it need to be prepared? How much necessary and optional course information can be supplied only by experts who must be brought into the sessions? Guest experts can visit at various points during the course, but their "arrival" times usually coincide with the analysis-of-an-application (higher) level of learning. For any lower learning levels (refer to Tables 4.2, 4.3, 4.4), the guest can be invited to contribute printed materials that the learners can study and then respond to in a "live" interactive session. In situations where the learning objectives are set at a high level, the guest can be invited to listen to the learners' critical reactions to her or his ideas and then confirm, correct and challenge them with new questions or additional examples of real-world problems or complex case studies.

Library services provide learners with computerized databases, sophisticated indexing services, useful materials and helpful librarians who can save you and your learners a lot of time in researching information. A responsive and anticipatory librarian on your team adds value and quality because she or he is knowledgeable about electronic information products and can help you choose authoritative material from indexes and the Internet, for example.

Teaching support services are essential if you have to keep records and manage the logistics of using a range of technologies. Will there be a technical person to set up all the sites you need and check that all the equipment is functioning perfectly? Will learners have access to information services after 4 o'clock each day? We discuss other implications of using technology in question 6.

### *QUESTION 5: How will I get variety in learning activities?*

We suggest that you think holistically and devise ways to appeal to the three thinking, feeling and doing domains of learning described by Bloom and his colleagues (see Tables 4.2 to 4.4). Also try to balance experience-based modes of learning, where learners are "dropped" into an experience first (the CE point of the Kolb cycle) and then have to analyze it, with information delivery modes, where you give a lecture of already analyzed information. Table 4.6 gives you and your learners a menu of "good food" choices. We also recommend that you consult authors such as Patricia Cranton, Dorothy

**TABLE 4.6:** VARIETY IN ACTIVITIES

| REGARDING COURSE CONTENT | |
|---|---|
| • As much as you can, use real-world problems as resources.<br>• Use both brain hemispheres, thus releasing intuitive and creative thinking, as well as analytical and synthetic thinking.<br>• Gather information from raw experience, not just from "distilled" knowledge from experts.<br>• Generate metaphors, analogies and images to help display and understand concept learning.<br>• Apply thematic and interdisciplinary treatments to the structuring of course content: look for ways to link content presented from varying points of view. | • Facilitate small peer groups, keeping the omniscient instructor out of the picture. Use learning partnerships to help learners reflect aloud on their learning methods and progress.<br>• Play—have fun. It's okay, and it definitely helps creative thinking.<br>• Design assignments to help learners explore library collections and enjoy a serendipitous approach to finding information.<br>• Try to experience unfamiliar ideas or to see familiar ideas in unusual contexts. |
| **REGARDING PEOPLE'S SELF-ESTEEM** | |
| • Be aware of body messages (such as tiredness, anxiety or fear) that may inhibit learning processes.<br>• Express the positive and negative feelings associated with learning.<br>• Recognize and use differences based on gender, ethnicity and age.<br>• Legitimize relaxed silences in groups, calling it thinking time (not dead air). | • Encourage learners to use first-person language to help them claim ownership of personal values, experiences and insights.<br>• Set learning objectives that relate to skill or knowledge development, and help integrate self-concept and self-esteem development too. |

MacKeracher, Peter Renner, Chet Myers and Thomas Jones, and Mel Silberman for more practical details.

*QUESTION 6: Which mix of technologies will best support the learning?*

The answers to this question depend as much on learner and instructor issues as they do on the learning levels and objectives of the program. We use the term *mix* because no technology gives the single miraculous answer.

Use five key approaches.

1. Keep in mind that technology does not, in and of itself, promote learning. It all depends on (1) how well you understand and manage the unique features and strengths and weaknesses of each technology, and (2) how you define the ideal mix of learning strategies and activities required to gain the best possible learning outcomes. You will find more details in Chapter 6.
2. Refer to the learning strategies we outlined in Chapter 3, and think about how each one might be implemented in a variety of activities throughout the course. For example, in a workshop on labor market trend analysis, you want to make extensive use of analytical and convergent thinking, but you also want to break new ground and encourage creative and divergent thinking. How can your participants best carry out these four types of thinking? How will you and the learners experience each type of thinking in progress? Will the thinking need to be done mostly in real-time to capitalize on the volatility of live conversation? Will you want to literally see the thinking unfolding by learners drawing diagrams? Will you want to display complex mathematical formulas and work on them during class time? Will you want to bring into the workshop some of Canada's leading experts in labor market analysis? Do you want the learners to be able to work on their own, in teams, on research projects? You can see what we mean by thinking about learning before thinking about technology.
3. Then you use your knowledge of the features, strengths and weaknesses of each technology to make a preliminary choice. Carry out a reality check: Do the learners have easy, frequent, reliable and affordable access to the technologies? Part 2 of our book gives you many hints to help you make decisions.
4. Finally, when you think you've settled on the most appropriate mix, give it one more check: Does it accommodate differences in learning styles? For example, have you considered those learners who prefer to first hear about or read abstract theories (the assimilator style), as distinct from those who first want to do something in the real world (the accommodator style)?
5. If at all possible, go over your intended design with some potential learners, or discuss it with a creative colleague.

We make just three points here. You will see guidelines for developing a learner's manual in Chapter 5 and detailed examples of course manuals in the Resource Kit.

*QUESTION 7: How will the learners know what to do?*

The first point is that we believe learners and instructor can all work from the same materials. This view reflects our values about how to treat adults as learners; there is no need to hide the instructor's rationale or intended strategies. If the learners are busy and happily involved with how the course activities proceed and their own progress, they won't have the time to go chasing after any details that you don't think are appropriate for them to see. Adult learners placed in positions of trust in a well-functioning course usually keep that trust. And any learner has a right to know the details about what they will be doing in a course.

The second point refers to how much detail you need to supply and when. We don't advocate that you always prescribe in advance every little detail about the course and then lay out those details in a highly detailed book. How much prescribing you do depends on your model of teaching, the kinds of learning objectives, and the availability of regular and fast communications. In Chapter 5 we explain how you can organize the detail you do think is necessary.

The third point refers to adult learners' needs to feel connected and competent to handle various situations. Prepare and distribute course materials in advance so that learners can arrive with some knowledge and be prepared to discuss the subject matter with the other learners. Well-organized and graphically attractive materials sent to learners ahead of time will encourage them to at least skim over the materials.

*QUESTION 8: What will I do?*

After all the above guidance, what do you see yourself doing? We believe in using precious (and expensive) class time for in-depth communication among all the course members, for analysis, critique and application of new ideas and skills. You can usually arrange learner access to all or most of the basic information they need, either from materials delivered as part of the course package, or from other sources. Chapter 5 contains more details on how to do this.

You will follow all the principles of adult learning (Chapter 3) if you focus on seven functions:

1. Create the climate and negotiate ground rules for working in the course or workshop.
2. Connect learners to peers and other resources.
3. Confirm new learnings and insights.
4. Correct misunderstandings.
5. Change the agenda or activities as necessary.
6. Challenge learners to more sophisticated thinking or applications.
7. Check for losses of attention.

These functions apply across all the learning activities that you and the learners decide are useful. In the Further Readings section, we list a number of books with practical guidelines on using such activities as role plays, case studies, structured discussions and project research.

*QUESTION 9: What kinds of problems might arise?*

Imagine that your learners at another location are so intent on their discussions that they forget to operate their audioconferencing equipment so that the instructor can call them back to the class. As the seconds tick by, the instructor remembers that the rural students have gathered in someone's house, but no one knows the phone number of a neighbor who could be asked to knock on the door and tell the students how to reconnect to the conference. And there is a minus-27-degree-Celsius blizzard storming around the house... What would you do to beat Murphy's Law? You have two minutes to make a decision. This scenario really happened to Liz. A very helpful police patrol car came to the rescue after she confessed the problem to a sympathetic dispatcher on the night shift.

We include this anecdote because Murphy has an extended family, and you could be visited by his relatives any day. And the "higher" the technology, the higher the probability that things won't work. Erin Keough, director of the Open Learning and Information Network of Newfoundland and Labrador, is an experienced designer and manager of distance education operations. She bluntly refers to the need for an "obsessive-compulsive attention to detail and a robust sense of humor." She sent us Malachy Mandeville's (1995) now famous "Aspirin, Anyone?", which you'll find in Chapter 10. Enjoy; it's all true!

Otherwise, our best advice is to discuss your ideas with colleagues either one-to-one or at conferences, and have your own continuous feedback and troubleshooting mechanisms in place. More often than not, it will be the little details that run you aground.

### *QUESTION 10: How will I know if things are working well?*

In today's world of public accountability and corporate need to show return on investment, evaluation is an inescapable task for educators and trainers alike. We outline here five factors to consider as you plan an evaluation strategy.

First, evaluation is an umbrella process; it focuses on a broad range of issues, rather than on the particular aspect of testing learners to assess their skill, attitude and knowledge acquisition. Two practical books by American program planning and training specialists (Angelo & Cross, 1993; Jacobs & Chase, 1992) are listed in the References so that you can explore the complexities of test construction and grading issues.

Second, the addition of technologies to a program always adds either direct or indirect costs, and the actual impact of the technologies may be quite different from the "hype" associated with them. You need to be brave and clear-eyed!

Third, an evaluation strategy is designed to gather data needed to make decisions about whether to (1) continue a program or (2) improve it. Anthony Carnevale, Leila Gainer and Ann Meltzer, American trainers and consultants in workplace training, explain that, if the decision relates to improvement, you need to gather data on the strengths and weaknesses of the workshop or course, who gained the most from attending and future marketing strategies. If the decision relates to the continuation of a program, you need to gather data on the extent to which the program objectives were appropriate for the original problem (Was the problem identified correctly in the first place?) and, if so, the extent to which the program objectives were met by the participants (Carnevale, Gainer, & Meltzer, 1990).

Fourth, many "evaluations" seek what are called "happiness ratings." You have probably completed a short questionnaire at the end of a workshop that asked you what you liked and disliked, and what things you would want to change, and so on. What is being sought here is your general reaction. That response is classified by Donald Kirkpatrick, one of the gurus of training evaluation in North America, as only the first level of evaluation. He specifies three more levels because, in his words,

> ... even though [the trainer] has done a masterful job of measuring the reaction of the group, [he or she] still has no assurance that any learning has taken place. Neither has [he or she] any indication that the behavior of the participants will change because of the training program. And still farther away is any indication of the results that can be attributed to the training program.
>
> *(Kirkpatrick, 1959, p.8)*

ADAPT KIRKPATRICK AND USE THESE QUESTIONS TO CLARIFY THE FOCUS OF YOUR EVALUATION.

- DID THEY LIKE IT? (LEVEL 1: REACTION)
- DID THEY LEARN ANYTHING NEW? (LEVEL 2: LEARNING)
- CAN THEY ACTUALLY DO ANYTHING NEW? (LEVEL 3: BEHAVIOR)
- DID THE COMPANY OR INSTITUTION GET A RETURN ON ITS INVESTMENT? (LEVEL 4: RESULTS)

Kirkpatrick's four levels of evaluation are: reaction, learning, behavior and results.

Our fifth and final factor builds on the fourth one and relates to the overall theme of clarity in evaluation. Regardless of the program evaluation level required, you need to design data-gathering tools that reduce "fuzziness," bias and answers that seek approval. To reduce fuzziness (you can't accurately assess how they felt or what they did), use only a few open-ended questions and look for how often (a frequency measure) or how strongly (an impact measure) something was experienced. For example, use scales from "almost always" to "almost never," or from "a lot" to "very little." To reduce bias and approval-seeking behavior, avoid leading questions, enable anonymous responses and provide honest alternatives in any multiple-choice questions. For example, avoid creating a situation where learners feel compelled to indicate that they or their instructor are paragons of virtue, and let them indicate the downside as well as the up, for example: "I couldn't operate the equipment very easily."

LEAVE 10 MINUTES AT THE END OF EACH SESSION TO ALLOW FOR OPEN DISCUSSION ABOUT WHAT IS WORKING WELL AND WHAT IS NOT WORKING WELL IN THE OPINION OF THE LEARNERS.

To increase your chances of clarity and accuracy in data collection, try pilot-testing the data-gathering tool, e.g., a questionnaire, and interviewing the participants and others who have a stake in your work. You may be surprised at the good things you hear, and you may get some new and constructive ideas for improvement.

## CONCLUSION

We've covered a lot of territory and tasks in this chapter: selecting a model of teaching, specifying levels and objectives of learning and addressing 10 key planning questions. We hope you feel more secure about the basics of how to plan an instructional response for what is always a complex set of factors in any training or educational setting. Now it is time to see some concrete details; to see how these ideas are implemented.

You will find more ideas in Chapter 5 and in the Resource Kit for this book.

# References

Angelo, T. A., & Cross, K. P. (1993). *Classroom assessment techniques: A handbook for college teachers*. San Francisco, CA: Jossey-Bass.

Bloom, B. S. (Ed.) et al. (1956). *Taxonomy of educational objectives: Handbook I, Cognitive domain*. New York, NY: David Mackay Co.

Carnevale, A. P., Gainer, L. J., & Meltzer, A. S. (1990). *Workplace basics training manual*. San Francisco, CA: Jossey-Bass.

Cranton, P. (1989). *Planning instruction for adult learners*. Toronto, ON: Wall & Thompson.

Cross, K. P. (1987). The role of schools. In R. M. Smith (Ed.), *Theory building for learning how to learn* (pp. 95-97). Chicago, IL: Educational Studies Press.

Gronlund, N. E. (1991). *How to write and use instructional objectives* (4th ed.). New York, NY: Macmillan.

Hannum, W. (1990). *The application of emerging training technology.* Alexandria, VA: American Society of Training and Development.

Jacobs, L. C., & Chase, C. I. (1992). *Developing and using tests effectively: A guide for faculty*. San Francisco, CA: Jossey-Bass.

Kirkpatrick, D. L. (1959, 1960). Techniques for evaluating training programs, parts 1-4. *Journal of the American Society of Training Directors, 13*(11 & 12), *14*(1 & 2).

MacKeracher, D. (1996). *Making sense of adult learning*. Toronto, ON: Culture Concepts.

Myers, C., & Jones, T. B. (1993). *Promoting active learning: Strategies for the college classroom.* San Francisco, CA: Jossey-Bass.

Percival, A. (1994). *Practising theory: A guide to becoming an effective adult education programmer.* Saskatoon, SA: University of Saskatchewan, Extension Division.

Pratt, D. (1992). Conceptions of teaching. *Adult Education Quarterly, 42*(4), 203-220.

Renner, P. (1988). *The quick instructional planner*. Vancouver, BC: Training Associates.

Silberman, M. (1990). *Active training: A handbook of techniques, designs, case examples and tips.* New York, NY: Lexington Books.

Sork, T., & Caffarella, R. (1994). Planning programs for adults. In S. B. Merriam & P. M. Cunningham (Eds.), *Handbook of adult and continuing education* (pp. 233-245). San Francisco, CA: Jossey-Bass.

# Chapter 5

# What Does the Real Action Look Like?

*It doesn't matter if you have a limousine or a compact car; they both need an engine, wheels, tires, gas and a driver to get into action.*

**THÉRÈSE LAMY,**
SED, MONTRÉAL, QUÉBEC

## INTRODUCTION

There are many forms of action in education and training; like cars, they need the same basic elements to get them moving. A well-designed manual for learners is the educational equivalent of a car. It is the vehicle to help a learner reach the destination with safety and efficiency. When you have finished this chapter, you will be able to explain with examples the functions of 10 core elements in a manual and identify three key themes in producing a manual.

This chapter enables you to see how the information in Chapters 2 to 4 gets transferred into practice, and integrates materials from Chapters 6 to 9. We believe that core elements of content and the creation process apply to the design of a learner's manual for any communications technology context, whether it is a two-page manual for a short training event or a more lengthy document for a semester-long course.

The chapter has three sections: a definition, core elements and helpful production hints.

## WHAT IS A LEARNER'S MANUAL?

What is a learner's manual? It is a document that provides a range of content and process information designed to cover all the aspects of the learning experience—from the first to the last day. An effective manual will help the learner feel competent and connected, without feeling that every minute of her or his time is rigidly prescribed.

This definition contains two key words: content and process. Content refers to what is being studied in the course or workshop, for example, pediatric nursing or conflict resolution skills. Process refers to how the learners and instructor work their way through the content, for example, role plays, seminars, library research or interviews with experts.

Two points need explanation before we proceed. First, the word *course* is used as a generic term to include workshops, seminars and other training events. Second, we focus on a print-based manual for use with one or more of

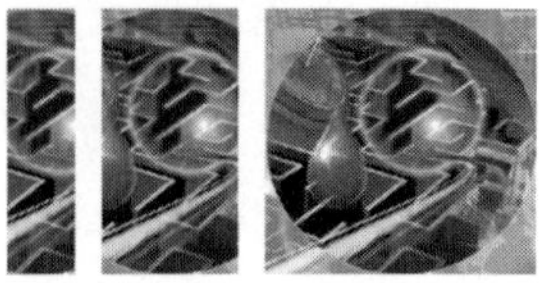

IF YOU ARE ABLE TO USE THE INTERNET OR SOME OTHER FORM OF COMPUTER-BASED SUPPORT, SOME ELEMENTS OF THE MANUAL CAN BE PROVIDED ELECTRONICALLY.

In the Resource Kit, you will see an example of a print-based learner's manual from the university environment and obtain references to manuals from other sectors.

the technologies in Part 2 of this book. Print is still the most widely used and accessible medium across a variety of training and educational settings. However, the same components need to be considered for a networked environment, as Margaret Haughey and Terry Anderson (1998) explain in their book, *Networked Learning: The Pedagogy of the Internet.*

Regardless of whether you are designing a manual for a three-day, job-skill upgrading workshop or a three-month graduate course, you will do well to use the core elements that we outline here. The "value-added" aspect is that a manual can be designed for use by both the learners and you, thus saving extra effort, as well as modeling "being up-front" with adult learners.

## WHAT IS IN A LEARNER'S MANUAL?

Carolyn Nilson (1989), a training consultant for North American companies, listed a key guideline for any publication that has to help learners steer their way through all the parts of a workshop or course without feeling overwhelmed by or deprived of information: "... [it] has to meet the 'necessary and sufficient' test—that is, only the necessary information and all of the sufficient information... [it] should never be an information 'dump' " (p. 175).

We could not agree more! A fine balance is needed; indeed, the issue of balance goes beyond the selection and organization of information to how that information is displayed. What does a "balanced" manual contain? The balance lies in what you explain up front, and what you leave to be negotiated during the course.

Table 5.1 shows the 10 elements that we believe meet Nilson's criteria. We now describe what each of these elements contains.

**TABLE 5.1:** CORE ELEMENTS OF A LEARNER'S MANUAL

| |
|---|
| **Contents Page** |
| **Part 1: General Guidance** |
| **1.** Introduction |
| **2.** Objectives |
| **3.** Topic structure |
| **4.** Learning process |
| **5.** Participant information |
| **6.** Resources |
| **7.** Learning assessment |
| **8.** Interpersonal communication skills |
| **Part 2: Specific Topics** |
| **9.** Topic 1, 2, 3, etc. |
| **Part 3: Feedback** |
| **10.** Course evaluation forms |

## Contents Page

We want to make just one point here, because you may not have access to sophisticated print production facilities and staff to do detailed clerical work. Arrange the contents page so that you can change any elements without having to alter the whole page sequence.

Gain flexibility by paginating each of the three parts in its own sequence. If you decide to include a few articles for reproduction within each topic and don't want to place them in a separate collection, the printing staff will expect you to mark every page in a non-copiable blue number to show the correct sequence. When you add or change readings, pagination changes can be made faster if each sequence is kept as short as possible. Make sure that all copyright clearance procedures are completed.

## Part 1: General Guidance

This part contains the information needed to answer the learner's initial "what, why, when, how and who" questions. More detailed discussion about the course content and process is contained in Part 2.

## Introduction

This is the learner's entrance into the course, and it should be short and sweet. By that we mean engaging, lively and anticipatory. Tell the reader in general terms about the course rationale, content and process. Include a quotation or an anecdote to grab attention and model an interactive style. The tone you set here is very important: it sets up certain reactions in the learner's mind and heart. You want those reactions to be energizing, especially if the learner has just sat down at the kitchen table at 10 p.m. after a long day.

## Objectives

Now the detail begins. Use, on average, four to six objectives to cover the whole course. We explained in Chapter 4 how to write objectives that are clear and specific about the intended outcomes. At this point, the reader may decide that this course is not what he or she expected, withdraw their registration and try another course—if that is an option. That's okay, better now than later.

Since you don't want to overwhelm the learner, include the specific objectives for each topic in Part 2 of the manual.

## Topic Structure

Here you indicate the landscape of the content and how the learner will travel over it. You don't want to overwhelm the reader with lots of topics, otherwise she or he will think it's a marathon. Use about six to eight broad topics, and, if necessary, use subtopics. Think about various visual ways to display the structure. For example, a diagram or concept map of topics drawn in non-linear directions is an effective way to show how the content is interlinked as a body of knowledge and/or skill. A key question is how to sequence the content, and from that, the topic structure, so that it makes practical sense to the learner.

You can sequence the content in a number of ways, depending on, for example, the rationale for the course and the needs of the learners. Derek Rowntree, an instructional designer based at The Open University in Milton Keynes, England, lists nine ways in which you can sequence the content. They are summarized in Table 5.2 (Rowntree, 1994, p. 96).

The chronological sequence is often used in survey courses, but it can be irrelevant and tedious for learners needing to "cut to the chase" and get up-to-date information. A problem-centered sequence, or a thematic one, keeps the

**TABLE 5.2:** CONTENT SEQUENCE METHODS

1. Random (no rationale at all)
2. Chronological (how things developed historically)
3. Place-to-place (separate areas within one broad area)
4. Concentric circles (each old topic folded into each new one)
5. Causal sequence (cause and effect)
6. Structural logic (foundation knowledge gained first)
7. Problem-centered (selection of key problems)
8. Spiral sequence (re-examine earlier content, but with more complexity)
9. Backward chaining (when it's useful to learn the last skill first)

focus on the key issues addressed in the course. If the course is skill-centered, you may need to use a backward chain sequence in which you teach "the last one first, then the second to last, and so on" (Rowntree, 1994, p. 96). For example, teach a radio dispatcher the key skills for responding to emergencies, then go back to the skill sets that enhance those responses. If the learners need to acquire certain skills or concepts first before applying them in practical settings, then you can decide if all the concepts get treated first before sending the learners out into the complexities of the real world, or if the concepts are introduced in parallel with the practical, real-world activity.

## Learning Process

In this section you tell the learner, in general terms, about what is involved in learning. They have a right to know what is expected of them, not just in terms of assignments, but also in terms of how learning happens and how they interact with peers in the course. Some learners, for example, may have no idea of the general, inside-their-head processes that produce good learning. Other learners may expect a course in which you give lectures and it is their job to listen, copy down and repeat. If you explain the basics about how your model of teaching translates into practice, the learners know what to expect and may even see an opportunity to improve their learning skills.

Our beliefs about productive learning and adult characteristics prompt us to recommend an explanation to learners that looks something like this:

> You are responsible for constructing your own meanings and interpretations, but we will jointly explore topics and test theories in real-life situations and also against our own practical knowledge. So, rather than only listening to other people's ideas and repeating them, you will be able to discuss concepts, theories and principles, examine the assumptions that you bring to this course, reflect on your own life experience, analyze paradoxes and ambiguities in knowledge, assess your learning, contribute actively to class discussions and get support from class members.

Is this explanation congruent with your values as a trainer or educator?

Because we believe that it is important to avoid spending valuable interactive class time in transmitting information, this section of the manual should also contain a note about how information acquisition and its processing are integrated: (1) before-class reading, thinking and exercises are designed to give a basic understanding of the new information; and (2) in-class, collaborative activities are designed to teach you to apply, analyze, evaluate and synthesize new knowledge (the higher learning levels of the Cognitive Domain that we outlined in Chapter 4).

IF YOUR REALITY DOES NOT INCLUDE MUCH TIME FOR PRE-CLASS INFORMATION ACQUISITION, BUILD TIME FOR IT IN THE CLASS.

Think about including an explanatory and reassuring note about the inevitable anxiety the learner may experience during the course. Such stress may occur when adults impose high standards on themselves; are expected to question their cherished assumptions, or even drop old, unhelpful attitudes; or rapidly reach a level of skill mandated by their employer. We believe that naming the inevitable stresses in significant learning goes halfway to alleviating them.

## Participant Information

If you are going to role-model a learner-sensitive approach and use collaborative learning strategies, you and all the participants need to know some basics about one another. In-class exercises can help, but reflective, written information is helpful too. We suggest that you:

1. Give information about yourself that is more than a perfunctory statement about your job description. The learners have a right to know what you bring to the course.
2. Provide one or two bio-data sheets that learners can quickly complete and return to you by fax, by hand or by e-mail. The sheets can ask for brief notes on prior experience with the course content, ideas on how each learner thinks she or he learns best, what he or she wants from the course, and how class peers might best help in the learning process.
3. Describe actual or potential guest experts who have been invited to the course, e.g., some brief bio-information.

## Resources

Print and resources in other formats, both essential and optional, should be listed. Other formats can include audio-visual and the Internet, but we suggest you provide a warning about the unrefereed quality of much of the Internet material (that it has not been reviewed by experts to decide whether it is good enough to be published). We also note that learners do not like to read too much material on screen and that downloading a lot of material to print and read is time-consuming.

IF GUEST EXPERTS ARE TO FORM PART OF THE RESOURCES, THEN A FEW NOTES ON EFFECTIVE INTERVIEWING MAY BE HELPFUL FOR THE PARTICIPANTS.

## Learning Assessment

This section should describe, in as much detail as possible, what kind of evidence of learning will be needed and when. We don't suggest that you decide every single detail, because that wouldn't help the learner act in constructive and responsible ways. What you can do is set out the basics and then negotiate with the class as a whole, or individually, at the appropriate time, the kind of assessment that will balance learner needs and academic standards.

Here are the basics from which you can choose, depending on the length and type of your course:

1. The number and sequence of, and rationale for, the assignments (Can the learner choose the topic? How do the assignments build on each other?).
2. The formal criteria to be used for measuring skill and/or knowledge development before, during and after the course.
3. A warning note about copyright and plagiarism.
4. Guidance about how the learner can reflect on and informally grade her or his work before sending it to you.

These basics help develop learner responsibility as well as many learning-to-learn skills. They also reflect one aspect of being learner-sensitive. For various good reasons, a learner may not be able to spend the optimum time on an assignment and therefore expects a lower grade. If you both know that, you will both save time and agony!

### Interpersonal Communication Skills

Not every learner is aware of what is involved in effective communication. The use of any communications technology emphasizes the need for interpersonal skills, because for each technology there is some reduction in the information available to help listeners and viewers interpret and respond in helpful ways.

At minimum, give advice on how to listen, speak, not dominate, show personal courtesies and get past the initial awkwardness of not being in the same geographic and/or time place as everyone else. Chapters 7 to 9 (Part 2) provide examples of such advice that are specific to each technology.

### Part 2: Specific Topics

Part 2 of the manual helps the learner work through each topic in the program.

Here are the five basic components:

- A short, engaging title, such as a question (the format we use in this book).
- An attention-getting introduction. Describe how the topic links with the previous topic. Be brief and use a quotation, a question, a real-world problem or a provocative comment to create a "need to know."
- Learning objectives that describe as accurately as possible intended learning outcomes. A narrative paragraph is more informal than objectives in point form, but either is appropriate depending on your circumstances.
- An outline of suggested basic activities for each session, on the understanding that these are not written in stone. If you decide to have the learners draft plans for activities in each class (with your guidance), then the details will have to be described in the prior class, or faxed or e-mailed to the learners at an appropriate time.

Try to design whole-class and small-group activities so that your role as instructor is to help learners confirm or correct their new learning, share experiences, discuss critically the results of their reading and thinking, and solve some real-world problems (see Chapter 4). When learners know that you are not the discussion traffic cop, you may be delighted with what you hear!

- A list of the resources the learners need for each session, with a separate listing of any additional resources that can be pursued later.

SEPARATE THE ACTIVITIES INTO THOSE THAT ARE CARRIED OUT (USUALLY ALONE) BEFORE THE WHOLE GROUP MEETS, AND THOSE LARGE- AND SMALL-GROUP ACTIVITIES THAT BUILD ON THE LEARNING DONE PRIOR TO CLASS. THE INDIVIDUAL, PRE-SESSION ACTIVITIES SUCH AS GUIDED READING OR REAL-WORLD INVESTIGATIONS CAN FUNCTION AT THOSE LOWER LEVELS OF BLOOM'S COGNITIVE DOMAIN, FOR EXAMPLE, THE ACTIVITIES CAN FOCUS ON THE UNDERSTANDING OF BASICS AND THE BEGINNINGS OF APPLICATION (REFER TO CHAPTER 4: LEVELS AND OBJECTIVES OF LEARNING).

The amount of detail in Part 2 will vary depending on your preferred model of interacting with learners, the practical reality of your training or educational environment and the capacity of the communications technology for fast and frequent interaction. The "necessary and sufficient" information you provide here is a matter of balance. This time the balance lies in what you indicate is pre-class and in-class activity (what the learner does independently and interdependently). The amount of detail you give here also depends on how often and easily you can talk with learners to negotiate aspects of the course process.

## Part 3: Feedback

We outlined general goals of evaluation in Chapter 4, so now it is time to provide some practical steps and hints. Evaluator Floyd Fowler (1993), based at the University of Massachusetts at Boston, reminds us how important it is to know exactly what needs to be assessed: "Deciding what is to be measured ... may seem simple and self-evident, but it is a step that is often overlooked, to the detriment of the results" (p. 95). Rosemary Caffarella (1994), an adult educator and program planner based at the University of Northern Colorado, suggests that there are seven basic steps to planning effective feedback. We believe that her steps are broad enough to apply across all training and educational settings.

1. Become very clear about why you need the evaluation done.
2. Specify who and what are under scrutiny—instructor, learners, cost-effectiveness, company goals?
3. Decide on which kinds of data will best respond to the need and be most easily collected.
4. Select the strategy for data collection and analysis.
5. Know how you will judge which data to use for the final analyses.
6. Look for data about failures.
7. Take care in how you present the results; again, balance is needed—use only "necessary and sufficient" data.

We now offer eight suggestions toward the production of a useful form or questionnaire for collecting data. The better-looking and more user-friendly the tool, the greater the chance that you will get more forms returned with thoughtful comments.

SOME INSTRUCTORS PROVIDE REPRINTS OF ARTICLES OR COPIES OF COMPANY POLICIES IN THE LIST OF RESOURCES IF THEY ARE AT ALL CONCERNED ABOUT THE LEARNERS' ABILITY TO ACCESS THE MATERIAL.

1. Divide the form into logical sections so that the learner can follow a train of thought from the specific to the general.
2. Give plenty of white space—don't clutter the page.

3. Enable honest, frank responses. The learner may have low self-esteem, or carry negative feelings, or have experienced problems during the course that bore no relationship to what you did. If they think that you expect only successful learners to respond, they will probably clam up.
4. Provide for the fast selection of one choice. Avoid many open-ended questions—they usually don't get answered.
5. Make room for spontaneous comments.
6. Look for how often the participants experienced certain things, or how useful they judge course components to be. Such scores are more valid than levels of enjoyment ratings.
7. Design "necessary and sufficient" questions that can be answered in total in 10 minutes. You can always interview participants later to flesh out their responses.
8. Pilot-test the form first with two or three people before you field-test it with a sample of expected respondents. Take note of their reactions; you are too close to see the questionnaire as they do.

Having outlined the functions of the 10 core elements in a manual, it is time to summarize the key points for producing a manual.

## HOW DO I PRODUCE THE BEST POSSIBLE MANUAL?

THERE ARE SOME EXCELLENT BOOKS PUBLISHED ON PRODUCING MULTIFORMAT MANUALS; WE LIST SOME OF THEM IN THE FURTHER READINGS SECTION.

We believe that teamwork, design and voice are the three key themes in producing a manual. The integrative goal of all three themes is style. Style goes beyond the "necessary and sufficient" criteria to include a strong interpersonal quality and an attractive appearance.

### Teamwork

We cannot stress enough the advantages of teamwork for the design and production of a manual. It is unrealistic to expect one instructor to have all the skill sets needed to turn out a high-quality package.

Table 5.3 shows the team skills needed to produce quality learning manuals.

NOT EVERYONE CAN HAVE A NINE-PERSON TEAM, BUT IF YOU'RE SERIOUS ABOUT QUALITY, A QUARTET OF INSTRUCTOR, LEARNING DESIGNER, EDITOR AND GRAPHIC DESIGNER IS A MINIMUM REQUIREMENT.

**TABLE 5.3:** TEAM SKILLS FOR QUALITY MANUAL PRODUCTION

1. Production manager: Oversees whole process and keeps people on deadlines.
2. Instructor/s: Provide/s content expertise.
3. Learning designer: Guides instructor and acts as learner advocate.
4. Editor: Ensures consistency and quality of communication in materials.
5. Librarian: Checks for resources access, accuracy, currency and duplication.
6. Multimedia producers: Design formats in addition to paper text.
7. Reviewers : External experts assess the content as written by the instructor.
8. Graphic designer: Renders text and other resources into consistent, reader-friendly layout.
9. Word processor: If the instructor is slow on the keyboard, the manager may assign a competent person to help.

## Design

As soon as they see your manual, learners will make some judgment about how you regard them, as well as what you think about learning and instructing. A manual that has its own subtle but insistent style will immediately create a positive impression.

Style, regarding appearance, means, for example, that the pages show

- text in a serif font (letters with little "feet")
- substantial margins (2-inch-wide margins, or one margin 2.5 inches and the other 1.5 inches), with only the left margin justified (text in a straight line)
- clear access devices into the text (headings, paragraphs)

At all costs, reduce the clutter; you don't have to use a large number of type fonts, for example, or cover the page with icons or clip art.

This book is an example of how a professional graphic designer transformed our manuscript into an effective communication tool. His skill makes the design almost transparent; you are aware only of how good the book feels. When you look more closely, you can see how the amount of white space avoids visual clutter, the headings and margin devices direct your attention, and the margin widths and typeface help your brain perceive relevant information.

Robin Williams, a graphic designer based in California, published, in 1994, a witty and now very popular guide, *The Non-Designer's Design Book,* which stresses the importance of being able to name the four basic principles of graphic design: contrast, repetition, creative but consistent alignment of text, and visual closeness of related items. Such books are helpful to the novice, even to help that person name the problem in a page layout; but you can never replace the skill of a professional graphic designer.

THE IRONY IS THAT IT TAKES NO EFFORT AT ALL TO CREATE A NEGATIVE IMPRESSION, AND EVERY EFFORT TO MAKE A GOOD ONE! WE RECOMMEND THAT YOU USE THE SERVICES OF A PROFESSIONAL GRAPHIC DESIGNER TO ESTABLISH YOUR "HOUSE STYLE" (THE LAYOUT OF YOUR COMPANY OR INSTITUTIONAL MATERIALS, SINCE THE RECOGNITION FACTOR APPLIES TO EDUCATIONAL MATERIALS). ONCE THE HOUSE STYLE HAS BEEN FIXED, USE IT AS A TEMPLATE. IF YOU CANNOT ENGAGE SUCH PROFESSIONAL SKILLS, TRY TO FIND EXAMPLES OF EXCELLENCE ELSEWHERE AND FOLLOW THEIR LAYOUT.

## Voice

Voice refers to the tone and directness with which you "talk" with learners. Often the biggest task for a learning designer in working with an instructor is to help her or him make the shift from "sage on the stage" to "guide on the side." Part of that change depends on how the learner is addressed.

Instructors sometimes have to be guided to use a personal, direct and informal style in their voice. Sentences or commands, such as, "The learners are expected to produce three papers for the instructor," do not help to break down the psychological distance between a new learner and the grade-giving instructor. It is much more productive to say: "You will write three papers, and I will guide you once you are ready to begin work." Here is another example of not recognizing the processes in adult learning, especially the ones associated with mistakes and anxieties. Rather than saying, "If you have a question, call the instructor at this number," say or write, "When you want to talk things over and ask questions, call this voice-mail number at any hour, and I'll return your call as soon as possible." The second "invitation" sends a subtle signal that questions are expected, not avoided or judged as a weakness.

KEEP YOURSELF IN MIND AS YOU DEVELOP THE MANUAL: WOULD YOU LIKE TO USE IT FOR THREE HOURS OR THREE MONTHS?

When a learning event is tied to a performance appraisal, it is particularly critical that the "advising voice" in the manual be separate from the "judgment voice" that appears when it is time to assess the learning. Learners deserve all the psychological space and practical help they can get to maximize their chance of success.

## CONCLUSION

In this chapter we explained the functions of the 10 elements in a manual and offered you three guidelines that work toward a stylish and balanced product. We hope you feel prepared now to apply the ideas about learners and learning that you read in Chapters 2 to 5 toward the effective use of the three technologies introduced in Part 2.

# References

Caffarella, R. S. (1994). *Planning programs for adult learners: A practical guide for educators, trainers, and staff developers.* San Francisco, CA: Jossey-Bass.

Fowler, F. (1993). *Survey research methods* (2nd ed.). Newbury Park, CA: Sage.

Haughey, M., & Anderson, T. (1998). *Networked Learning: The pedagogy of the Internet.* Montréal, QC: Chenelière/McGraw-Hill.

Nilson, C. (1989). *Training program workbook and kit.* Englewood Cliffs, NJ: Prentice-Hall.

Rowntree, D. (1994). *Preparing materials for open, distance and flexible learning: An action guide for teachers and trainers.* London, UK: Kogan Page.

Williams, R. (1994). *The non-designer's design book: Design and typographic principles for the visual novice.* Berkeley, CA: Peachpit Press.

# PART 2

# WHAT ARE THE KEY ISSUES IN USING THE TECHNOLOGIES?

In Part 1 we described key points about learners and how they learn and highlighted essential features of the classroom environments we can create to enable them to achieve their learning goals. Part 2 is designed to link these more theoretical concepts to the practical realities of the Information Highway.

In Chapter 6 we explore the meanings of the term *Information Highway* and their implications for instructors. In Chapters 7, 8 and 9, the opportunities offered by audio and audiographic, networked and compressed video learning technologies, respectively are examined. Each chapter consists of five sections:

- A brief *Introduction* states the learning goals that underlie the chapter.
- The *Description* sets out the physical elements of the technology in print and through diagrams.
- The *Special Features* section describes the benefits that can be achieved by using that mode of learning and highlights topics relevant to the appropriate instructional use of the technology.
- *Appropriate Use* summarizes techniques that instructors can use before, during and after their use of technology in the classroom to optimize learning.
- *Success Stories* are drawn from the public and private sectors and are based on more lengthy materials provided in other books in the Series.

Chapter 10 "brings it all together" by featuring what we consider to be the 10 most important points made in the book and ends with a lighthearted summary of the perils that befall us all, no matter how we try to avoid them!

*References* are provided at the end of each chapter, and a *Further Readings* section is provided at the end of Part 2 as a gateway to the rich literature on each type of learning. A *Contact Name* is provided for each success story.

# Chapter 6

# How Do We See the Information Highway?

*The potential of the Information Highway for learners around the world is enormous. In partnership with our learners, we instructors need to create a vision of how that potential becomes reality.*

BARBARA SPRONK,
INTERNATIONAL EXTENSION COLLEGE,
CAMBRIDGE, ENGLAND

## INTRODUCTION

The Information Highway offers us a number of different technical tools that, when used appropriately, can support the learning models and methods described in Part 1. By taking advantage of the Information Highway, we will be able to achieve a number of benefits for our learners.

We can improve access for learners isolated by geography: Audio Learning (Chapter 7) is ideally suited to achieving that purpose because telephones are readily available in many parts of the world. We can improve learner access to scarce expertise: Networked Learning (Chapter 8) is a particularly strong means to that end because experts and learners do not have to be on-line at the same time. We can serve new groups of learners: Those who have a high need for social presence and who find other technologies inhibiting are often ideally served by Compressed Video Learning technologies (Chapter 9).

Increasingly, we are able to draw upon more than one of these technologies in a seminar or course depending on the needs of our students. Chapter 10 will synthesize points made throughout the book on this issue.

When you finish reading this chapter, you will know how the term *Information Highway* is defined and some of its social, economic and educational implications for you as an instructor. You will have explored eight opportunities that Information Highway technologies offer and reviewed the key factors and issues for choosing among the technologies.

## WHAT DOES THE INFORMATION HIGHWAY MEAN FOR INSTRUCTORS?

Classroom instructors are finding meanings for the term *Information Highway* in collaboration with many other public and private sector groups in society. Interested stakeholders include the educational, artistic and creative communities; telecommunications, broadcasting and information technology industries and institutions; and consumer and labor organizations. One forum for discussion among these groups in Canada, as in many other countries, has been a public policy process.

In 1994, Industry Canada established an advisory group, the Information Highway Advisory Council (IHAC), to recommend to the federal government how to deal with 15 policy issues arising from the Information Highway. Learning and training issues were addressed by IHAC, which itself was counseled by an 11-member Learning and Training Working Group. Its work, and that of similar bodies in other countries, is an important context for our future classrooms.

DEFINITION The term *Information Highway* has a specific technical meaning. IHAC defines the term according to current practice in Canada and other countries.

> The term [Information Highway] flows from the convergence of once-separate communications [telephone and television] and computing systems into a single global network of networks.
>
> *(IHAC, 1995, September, p. 2)*

In other words, the conversion of all communication signals to the digital format will make it possible for telephones to become television terminals and for television sets to become computers—and vice versa.

Different words are used to refer to this same set of converging technologies. In the United States, for example, Chris Dede (1994), a professor and researcher at George Mason University Graduate School of Education in Fairfax, Virginia, notes that the term *National Information Infrastructure* is employed, while in the United Kingdom, Information Superhighway, or Superhighways for Education, are the more common language (Department for Education and Employment, 1995). We believe they all share the common technical meaning we presented earlier in this section and give rise to the same social, economic and educational connotations.

For us, the Information Highway is more than the Internet. It consists of all the distributed, interactive technologies, including audioconferencing, computer Networked Learning and compressed videoconferencing. Internet advocates predict that it will soon support Audio, Audiographic and Compressed Video Learning, as well as Networked Learning through computers, and that telephone and television networks will be overtaken or bypassed by the Internet. However, telephone and television network suppliers are rapidly developing competing products for their networks and are planning to interconnect their networks to the Internet. Thus, instructors and learners will have, in theory, an ever-widening range of technical infrastructures available. In practice, the range may be limited by institutional policies and budget or geography.

A critical technical issue related to the effective use of the Information Highway for learning, especially on the Internet, is the ability to locate content. User-friendly, accessible software systems are essential. Browsers and search engines enable users to navigate the Internet to find the content they want. You may already be aware of how computer-based library services, for example, have changed, and how your own research skills are adapting in order to locate content on the Information Highway.

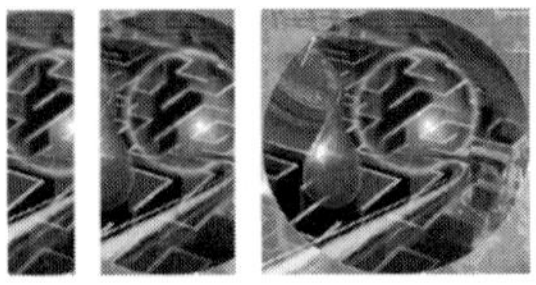

IF YOU HAVE THE CHANCE TO CHOOSE AMONG DIFFERENT NETWORKS, CONSIDER FACTORS SUCH AS RELIABILITY AND SERVICE SUPPORT. RIGHT NOW, WE WILL EXAGGERATE TO MAKE A POINT: "NOBODY IS IN CONTROL" OF THE INTERNET, SO THERE IS NO ONE SERVICE AGENCY THAT TROUBLESHOOTS PROBLEMS. YOU CAN, HOWEVER, TURN TO YOUR TELEPHONE OR CABLE COMPANY AS A SOLE VENDOR ACCOUNTABLE TO YOU FOR RELIABLE SERVICE.

IMPLICATIONS Let's examine some of the social, economic and educational implications of this new technical environment.

New social relationships are possible on the Information Highway between the producers and consumers of content. Historically, subject matter experts wrote books, which were available for private purchase from bookstores or for public use through libraries. Most learners would not expect to come in contact with such experts until graduate school, at the earliest. Now, subject matter experts may well have public e-mail addresses, may respond to questions submitted on the Internet and may give guest lectures in audio or video learning sessions.

The social distinction between the provider (instructor) and consumer (learner) categories is blurring. Both report that the absence of visual cues in environments such as Audio or Networked Learning break down some of the power that body language can impose on a group. Learners report being less intimidated about participating in discussions when they don't "feel the professor staring down at them."

The social relationship between learners is also changing. Special-needs learners, for example, can be part of a classroom environment using any of several technologies. They can also be linked with one another across great distances, a particularly important feature if there is no peer in their community with the same challenge. "The opportunity to share hopes, dreams and frustrations with others sharing the same physical and mental limitations was very important for the six students who participated," reports Susan Alcorn MacKay, Coordinator, Special Needs Center, Cambrian College (Roberts, 1998).

The economic implications of the Information Highway are also important to consider. Improved economic competitiveness and job creation are goals the Information Highway can help realize in several ways. One, noted by IHAC, is that jobs will be created in the information and communications sector if education and business make more use of Information Highway technologies. Second, learning and training productivity gains are achievable through the appropriate use of technology. Third, since there is a documented relationship between high levels of education, literacy and economic success, improved education and training systems will strengthen private sector activity and national economic strength. The government of the United Kingdom, in launching its "Technology Foresight" inquiry, is typical of many governments that are exploring the contribution science, engineering and technology can make to the competitiveness of businesses. Eddie Brittain (1996), an official in the Department for Education and Employment in London, England, notes that learning technologies can facilitate efficient knowledge transfer in science, engineering and technology between the public and private sectors, which in turn will enhance national economic competitiveness.

Lastly, since this book is largely devoted to the educational implications of technology, we should focus on the appropriateness of the highway metaphor. As colleagues such as Heather Menzies (1996) at Carleton University in Ottawa have pointed out, the word *highway* connotes speed, linear travel, volume and efficiency. Some might add gridlock and traffic jam to that list! It is therefore not an accurate metaphor for learning, since most learning takes place in a non-linear fashion that is not always best measured by its efficiency.

The highway metaphor is also not applicable to all the technologies that make up the Information Highway. Telephone lines and television channels, for example, are separate roads, with highly variable capacities to support volume and speed. The difference between unpaved country lanes and multilane autobahns comes to mind. Moreover, the Internet is a highly decentralized and sometimes slow structure—hence the coining of the term [World Wide] Web to describe one of its components.

In spite of these limitations, we have chosen to use the term *Information Highway* in this book and in this Series because we believe that the metaphor is a useful shorthand to describe the technical trend to network convergence—toward an integration of information and communications services that will provide a new and more powerful road to support learning. We therefore make four practical assumptions about linking the classroom and the Information Highway:

- The telephone, computer and television are becoming more similar and interconnectable across small or great distances.
- They are becoming more and more common in every classroom, thus blurring the conventional distinction between classroom and distance learning.
- They offer exciting learning opportunities if used appropriately.
- The key to their effectiveness as learning support tools is that they are used in ways that facilitate human interaction and active learning.

## WHAT OPPORTUNITIES DOES THE INFORMATION HIGHWAY OFFER IN THE CLASSROOM?

As instructors ourselves, we believe that these practical beliefs point the way to a number of opportunities in our classrooms. We highlight eight; you may well think of others. The eight are competencies, timing, learner expectations, new roles, access, cost, competition and partnerships.

COMPETENCIES First and foremost, we have the opportunity to learn new ways of teaching and learning and to participate actively in the debate about the roles of Information Highway technologies in the classroom once we acquire the knowledge and skills to use them effectively. Two colleagues indicate the depth of the opportunity and the critical role that knowledgeable instructors can play.

Gilles Séguin, director of Membership Services at the Association of Canadian Community Colleges (ACCC), reports

> ... [that] the estimated 30,000 faculty in Canadian community colleges want more information about the Information Highway and its impacts on learning and the role of professors. We know that change is coming and we want our members to feel that they are affecting the change—not being overwhelmed by an outside force over which they have no control.

David McIntyre, coordinator of The Conference Board of Canada's Canadian Training Directors Forum, believes that "educators and trainers have not 'bought in' to the idea that the Information Highway will be a primary delivery vehicle for lifelong learning because there has been too much glitter and not much practical use." He adds: "I have seen too many examples in corporate environments where technology became more important than the learning goal, with the result that the learning process was ineffective and outcomes were less than hoped for."

TIMING The need for learning how to use technologies appropriately is urgent given the existing infrastructure and the pace at which new facilities are being installed.

Statistics Canada data show that almost 100 percent of Canadian households have had telephones, radios and television sets for several years. Households are rapidly acquiring computers, as the comparison of statistics between 1995 and 1996 shows (see Table 6.1). The data show the average number of households with computers and demonstrate the strong effect of both income level *and* the presence of children aged 18 or under in the house (Statistics Canada, 1996 and 1995).

**TABLE 6.1:** PERCENTAGES OF CANADIAN HOUSEHOLDS WITH COMPUTERS

| Income Level | 1996** | | 1995*** | |
|---|---|---|---|---|
| | Average* | Children+ | Average* | Children+ |
| Average | 31.6% | 44.6% | 28.8% | 40.4% |
| < $10,000 per annum | 16.3% | 26.3% | 13.6% | 22.2% |
| > $70,000 per annum | 56.2% | 65.0% | 52.7% | 60.9% |

* From Table 1, Catalogue 13-218 ** 1995 income
\+ From Table 4.8, Catalogue 13-218 *** 1994 income

Source: Statistics Canada.

These Canadian data are indicative of trends in other countries. Germany has approximately the same level of computers in the household, while Australia has a much higher level. Ralph Leonard, senior consultant at Australia's Open Learning Technology Consortium, reports that 60 percent of Australian homes with children have computers, and that the average for all homes is 47 percent. Consulting Associate Elizabeth Katz in Connecticut, and her Bridgewater Research Group colleagues Bill Weimer in North Carolina and R. Grant Tate in The Netherlands, cite statistics indicating that computer sales to the home outstripped those to the workplace for the first time in 1994 (Katz, Tate, & Weimer, 1995).

Schools, colleges, universities and workplaces vary in their capacity to match these household statistics, particularly with respect to their ability to purchase the hardware. Do you think there are enough computers in your classroom or training center?

Vendors of networks are doing their utmost to make available the networks—the Highway—required to link whatever hardware does exist. In Canada, for example, Stentor's Beacon Initiative envisages providing broadband multimedia services to 80 to 90 percent of Canadian homes and businesses by 2005. Stentor announced in March 1996 that it was donating satellite time and other resources so that every school in Canada could be linked in an initiative called SchoolNet, described by our colleagues Margaret Haughey and Terry Anderson in their book *Networked Learning: The Pedagogy of the Internet* (1998). In a press conference distributed by videoconferencing, Stentor's Robert Milne (1996) noted that "distance should not be a barrier to education."

Cable companies are bringing complimentary cable service to schools in both Canada and the United States. Notes Shari Baldwin, herself a former teacher and now executive director of the Canadian Cable in the Classroom program, "Cable operators and programming services like *Newsworld*, *TSN*, *RDI*, *YTV* and Canadian educational broadcasters are working together to bring copyright-cleared, commercial-free, educationally relevant French and English television programming free to schools across Canada. Instructors can tape the programs and use them to support their curriculum and their students' learning needs."

LEARNER EXPECTATIONS As a result of this rapid deployment of technical facilities, learners will increasingly expect technology to be available in their places of learning. Anna Stahmer (1995), Toronto co-publisher of a learning technology newsletter *The Training Technology Monitor*, notes that workplace trainers are moving rapidly into the use of technology, including non-network-based methods. "The move ... will not remain an option for trainers to choose or reject. It will become a reality as a result of pressure from learners themselves" (p. 55). Elizabeth Katz (1995) and her colleagues at the Bridgewater Research Group note similar trends, as does the American Society for Training and Development (1996) in its annual survey of the use of training technologies in large and medium-sized American businesses.

Instructors are uniquely positioned within their organizations to understand changing learner expectations and to assist their public and private sector employers to respond appropriately.

NEW ROLES Instructors and learners usually take on new roles when they use learning technologies effectively. Typically, the changes focus on de-emphasizing the lecture format, which is centered on delivery of the instructor's knowledge, and on increasing the use of other formats that develop the learner's capacity to acquire and create knowledge. Robert Yee (1996), an instructor at the Toronto-Dominion Bank in Toronto, Ontario, reports that, when he first used multimedia technology, "The hardest part was giving up control" (p. 1). Many instructors come from a line job or a teaching environment where knowledge of content was their strength. As a result, notes Anna Stahmer (1995), "trainers [*sic* instructors] have rarely been exposed to tutoring, counseling by telephone or e-mail, or management of learner files through computer analysis—skills essential for effective support of technology-based learning systems" (p. 53). As we shall see in subsequent chapters, however, instructors and learners alike readily adapt to, and feel liberated by, adding new roles to their existing repertoire of learning behaviors.

ACCESS Access is a key fifth opportunity. How do you meet the needs of learners who do not have technology in their homes but who must hand in assignments by e-mail or in a word-processed format? How do you and your learners access resources if you are in the 10 to 20 percent of the country that Beacon will not serve? Erin Keough, director of the Open Learning and Information Network in Newfoundland, notes that the "digital divide" is real. "We know that the type of infrastructure available to instructors and learners will vary. We need to ensure that planning for the Information Highway includes planning for diversity in capacity. Instructors will need to be well versed in all types of learning technologies, not just the high-end ones available in urban areas." Our choice of technology will be constrained by where we live, institutional commitment to the use of technology and many other factors. Some may feel that our use of the word "choice" is idealistic in their context. Our colleagues Andrew Clement, Faculty of Information Studies, University of Toronto, and Leslie Regan Shade, information technology consultant based in Ottawa, are concerned about this issue of equitable access (1996).

COST The cost of Information Highway technologies is highly context-specific. Moreover, public and private sector experiences of this issue are not always the same. In researching her book on Compressed Video Learning for this Series, Judy found that companies such as the Insurance Corporation of British Columbia, a Crown corporation providing motor vehicle insurance products and claims services to citizens of that province, find videoconferencing to be highly cost-effective because it saves travel dollars, while a board of education such as the one in Huron County, Ontario, can only afford the technology by selling surplus time to local businesses (Roberts, 1998). Workers' wages can be saved if Networked Learning is more time-efficient than the conventional classroom approach, but there are no similar "wage savings" attached to Grade 10 students' time. We therefore need to examine all the factors in our own cost context and not rely too heavily on the numbers in someone else's business case.

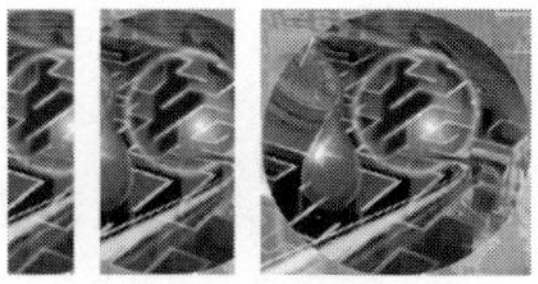

TONY BATES, DIRECTOR OF DISTANCE EDUCATION AND TECHNOLOGY IN CONTINUING STUDIES AT THE UNIVERSITY OF BRITISH COLUMBIA IN VANCOUVER, IN HIS BOOK, *TECHNOLOGY, OPEN LEARNING AND DISTANCE EDUCATION* (1995), PROVIDES USEFUL STRATEGIES FOR DEVELOPING A COST FRAMEWORK FOR DIFFERENT TECHNOLOGIES.

COMPETITION Technology eliminates barriers of time and place for learners, and opens institutions up to competition from around the globe. Education and training are becoming international in scope. Tom Prebble (1996) of New Zealand's Massey University notes that "traditional institutions are facing a competitive threat from purpose-built high tech agencies and governments and funding agencies are pressing for improved efficiency" (p. 3). He adds that "if conventional educational institutions can use new technologies to enhance the educational experience of students both on and off campus, they are likely to remain the educational destinations of choice for a great many would-be students" (p. 20). We do not address the complex issue of institutional restructuring; however, we do position you to be competitive by helping you acquire the skills you need to use technology appropriately. By acquiring such skills, you are also well positioned to survive job loss or change.

PARTNERSHIPS Partnerships are a common feature of learning on the Information Highway. One type of partnership, which we described in Part 1, is that which is found among instructors and other professionals. The need for a strong alliance between the content expert and learning design specialist is particularly important (see Chapter 5). Another type of partnership is that which is found among content experts. Team teaching among instructors is becoming "virtual team teaching" as instructors from several institutions use technologies to share teaching responsibilities in one course. Contact North/Contact Nord or EuroPACE 2000 exemplify a third partnership, one that exists among several types of educational institutions whose primary goal is to reduce the cost of technology through the establishment of consortia. Lynette Gillis, Ruth Pike and Cathleen Gibson (1996), evaluators of the Interactive Learning Connection—University Space Network Pilot Project in Ontario, note that this type of partnership represents "a way to possibly enhance the quality and the reach of learning by sharing the financial, material, and intellectual resources of our learning institutions" (p. 21).

CONCLUSION This is a brief overview of some of the opportunities of the Information Highway for you, the instructor. Other significant issues that other colleagues have raised include the importance of user needs in driving the deployment of technology (Cukier, 1995), the use of networks by communities (Balka, 1996), the need to manage negative impacts such as possible job loss, the protection of intellectual property, and the need for research to assist instructors. However, as Veronica Lacey, co-chair of the IHAC Working Group on Learning and Training indicates, the opportunities and possible benefits outweigh the perils. "IHAC adopted the principle that lifelong learning should be a key design element of the Information Highway. That vision encompasses change in every aspect of how we currently promote and facilitate learning in the classroom, workplace and home. Instructors, in partnership with learners, should be at the forefront of that change process."

This book, and others in the Series, concentrates on launching a process through which you can acquire the knowledge needed to master technology in the classroom and participate in the debate about the Information Highway. Further Readings at the end of this book will enable you to pursue these and other issues.

## HOW DO I CHOOSE APPROPRIATE TECHNOLOGY?

Now that we have defined the technical meaning of the term *Information Highway,* some of its social, economic and educational implications and the opportunities that it presents in the classroom, let's consider how to choose among, or integrate, them appropriately to meet learner needs. Right now, this may mean combining separate pieces of equipment such as those described in Chapters 7 to 9. In future, the issue may become one of activating various features on a single piece of equipment such as the computer or television set. Depending on the richness of your environment, that future may already be here! Regardless, as Tom Prebble of Massey University's Extramural Studies notes, "Matching technologies with purpose is critical."

Some of you may not yet be in a position to choose; your organization may have committed itself to one particular technology. You may want to skip this section and come back to it when the issue of choice is more relevant to you.

In Part 1 we examined some of the factors related to learners and learning that will affect your choice. Table 6.2 presents some of the key factors from those chapters in checklist format.

**TABLE 6.2:** CHECKLIST FOR CHOOSING APPROPRIATE TECHNOLOGY: LEARNING ISSUES

- ☑ Learner characteristics such as age, gender and special needs
- ☑ Learning principles to be followed
- ☑ Learning strategies to be adopted
- ☑ Teaching model to be used
- ☑ Level of learning desired
- ☑ Content characteristics
- ☑ Degree of collaborative learning required

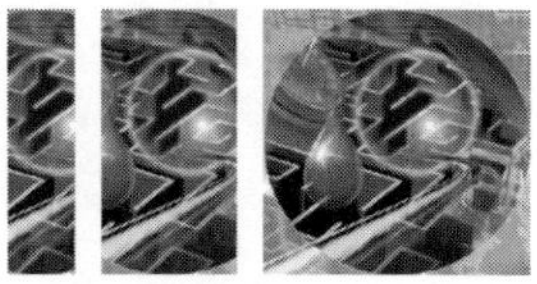

THINK LEARNERS FIRST, THEN ADMINISTRATION AND LOGISTICS.

In this section we highlight three administrative and logistical issues that will influence your choice of technology: human resources, physical facilities and cost. They are summarized in Table 6.3.

**TABLE 6.3:** CHECKLIST FOR CHOOSING APPROPRIATE TECHNOLOGY: ADMINISTRATIVE ISSUES

- ☑ Human resources
  - ☑ Instructional design
  - ☑ Technical support
  - ☑ Learner support
  - ☑ Evaluation
  - ☑ Coordination
- ☑ Physical facilities
  - ☑ In the room
  - ☑ In the building or community
- ☑ Cost
  - ☑ Capital costs
    - ☑ Equipment
    - ☑ Renovations
    - ☑ Service contract
    - ☑ Replacement
  - ☑ Operational costs
    - ☑ Time for training
    - ☑ Usage charges
    - ☑ Maintenance

RESOURCES People and facilities are two critical types of resources.

Categories of personnel resources are similar no matter what type of technology you use. As an instructor, you will be functioning as part of a team (whose members could be at different locations) whose common goal is to facilitate learning. However, as you will appreciate in succeeding chapters, the amount of time required from these team members will vary depending on the type of technology you use. In this overview, therefore, we describe each function generically.

Assuming that you are functioning as the content expert, the other key members of the team are:

- Instructional design staff: This specialist helps you plan the best course of action to achieve the learning goals required in your course or workshop. You may want to re-think your goal of driving on the Information Highway if such support is not available. "Companies, as well as schools, colleges and universities, are increasingly realizing the critical role which instructional design plays," notes Lyndsay Green, Toronto-based co-publisher of *The Training Technology Monitor*. "People are increasingly comfortable with technology, which now generally works reliably, so the challenge lies in developing processes that support learning in the best way possible."

IF YOU ASSUME A SUPPORT ROLE SUCH AS TUTORING, THEN AT LEAST ONE OTHER PERSON NEEDS TO BE ADDED TO THE TEAM AS A CONTENT EXPERT.

- Technical support personnel: Any technology requires some technical support from time to time. Make sure that it is available—don't think that you can do it all yourself. Such support can take many forms. Sometimes a highly skilled technician is needed, but other times another instructional colleague or a learner may well be able to operate and troubleshoot hardware or software. Some technologies require several types of technical support, while others are less demanding of human resources.
- Student support staff: Jane Brindley (1995), a psychologist and distance education consultant based in Sudbury, Ontario, is one of many respected practitioners who believe that learner support systems are critical to success. While there is some debate about precise definitions, Alan Tait (1995), a senior counselor at The Open University's Regional Centre in Cambridge, England, and other international researchers agree that such systems commonly include tutoring, counseling and library support and share a common element of customizing learning to the needs of individual learners.

IDENTIFY A TEAM COORDINATOR TO KEEP THE WORK ON SCHEDULE.

- Coordinators: As we will see in many of the success stories in Chapters 7 to 9, projects using technologies such as Audio, Audiographic and Video Learning frequently have community or regional centers where learners come to access the technology. Site coordinators typically provide both technical and student support functions at these centers. Such centers are less commonly used in Networked Learning.

Chapter 5 and the materials in the Resource Kit provide valuable guidance on this topic.

- Evaluation expertise: In the initial stages of using learning technologies, you need to determine whether you and the learners in your session are adjusting appropriately to the technology and meeting one another's expectations.

Physical facilities in both the classroom and the community are the other important resource influencing your choice of technology.

- An ergonomically appropriate physical environment. For example, if there is nowhere to put the television set for a Video Learning session where light does not reflect off the screen, or if there are no curtains or blinds on the windows, you may not want to try Video Learning as the room limitations could be overwhelming. If the room has the potential for good audio quality, perhaps the agenda and learning plan can be modified to suit that approach.
- The necessary technical installations in the building and the community. Digital telephone lines are not yet available in all learning and training environments throughout the world. You have to use technologies that can be efficiently supported in the buildings and communities where you and your learners are located. Audio and audiographic technologies (see Chapter 7) require POTS—plain old telephone service—to function. Just check to ensure that access to the public telephone network is suitable and fast if you use POTS.

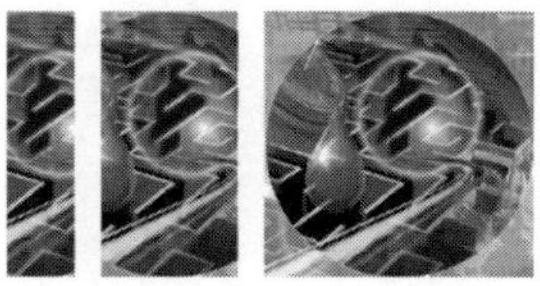

ORGANIZING PEOPLE AND FACILITIES IS AN INESCAPABLE TASK. FOR EXAMPLE, BALANCING LEARNING DESIGN NEEDS FOR THE VISUAL PRESENCE OF VIDEO LEARNING WITH THE PRACTICAL REALITY THAT LEARNERS CANNOT BE PRESENT AT THE SAME TIME IS NOT SIMPLE. MASSEY UNIVERSITY WAS NOT INITIALLY SUCCESSFUL IN ITS ATTEMPTS TO USE AUDIO AND VIDEO LEARNING, BUT HAD GREAT SUCCESS WITH AUDIOGRAPHIC LEARNING. THE DIFFERENCE, REPORTS TOM PREBBLE, WAS IN THE LEARNER CHARACTERISTICS. THE AUDIOGRAPHIC COURSES WERE OFFERED TO TEACHERS AND PRINCIPALS WHO FOUND IT FAIRLY EASY TO GET TOGETHER AT THE SAME TIME, A REQUIREMENT OF AUDIOGRAPHIC LEARNING. THE TARGET AUDIENCES FOR THE OTHER TWO TECHNOLOGIES, WHICH ALSO REQUIRED THAT LEARNERS IN DIFFERENT PLACES BE AVAILABLE AT THE SAME TIME, DID NOT HAVE SCHEDULES THAT COULD BE EASILY COORDINATED (PREBBLE, 1996, PP. 14-15).

COST The second important factor is cost, both capital and operational. Is the technology that you want to use affordable? Since cost varies enormously depending on your location, we describe four capital cost items (equipment, renovations, service contracts and replacement) and three types of operational expenses (time, usage and maintenance) that you can customize to your own situation.

We should explain why we do not cite specific numbers in this section, nor try to compare the costs of one technology to another. First, cost varies so much by jurisdiction within even one country that it is hazardous to cite specific numbers. The situation is even more complex when dealing with comparisons across countries. Second, many of the people we contacted in preparing the success stories considered their cost information to be proprietary and could not share it. Third, vendors are reluctant to cite costs as prices and models are constantly changing. We therefore provide you with the categories you need to consider and recommend that you research your own cost figures.

Capital costs include:

- Equipment. You need to know the price ranges of the various technologies so that you can responsibly balance the learning objectives you wish to facilitate with the cost of doing so.
- Renovations. Each technology will probably require some renovations to an existing room, since the room wasn't likely originally designed to accommodate a learning technology. Whether it is improving room acoustics for Audio Learning or wiring for Networked Learning, construction costs may have to be incurred to ensure that you and the learners have a positive experience with technology.
- Service contracts. Most vendors offer service contracts as part of their capital cost quotation. Such contracts offer the advantages of a fixed

annual cost that can be amortized as a capital budget item. Depending on how frequently you think you will need service and how your institution treats capital budgets, however, you may be better off financially paying for service support as an operational item (see below).

- Replacement. All equipment breaks down or becomes obsolete, so your budget should provide for replacement costs. The difficult question is deciding how long your technologies can remain effective without continuous upgrades.

MANY INSTITUTIONS ARE LOOKING TO SHARE COSTS WITH PARTNERS, WHICH MEANS THAT INSTRUCTORS NEED TO BE FLEXIBLE IN THEIR REQUIREMENTS FOR HOW THE ROOM IS SET UP AS IT MAY HAVE TO CHANGE FROM HOUR TO HOUR DEPENDING ON THE USER.

Operational costs include:

- Your own time and that of learners. A critical time factor relates to mastery of equipment. Will it take you and/or your learners so long to learn how to use the technology effectively that it becomes impractical for your application? Learning how to master complex computer processes may be feasible in a semester-long college or university course, but may be totally impractical for a one-day corporate training event.
- Long-distance or other usage costs. All of the distributed technologies described in this book and in the Series require payment of network fees (usually your long-distance bill) for the time they are used, although practice may vary depending on your organizational setting. Postsecondary professors, for example, have generally had unlimited "free" use of many parts of the Internet—especially e-mail links to one another around the world. However, individual corporate trainers have to pay an Internet Service Provider for such a service. A partnership between a university professor and a corporate trainer may therefore have significantly different cost implications for the amount of time they spend sending each other e-mail messages. Some feel that this cost differential is rapidly being eliminated and will soon cease to be a relevant factor.
- Maintenance. As mentioned earlier, you may want to treat equipment maintenance as an operational cost item. You can do this by paying for "service on demand" from your vendor or by having your own skilled maintenance technicians.

IF YOU DO NOT HAVE ADEQUATE TECHNICAL TRAINING SUPPORT, THE TIME FACTOR ESCALATES. NO LEARNER OR INSTRUCTOR WILL EASILY TOLERATE TIME WASTAGE.

## CONCLUSION

The Information Highway is a trendy shorthand to describe the fact that telecommunications and computing networks, which were previously separate, are converging. Although some are unhappy with it as a metaphor, others find it a useful focus for mobilizing public and private sector interest in the roles these networks can play as tools for learning and prosperity. The pace at which this "network of networks" is being deployed is astonishing and continues regardless of debates about access, affordability and other issues relevant to public and private sector learning stakeholders. Instructors continually face the task of skills upgrading in order to assess the promise and limitations of these technologies.

# Chapter 6

Now that we have introduced the meaning of the term *Information Highway*, its implications for learning, the opportunities it offers in the classroom and its resource requirements, we can move on to consider Audio and Audiographic Learning.

# References


American Society for Training and Development (1996). Industry report 1996: Our annual statistical snapshot of employer-provided training. *Training, 33*(10), 37-39.

Balka, E. (1996). *Computer networking: Spinsters on the web*. Ottawa: The Canadian Research Institute for the Advancement of Women (CRIAW).

Brindley, J. (1995). Learners and learner services: The key to the future. In J. M. Roberts & E. M. Keough (Eds.), *Why the Information Highway? Lessons from open and distance learning* (pp. 102-125). Toronto, ON: Trifolium Books Inc.

Brittain, E. (1996). Technology for adult learning. In *Adult Learning and Technology in OECD Countries*, Paper No. 14. Paris, FR: Organisation for Economic Co-operation and Development.

Clement, A., & Shade, L. R. (1996). What do we mean by 'Universal Access'? Social perspectives in a Canadian context. Proceedings of INET. http://info. isoc.org/whatis/conferences/inet/96/proceedings/f2/f2_1.htm

Cukier, W. (1995). *Technology-enabled learning and training: Defining user needs*. Ottawa, ON: Information Highway Advisory Council, Working Group on Learning and Training and Industry Canada.

Dede, C. (1994, October). *The technologies driving the National Information Infrastructure: Policy implications for distance education*. Paper commissioned by the Southwest Regional Laboratory. Fairfax, VA: George Mason University, Graduate School of Education.

Department for Education and Employment. (1995). *Superhighways for education*. London, UK: Government of Great Britain.

Gillis, L., Pike, R., & Gibson, C. (1996). *Innovations in course delivery for a distributed university: The evaluation of the Interactive Learning Connection—University Space Network Pilot Project*. Toronto, ON: Knowledge Connection Corporation.

Haughey, M., & Anderson, T. (1998). *Networked learning: The pedagogy of the Internet*. Montréal, QC: Chenelière/McGraw-Hill.

Information Highway Advisory Council. (1995, September). *The challenge of the Information Highway*. Ottawa, ON: Industry Canada.

Information Highway Advisory Council, Working Group on Learning and Training. (1995, December). *Making it happen: Final report of the Learning and Training Working Group*. Ottawa, ON: Industry Canada.

Katz, E. J., Tate, R. G., & Weimer, W. A. (1995). *Survey of telematics for education and training. Vol.II: United States*. Heerlen, The Netherlands: European Association of Distance Teaching Universities.

Menzies, H. (1996, February 10). *The medium, the message and librarians as the messengers*. Speech to the Ontario Library Association.

Milne, R. (1996, March 27). *Globe & Mail*, p. B4.

Prebble, T. (1996). Matching technologies with purpose. In *Adult Education and Technology in OECD Countries*, Paper No. 10. Paris, FR: Organisation for Economic Co-operation and Development.

Roberts, J. M. (1998). *Compressed video learning: Creating active learners*. Montréal, QC: Chenelière/McGraw-Hill.

Stahmer, A. (1995). Learners in the workplace. In J. M. Roberts & E. M. Keough (Eds.), *Why the Information Highway? Lessons from open and distance learning* (pp. 41-59). Toronto, ON: Trifolium Books Inc.

Statistics Canada. (1996, October). *Household facilities by income and other characteristics 1996*. Catalogue No. 13-218. Ottawa, ON.

———. (1995, October). *Household facilities by income and other characteristics 1995*. Catalogue No. 13-218. Ottawa, ON.

Tait, A. (1995). Student support in open and distance learning. In F. Lockwood (Ed.)*Open and distance learning today* (pp. 232-241). London, UK: Routledge.

Yee, R. (1996). Distributed multimedia used for training. *The Training Technology Monitor*, *3*(4), 1-2.

# Chapter 7

# Audio and Audiographic Learning: Why Are They the Cornerstone of the Information Highway?

*What telewriter? ... we've been doing this for so long now we hardly notice it any more!*

GRADE 12 PHYSICS STUDENT,
RED BAY, LABRADOR

## INTRODUCTION

In this chapter we explain the basics of audio and audiographic technologies. You will be able to identify their key opportunities, strengths and limitations. You can focus on (1) preparation, (2) delivery techniques related to task and social behaviors and the use of the voice and (3) evaluation. Finally, you will read selected success stories from our colleagues.

## HOW DO AUDIO AND AUDIOGRAPHIC LEARNING WORK?

Audio Learning (AL) occurs when learners and instructor use telephone technology to engage in discussions, exchange messages or access experts as part of a formal or informal learning process. All such interactions occur in real-time: the learners and instructor are present at the same time and must coordinate their schedules.

Audiographic Learning (AGL) occurs when learners and instructor use telephone and graphics technologies to facilitate dialogue, exchange messages and access experts as part of a learning process. Graphics technologies, or devices, are pieces of equipment that create, store and send visual materials such as handwriting, drawings and still pictures. All such exchanges occur in real-time: the learners and instructor are present at the same time and must coordinate their schedules.

As Figure 7.1 shows, the technical system required for AL has three components. Let's look at each component in more detail.

1. A telephone is required, either the telephone handset used in your home or workplace by individuals, or a speakerphone (group audio terminal is another term), which a group of learners can use in a seminar or classroom environment. Several types of group audio terminals have been designed specifically for education and training applications.

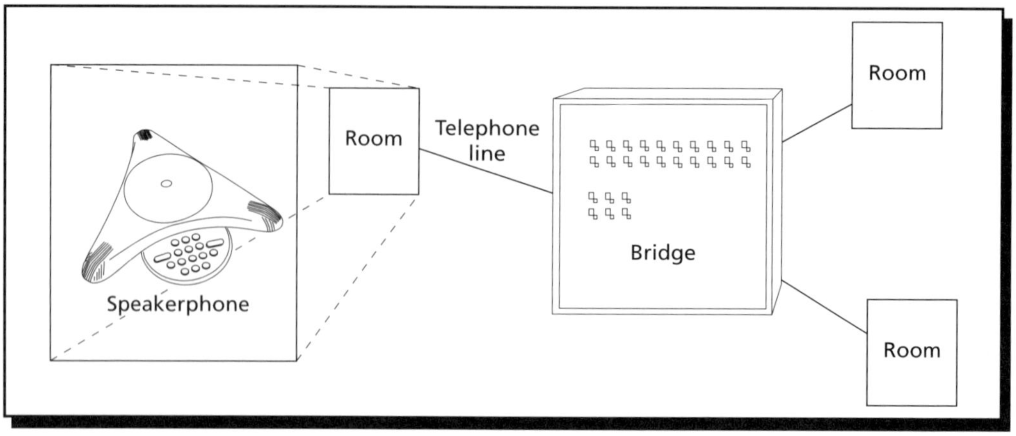


FIGURE 7.1: Three technical components of Audio Learning

2. The telephone network that links these telephones generally consists of standard dial-up telephone lines.
3. The mechanism by which three or more telephone calls are linked is called a bridge. Telephone companies and other vendors provide this mechanism as part of their conference-call service. Many consortia and institutions have purchased their own bridge so they can tailor this service to specific learning needs or to save money.

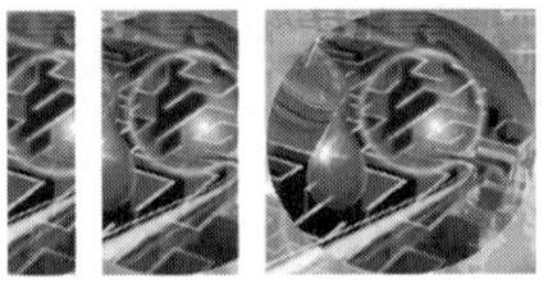

THE LEARNING PROCESS IS GREATLY FACILITATED IF AN OPERATOR TRAINED IN LEARNING APPLICATION NEEDS IS ON-LINE, OR ON CALL, THROUGHOUT A SESSION.

This technical arrangement, in which telephones or speakerphones and a bridge are used, is called an audioconference.

AGL adds a fourth technical component, a graphics device (see Figure 7.2).

4. A graphics device such as a tablet or whiteboard, with its related software, allows anyone in the conference to handwrite or type text and draw graphics that are seen in all locations in the conference. When this fourth device is added, the technical configuration is called an audiographic conference. Figure 7.3 illustrates two of the more commonly used devices.

Some types of equipment, such as the Optel Telewriter, work on the same line as the telephone handset and speakerphone and go through the same bridge. Others, such as the SMART 2000 whiteboard, require a second phone line and a second bridging device.

Regardless of which system is used, the process by which they facilitate interaction in AGL is similar.

1. The instructor and learners can talk with one another using their telephones, and they can keyboard messages on the computer or draw on the tablet or whiteboard. Some systems permit the visuals to be transmitted simultaneously with voice, while others require the person who is speaking to pause when the graphics are transmitted.
2. Learning materials can be prepared, saved on computer disk and copied to all sites in advance. On-line commands during the session cause each AGL unit to bring the required materials onto the screen. The graphics can then be annotated from any site to highlight key points using the pen or keyboard.

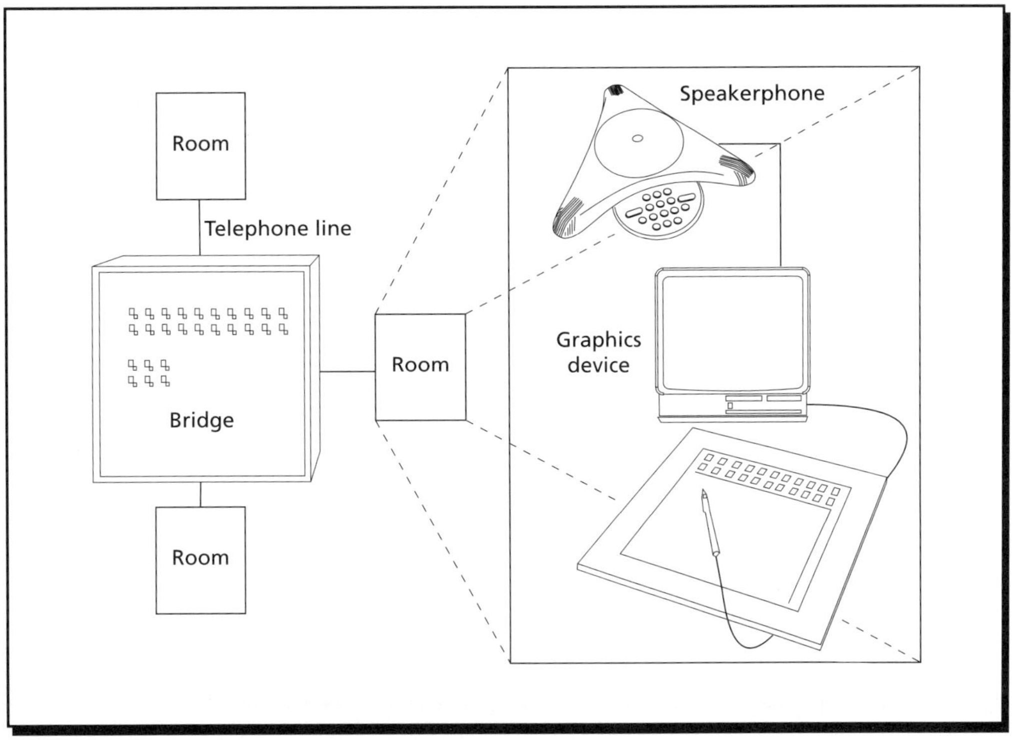


FIGURE 7.2: Four technical components of Audiographic Learning

3. Material created on-line during the class can be saved and added to previously prepared materials for use in future sessions.

This basic system can be enhanced, depending on the type of AGL system, with a document scanner, camera or VCR. Graphics can be prepared using a variety of graphics software packages or, if you have a scanner, from sources such as slides, pictures, 3-D objects, transparencies and other formats.

FIGURE 7.3: Two different types of audiographic devices: The Optel Telewriter System photo furnished by Optel Communications in New York (left); Rear Projection SMART Board photo courtesy of SMART Technologies Inc. (right).

FIGURE 7.3 SHOWS TWO TYPES OF GRAPHICS EQUIPMENT THAT CAN BE USED BY A GROUP OF LEARNERS AT A SITE. BECAUSE TECHNOLOGIES ARE CONVERGING ON THE INFORMATION HIGHWAY, COMPUTER SOFTWARE, CALLED GROUPWARE, IS BEING DEVELOPED THAT CREATES THESE SAME AL AND AGL ENVIRONMENTS THROUGH A DESKTOP COMPUTER.

## WHAT ARE AL AND AGL'S STRENGTHS? WHAT ARE SOME KEY ISSUES?

In Table 7.1 we highlight 10 strengths offered by AL and AGL and then describe eight key issues. The text following Table 7.1 briefly explains each point.

**TABLE 7.1:** STRENGTHS AND KEY ISSUES OF AL AND AGL

| STRENGTHS | KEY ISSUES |
|---|---|
| • Near universality | • Quality of equipment |
| • Affordability | • Appropriateness |
| • Flexibility | • Advance preparation |
| • Cornerstone of live interaction | • Scheduling |
| • Choice of technical configurations | • Connectability |
| • Learner support | • Integration of voice and visual elements |
| • Socialization | • Voice-only in AL |
| • Special needs learners | • Data transmission in AGL |
| • Service providers and partners | |
| • High user satisfaction | |

NEAR UNIVERSALITY Telephone signals, the technical basis of AL and AGL, are available virtually everywhere in the world through regular telephone lines or radio. They are also becoming available on the Internet.

AFFORDABILITY The capital and operating costs of the equipment and networks needed to support Audio and Audiographic Learning are typically among the lowest of any of the technologies available on the Information Highway, especially if discount rates are being offered to reduce the long-distance costs.

FLEXIBILITY AL and AGL equipment is portable and can be readily moved. AL, combined with print, 35-mm slides, overhead transparencies and other on-site tools, can support a wide range of learning activities such as peer discussions, panels and interviews with experts. When AGL technologies are added, the choice is further expanded.

CORNERSTONE OF INTERACTION The interactive techniques required for effective AL are the basis for most of the interaction strategies advocated for AGL, Video Learning and even some aspects of Networked Learning. Janice Cooper, Acting Director, Telemedicine Centre, Memorial University of Newfoundland in St. John's, notes: "In my experience, learning interactive techniques appropriate to AL develops skills that are transferable to other technologies: it is a lot easier to use some of the newer technologies if you have a foundation in AL."

CHOICE A wide variety of types of speakerphones and graphics devices are available, enabling instructors to choose those best-suited to their learning objectives and financial resources (see Figures 7.1 to 7.3).

LEARNER SUPPORT AL and AGL offer learners the opportunity to talk to their peers about the print materials they have been reading individually or other topics relevant to their learning. Interaction can enhance self-esteem and support learners who face adverse personal, professional or social learning conditions.

SOCIALIZATION Some learners need the social contact that real-time technologies such as AL and AGL provide. If they do not want to use the individualized approach of Networked Learning at home or in their office, they can choose these group-based technologies.

SPECIAL NEEDS LEARNERS AL has been used to enable children to participate in classes while they are in hospital or at home convalescing. The Canadian Cancer Society (Ontario Division) uses AL in its Cancer Connection program to train and support telephone visitors of cancer patients, who then provide individualized telephone support to patients when no in-person support is available. Freda Finley, coordinator of Patient Services in Toronto, says that "learning by phone when you are going to deliver the service by phone is a bonus. It would be hard to learn telephone counseling techniques in the classroom."

SERVICE PROVIDERS AND PARTNERS Many public and private sector consortia provide multi-purpose provincial and state networks so that individual institutions and businesses do not have to mount expensive in-house systems. (See pp. 82 to 87 in this chapter for examples, as well as Donald MacDonald's book in this Series.)

HIGH USER SATISFACTION Marquis Bureau, founding president of Le Collège des Grands Lacs in central and southwestern Ontario, notes that learners at the Collège prefer AGL to Video Learning because "it is more user friendly and more accessible to all of them during classes. In other words, the AGL technologies allow for more participation and interaction between participants." The lack of visual contact is not the impediment to acceptance that many instructors fear.

The eight key issues highlighted in Table 7.1 can become serious limitations if they are not addressed properly. Here are some suggestions as to how to do so.

QUALITY OF EQUIPMENT Selecting the highest possible quality of equipment your budget can afford is important. Straining to hear on inadequate technology impedes learning and adversely affects group social processes. Consult other owners of the equipment before you buy. If your existing equipment is inadequate, campaign vigorously to have it replaced.

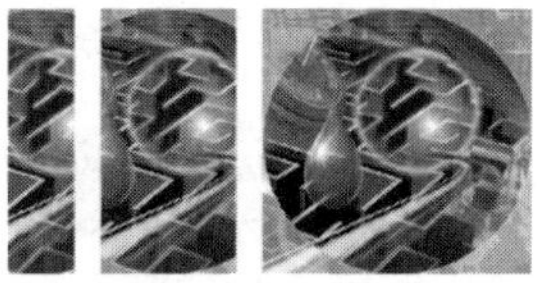

TEST THE EQUIPMENT IN YOUR ENVIRONMENT BEFORE PURCHASING IT TO ENSURE THAT BOTH THE EQUIPMENT AND YOUR TELEPHONE NETWORK ARE OF SUFFICIENT QUALITY. LEASE-PURCHASE ARRANGEMENTS CAN USUALLY BE MADE.

APPROPRIATENESS There are a variety of speakerphone and graphics equipment designs to choose from (see Figure 7.3), for example, a central speakerphone versus individual microphones style of group audio terminal, or a writing tablet versus a whiteboard style of graphics device. Carefully consider your needs before purchasing. For example, if your room environment is noisy, you will not want a sensitive microphone that will transmit the background noise.

ADVANCE PREPARATION As an instructor, you will need time to review the learning and learner issues raised in Part 1 and adapt them to the content,

GRAPHICS DEVICES CAN WORK ON THE SAME LINE AS THE TELEPHONE, OR THEY MAY REQUIRE A SECOND LINE. AS THE TWO-LINE SYSTEM GENERALLY SUPPORTS THE REAL-TIME TRANSMISSION OF COMPLEX VISUAL MATERIAL, THE TYPE OF GRAPHICS YOU WANT TO TRANSMIT AND THE OPERATING COST OF USING TWO LINES ARE FEATURES TO BE CAREFULLY BALANCED.

CAREFULLY RESEARCH THE NETWORKS YOU NEED TO LINK WITH, AND PURCHASE EQUIPMENT THAT IS COMPATIBLE WITH THEM.

REMEMBER TO USE ALL THE COLORS AVAILABLE IN AGL SYSTEMS. COLOR INFLUENCES THE THREE HUMAN RESPONSES OF STIMULATION, RELAXATION AND FOCUS DESCRIBED IN CHAPTER 2.

learners and technologies in your environment. Be generous in allowing yourself time to address these three issues as you may find it difficult to "design as you go" during class time. The essential point here is to use the real-time strengths of the technologies and the learning and teaching principles in Chapters 3 and 4 to create classrooms that facilitate collaboration and learning. Ideally, you should use the equipment as often as necessary before you start teaching so that it is "transparent" to you; in other words, so that you can operate it without thinking. You can then help create that transparency for learners based on your own experience.

SCHEDULING The great strength of AL and AGL is that, unlike audiocassettes, they allow learners and instructor to talk to one another in real-time. The design implication arising from this feature is that you should consider your learners' schedule as you plan your sessions. How often is it practical for them to meet? Is one three-hour session more feasible than three one-hour sessions? What are the learning design implications of the schedule choice? Time of day will probably affect the long-distance rates your institution pays, so learner convenience needs to be balanced against cost.

CONNECTABILITY The different types of audiographic equipment currently in use do not necessarily "talk to each other," which restricts the ability of classrooms to be linked. Vendors are aware of this limitation, however, and are working to resolve it.

INTEGRATION OF VOICE AND VISUAL ELEMENTS The combination of voice, text and graphics can accommodate a wide variety of learning styles. Integration is key: the visual elements should support and enhance the voice component, not duplicate or distract, and vice versa. In AL, the visual elements are typically paper-based text, 35-mm slides or overhead transparencies. In AGL, computer keyboard or stylus drawings on some type of screen can also be used to convey visual information. The biggest limitation of AGL from this perspective is its inability to transmit moving visual images.

VOICE-ONLY IN AL The lack of a visual element in AL is a barrier to learning some types of content, such as surgical techniques. Some learner and instructor learning styles do not adapt well to this "single channel" modality of relating to others in a linked classroom environment.

DATA TRANSMISSION IN AGL Some types of AGL equipment, especially those that function on a single telephone line, can't readily transmit complex graphics in real-time over a voice-quality, analog telephone line. While preparing and downloading visuals in advance of the class deals with this problem, it is not always feasible to do so.

## HOW DO I USE AL AND AGL APPROPRIATELY?

### Preparation

When applying the CARE learning principles and strategies outlined in Chapters 3 and 4 to AL and AGL, we try to create classrooms that build on the interactive and real-time strengths of the medium. Our preparation framework (see Table 7.2) features six points. Let's consider each briefly.

**TABLE 7.2:** PREPARATION FRAMEWORK FOR AL AND AGL

- A learner's manual
- Visuals
- Lead time
- Learner characteristics
- Ergonomics
- Comfort with the equipment

A LEARNER'S MANUAL This document is critical for both instructors and learners, particularly in longer learning events such as semester-long courses. However, it is a necessary tool even in a one-day training event. As we explained in Chapter 5, it should (1) contain clear directions so that everyone has the correct resources when they need them, (2) sequence the learning activities so that what learners do in the AL or AGL conference builds on what they have previously learned and (3) provide a variety of activities, both on- and off-line, because differences in learning styles may mean that some learners may not feel entirely comfortable all the time that they are on-line.

A sample manual is provided in the Resource Kit.

VISUALS Visuals you plan to use should be reproduced, if possible, in the manual to eliminate the need for learners to be so busy copying a graphic that they cannot participate in the discussion. Visuals should enhance and support the learning goals and be well integrated with the learning objectives. Chapter 9 on Compressed Video Learning describes several important features of putting together effective visuals that are relevant to preparing audiographic visuals (see also Donald MacDonald's book in this Series).

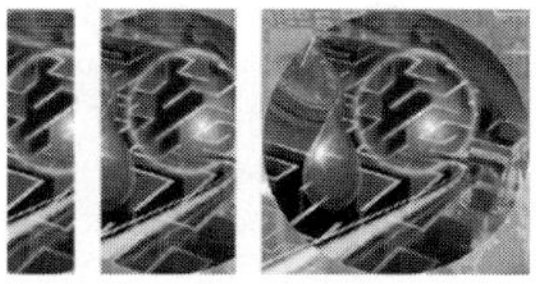

A WELL-DESIGNED AL OR AGL SESSION CAN FAIL IF THE GRAPHICS ARE NOT PROPERLY PREPARED. SQUINTING TO READ CROWDED SLIDES OR ILLEGIBLE HANDWRITING OR BEING BORED WITH UNNECESSARY VISUALS DETRACTS FROM EFFECTIVE LEARNING.

LEAD TIME Allow plenty of time to prepare the visual materials for the learner's manual and, if relevant, the audiographic system, to copy and distribute them to the sites, to learn how to use the equipment and generally to be ready for your session.

LEARNER CHARACTERISTICS Factors such as gender or culture could affect the amount of AL you should build into your learning or training event, as well as the type of interaction you can expect. Many women and certain cultural groups have collaborative learning preferences, for example. It is therefore useful to ask yourself several questions: Who are the participants? What interactive traditions do they have? How great is their need for visual cues? What is their prior experience and knowledge of the content? Appreciating participants' learning styles and prior knowledge enables you to adjust your approach, to choose an appropriate vocabulary, to ask relevant questions and to make understandable references.

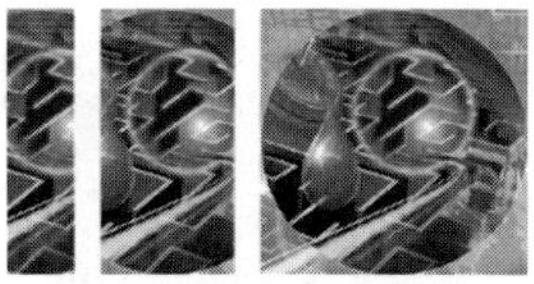

A GOOD AUDIO-VISUAL DEPARTMENT CAN SAVE YOU A LOT OF TIME AND EFFORT. THE DEPARTMENT CAN PROVIDE YOU WITH DETAILED TECHNICAL SPECIFICATIONS THAT ARE BEYOND THE SCOPE OF THIS CHAPTER.

ERGONOMICS The room should be comfortable in terms of temperature, color, sound quality, lighting and type and layout of chairs and table. A simple technique such as putting sound-absorbing felt on a table or desk can improve sound quality for very little cost. For psychological and logistical reasons, avoid crowding people around tables.

BE SURE YOU KNOW THE TROUBLESHOOTING TELEPHONE NUMBER TO CALL IF PROBLEMS OCCUR IN YOUR SESSION.

COMFORT WITH EQUIPMENT Learning will be impeded if the equipment is not transparent, so plan for time at the outset when learners can "play" with the equipment before serious learning activities begin. Even in a one-day event, this is worth doing. Learners generally need very little practice before they feel comfortable with the technology.

## Delivery

We cover three topics in this section: task and social behaviors, the use of the voice and pitfalls.

Once the learning event has actually started, a number of task and social behaviors can enhance or detract from the focus on learning. Table 7.3 summarizes task behaviors related to AL. In AGL environments, those same task protocols should be followed and those shown in Table 7.4 should be added. Table 7.5 describes selected social behaviors that foster learning and are common to both technologies.

**TABLE 7.3:** AUDIO LEARNING TASK CHECKLIST

- ☑ Expect and facilitate learner contributions: encourage focus and clarity.
- ☑ Establish an agenda for the session.
- ☑ Refer to session objectives whenever necessary.
- ☑ Respond to learner contributions as substantively as possible.
- ☑ Build relationships between ideas.
- ☑ Correct misunderstandings in knowledge quickly.
- ☑ Use images and metaphors to help learners understand ideas.
- ☑ Restrict your contributions, and those of learners, to 10-minute segments if the lecture format is being used.
- ☑ Listen more than you talk.
- ☑ Encourage learners to bypass you to talk to one another.
- ☑ Ask questions to guide creative and critical thinking.
- ☑ Suggest a change in the agenda if things are not working out.
- ☑ Ask learners to draft agendas so you know what they think they need.
- ☑ Get help quickly to remedy poor technical conditions.

GRAPHICS CAN SUPPORT MANY DIFFERENT INTERACTION STRATEGIES, INCLUDING REPORTING ON SMALL-GROUP ACTIVITIES, SOLVING PROBLEMS, DISCUSSING ASSIGNED TOPICS, LEADING A SEMINAR, EXPLAINING A COMPLEX CONCEPT, AND ASKING QUESTIONS OF ONE ANOTHER, INVITED GUESTS AND VISITING EXPERTS.

**TABLE 7.4:** AUDIOGRAPHIC LEARNING TASK CHECKLIST

- ☑ Use the pen, tablet and whiteboard in the same way you would a chalkboard.
- ☑ Keep the graphics legible.
- ☑ Use as many of the functions as possible yourself and encourage learners to do likewise. Visual variety enhances learning: erase, change colors, change the width of the lines, use the pointer function, zoom to magnify images.
- ☑ If available, use the keyboard for text and for captioning and encourage others to do likewise.
- ☑ Create graphics that need to be altered during the session to create involvement among the learners.
- ☑ Regularly store materials on disk and keep backup copies to minimize the chance of losing them because of technical malfunction.

**TABLE 7.5:** AL AND AGL SOCIAL BEHAVIORS CHECKLIST

- ☑ Introduce yourself by name and site, and remind learners to do the same, until the group recognizes one another's voices.
- ☑ Exchange pictures of one another to aid in visual imaging if that is important to the group.
- ☑ Create a social presence and tone in the session that are comfortable for you and your particular group of learners.
- ☑ Be as relaxed as possible: an easy atmosphere promotes group learning.
- ☑ Be aware of your voice quality: a lower pitch and slower speaking pace are reassuring.
- ☑ Leave time for learners to comment on proceedings and express their frustrations before problems get out of hand.
- ☑ Value the knowledge and experience of the learners.
- ☑ Correct people tactfully.
- ☑ Use silence as a learning process because people need time to reflect: AL and AGL are not broadcast radio where every second of airtime must be filled.

The last point in the checklist in Table 7.5 is worth reinforcing for two reasons. First, aboriginal learners, as well as other cultural groups, value silence as an important part of communication. Second, all learners need time to perform tasks such as reaching for a microphone, gathering their thoughts together or moving their chair closer to the table.

Another important delivery technique relates to your voice. How you use your voice in the session will affect how actively learners engage in the process. Here are a few points about preparation, volume, tone, pauses, rhythm, enthusiasm and clarity that you should keep in mind in order to be an effective learning facilitator in the audio or audiographic environment.

VOLUME Even though your voice is being transmitted by a microphone, it is important for you to project well, since any microphone needs a good, clear signal. Try breathing deeply as a way to increase the level of your voice without raising the volume. You don't want to sound as though you are yelling across a desert.

TONE Try to find a low tone with which you are comfortable so that your voice does not sound tight. Tense, high-pitched voices are difficult to listen to for any length of time. Breathing deeply will assist with tone as well as with volume.

PAUSES Waiting a few seconds (15 is a good target) for a reply to your question or to make a comment after someone else has intervened is a good idea for two reasons. First, the equipment may be voice-switched and may not permit two people to speak simultaneously. Second, people need time to reflect and to reach for their microphones.

A pause can extend a creative silence; a "thinking space" can be an attention-getter as well as a useful learning strategy. When you want to use a "thinking space," inform your learners: "Let's take three minutes of silence so that you can jot down …" Creative silences can also provide time to "rest one's ears and brain" because talking and listening without body language cues is tiring.

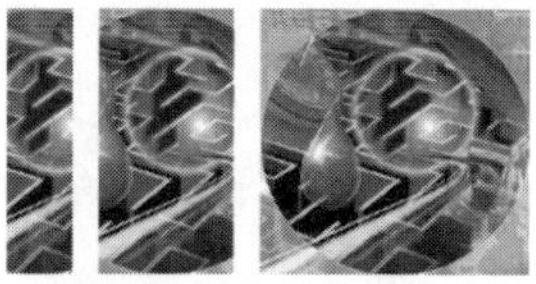

FIFTEEN SECONDS CAN SEEM LIKE A LONG TIME. TO HELP YOURSELF AND YOUR LEARNERS TO ACQUIRE A SENSE OF 15 SECONDS AS AN INTERVAL, MAKE USE OF CLOCKS WITH A SECONDS HAND. IF THE ROOM DOES NOT HAVE SUCH A CLOCK, BRING ONE FOR AT LEAST THE FIRST FEW SESSIONS, UNTIL YOU BECOME COMFORTABLE WITH TIMING THE PAUSES. IF YOU FEEL THAT CLOCKS ARE CREATING A DISTRACTING SENSE OF "ALWAYS WATCHING THE CLOCK," COUNT SLOWLY IN YOUR OWN MIND TO AT LEAST 15. BE TIME AWARE, NOT TIME CONSTRAINED.

> As a facilitator, I realize that I still talk too fast or refer too hastily to articles in the reference materials. I need to pause more and visualize my class. I also found it very hard to let the discussion develop and not jump in with my comments.
>
> *Colleen, a student-facilitator in New Brunswick*

RHYTHM For many people, this type of technical environment creates a fair amount of nervousness and a tendency to talk very quickly in a monotone. It is important to speak at a moderate rate and to vary both your tempo and your intonation. You and your learners can alter the pace of all the contributions by changing the tone of your voices and by modifying the "declarative sentence structure" sequence through the use of pauses, questions and examples. As we noted in Chapter 2, "rapport talk" is needed much more than "report talk."

Seek learner reactions to the session at regular intervals. Alter the pace of your presentation accordingly. Remember that print materials can convey the bulk of your content. It is important, therefore, when planning your session, to develop a structure that varies both pace and rhythm and to check during the session to see if the plan is working. For example, you could:

- limit the number of concepts discussed
- use an inquiring tone of voice to enhance your "presence"
- link the concepts; anchor them in prior learning
- make linkages with other parts of the course or with events in the workplace
- use many voices to provide variety and promote collaboration

ENTHUSIASM If you are bored with the subject or the teaching process, you can be sure that the participants are bored as well. Enthusiasm and passion for the subject matter are contagious, especially in Audio Learning where voices tend to give away feelings. Give learners enough time to identify and share their enthusiasm too.

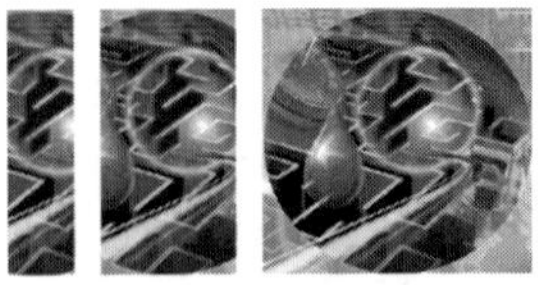

MOST OF THE COMMENTS IN THIS SECTION HAVE BEEN DESIGNED AS GUIDES FOR INSTRUCTORS. HOW CAN YOU SHARE THEM WITH LEARNERS SO THAT THEY CAN CONTRIBUTE EFFECTIVELY?

CLARITY The quality of the learning experience is enhanced if everyone articulates words clearly and pronounces them correctly.

References are provided at the end of this chapter that share ideas about effective use of the voice for learning, for example, Derek Rowntree's (1994) book on producing audiocassettes.

Our third topic on delivery relates to avoiding common pitfalls.

It is really important to monitor how efficiently you and the group are using the interactive capacity of AL and AGL. It is, after all, the interactive time that you are buying—a lecture could be delivered by audiocassette or print. Table 7.6 presents four indicators to watch for and avoid; our text proposes steps to improve the situation.

EXCESSIVE RELIANCE ON THE LECTURE MODE If you find yourself talking (lecturing) for more than 10 minutes, revise your strategy. Most people cannot use their voice effectively enough to sustain learner attention for more than 10 minutes. Moreover, people read faster than they listen, with the result that print is more cost-effective than AL or AGL for transmitting content.

**TABLE 7.6:** FOUR COMMON PITFALLS IN AL AND AGL

- Excessive reliance on the lecture mode
- Low level of learner participation
- Complex graphics
- Too many learners per graphics unit

Here is an example of a good session agenda that includes a number of learning activities and avoids the use of the lecture.

**TABLE 7.7:** SAMPLE AGENDA FROM GRADUATE ADULT EDUCATION CLASS, UNIVERSITY OF NEW BRUNSWICK

| | |
|---|---|
| **6:30 – 6:50** | Link up the sites |
| | Who's here? Happy Halloween! |
| | Review any questions |
| | Comments from your facilitators regarding tonight's activities |
| **6:50 – 7:35** | Off-line group activity |
| **7:35 – 7:50** | Break |
| **7:50 – 9:15** | Reports and critical responses to group activity |
| **9:15 – 9:30** | Wrap-up |
| | Final analysis from Instructor |

TAPE-RECORD ONE OF YOUR SESSIONS TO VERIFY YOUR IMPRESSION OF THE LENGTH OF TIME YOU ARE SPENDING LECTURING AND TO LISTEN TO YOUR VOCAL TECHNIQUES.

LOW LEVEL OF LEARNER PARTICIPATION Whatever the reason, this is not a good sign. Assuming that the issue is not about excessive lecturing or other instructor-related behavior, find out what the problem is and try to solve it.

Common challenges and solutions include:

- Learners don't feel comfortable with the equipment—build in more practice time.
- Learners don't feel they have enough time to respond—prolong the silence after you pose a question, or give generous time off-line for small-group activities so that issues can be thought through.
- Learners don't feel that they have any significant responsibility for creating a "good" session—give them some.
- Questions are too complex—focus on only one issue in each question.
- Poor interpersonal dynamics at a particular site—talk with that site off-line or talk to some learners at that site individually.

IF YOU HAVE A LARGE GROUP AND ONLY ONE GRAPHICS UNIT, ENSURE THAT THERE IS SUFFICIENT AUDIO-ONLY INTERACTION. ALSO, ROTATE ACCESS TO THE GRAPHICS UNIT SO THAT ALL MEMBERS OF THE GROUP STAY INVOLVED AND DON'T FEEL DISENFRANCHISED BECAUSE A CLIQUE OF LEARNERS MONOPOLIZES THE GRAPHICS UNIT.

COMPLEX GRAPHICS Illustrations that contain a lot of information are confusing and do not enhance learning. Find ways to break them down into "digestible bites" or to present them in print. Full screens of small print are hard to read.

TOO MANY LEARNERS PER GRAPHICS UNIT While ways can be found to ensure that a group of 20 to 30 learners can see a television monitor or whiteboard when graphics are received at a site, it is challenging to enable more than five or six learners to share a tablet or whiteboard that originates graphics. The advantage of having the graphics to support the learning objectives compared with the disadvantage of a low level of group participation has to be carefully considered.

### Evaluation

Evaluation results consistently record high levels of instructor and learner acceptance of Audio and Audiographic Learning. Peter Cookson (1995), a professor at Athabasca University in Alberta, cogently summarizes some of this research. Typical instructor and learner comments follow.

Shirly Ellis, an instructor at Cambrian College in Sudbury, Ontario, facilitates courses for The Insurance Institute of Canada using the Contact North/Contact Nord network. She reports strong support for AL among her students. Melissa's comment is typical, Shirly tells us.

> ... I personally have a better grasp of the text material when taking a course by teleconferencing [sic AL] as opposed to correspondence .... I find my study habits are better because I have committed myself to attend a "classroom" setting once a week. I know that when I have taken a course by correspondence, my motivation/self-discipline wasn't always what it should have been ... I like the scheduling teleconferencing offers.
>
> *Melissa, a learner*

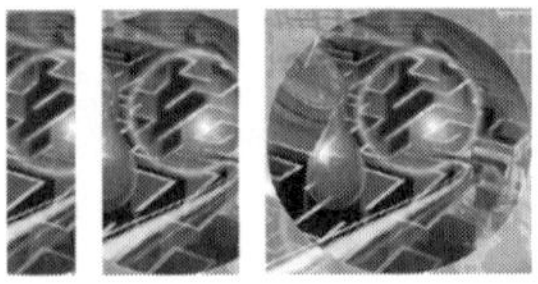

VISIT THE OPEN LEARNING TECHNOLOGY CORPORATION LTD.'S WEB SITE IN AUSTRALIA FOR A COMPREHENSIVE SET OF EVALUATION STUDIES. IT IS AN EXCELLENT DATABASE IF YOU WANT TO PURSUE THE AUDIO OR AUDIOGRAPHIC EVALUATION LITERATURE IN MORE DEPTH.

Donna Mese, an instructor and course author in the Early Childhood Education Program at Cambrian College, reports that her first reaction to AL was "excitement ... It is exciting to reach people who otherwise would not have access. ... Still today, I am amazed at how quickly students adapt."

Research also indicates no significant difference in learning outcomes, as measured by exam marks, between learners in conventional classrooms and those in audio or audiographic classrooms. Peter Cookson (1989) summarized research for the 1970s and 1980s in an article published in *The American Journal of Distance Education.*

## WHO IS USING AL AND AGL SUCCESSFULLY?

Schools, colleges, universities and employers are all successful users of AL and AGL. We cite one example from each sector and refer you to Donald MacDonald's book in this Series, *Audio and Audiographic Learning: The Cornerstone of the Information Highway* (1998), where each example is described in more detail.

### Enriching Senior High School Curriculum

*Small Schools Project, Department of Education, Newfoundland and Labrador*

The Department of Education, Government of Newfoundland and Labrador, has been using AL and AGL technologies to deliver senior high school courses to small schools located in rural and remote communities in Newfoundland and coastal Labrador since 1988. These sites are shown in Figure 7.4.

These courses are offered using services and technologies managed by the Telemedicine Centre, Memorial University of Newfoundland, in partnership with school districts and the Programme Development Division of the Department of Education.

In the 1995-96 school year, the Department offered 10 courses in advanced mathematics, physics, chemistry and French. There were in excess of 800 course enrollments in 74 small schools. The Department and participating school districts allocated 14.5 teaching units to the project and could use any of nine instructor sites in various schools, board offices and at the Telemedicine Centre. Operating on a six-day cycle and a common school calendar, the schools integrated AL and AGL into a regular school day; school administrators have been extremely cooperative regarding scheduling.

Evaluation instruments are prepared a year in advance and sent to schools during the summer. After students complete the various assessments, they are sent to the appropriate instructor by facsimile machine; results are returned the same way. Evaluations indicate that these students perform as well as their counterparts who are taking the same courses with direct-teacher instruction.

In 1996-97, a chemistry course was offered for the first time, four additional sites were added and one more instructor joined the team.

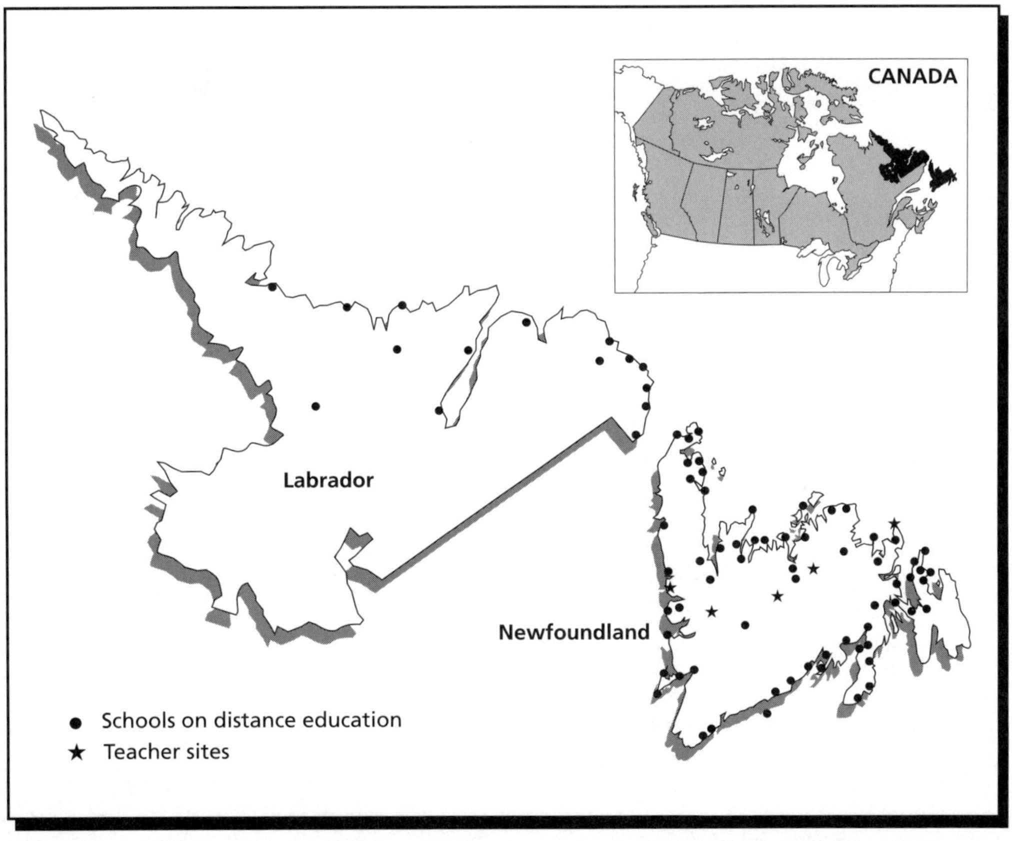


**FIGURE 7.4: Map of Small Schools Project sites in Newfoundland and Labrador**

The Resource Kit contains an example of a Participant Feedback form from an AL course. The Kit provides a number of other evaluation forms you might like to review and adapt to your own needs.

A reference to this handbook is provided in the Resource Kit.

## Serving Mature Learners

*Cambrian College of Applied Arts and Technology, Sudbury, Ontario*

Cambrian College in Sudbury, Ontario, serves the large catchment area in Northern Ontario shown in Figure 7.5. Collaborating with the distance education network called Contact North/Contact Nord, the College offers a one-year certificate and a two-year diploma program through AL. Learning activities and course materials for the 23 courses and four field placements are fairly similar.

Approximately 23 students enrolled in the Health, Safety and Nutrition course in the diploma program offered in the fall 1996 semester. The learners were distributed over 10 sites, some of which were in aboriginal communities. Weekly one-hour learning sessions, videotapes, a textbook and a book of Ontario government legislation were the primary resource materials. Learner support documents included a study guide and a student handbook on teleconferencing.

Donna Mese, instructor, course author and coordinator of the program, shares three lessons learned. The first relates to the lack of visual contact: "I learned to communicate with my students in a different way. I really worked hard at encouraging the students to talk a lot. In fact, they actually talk more

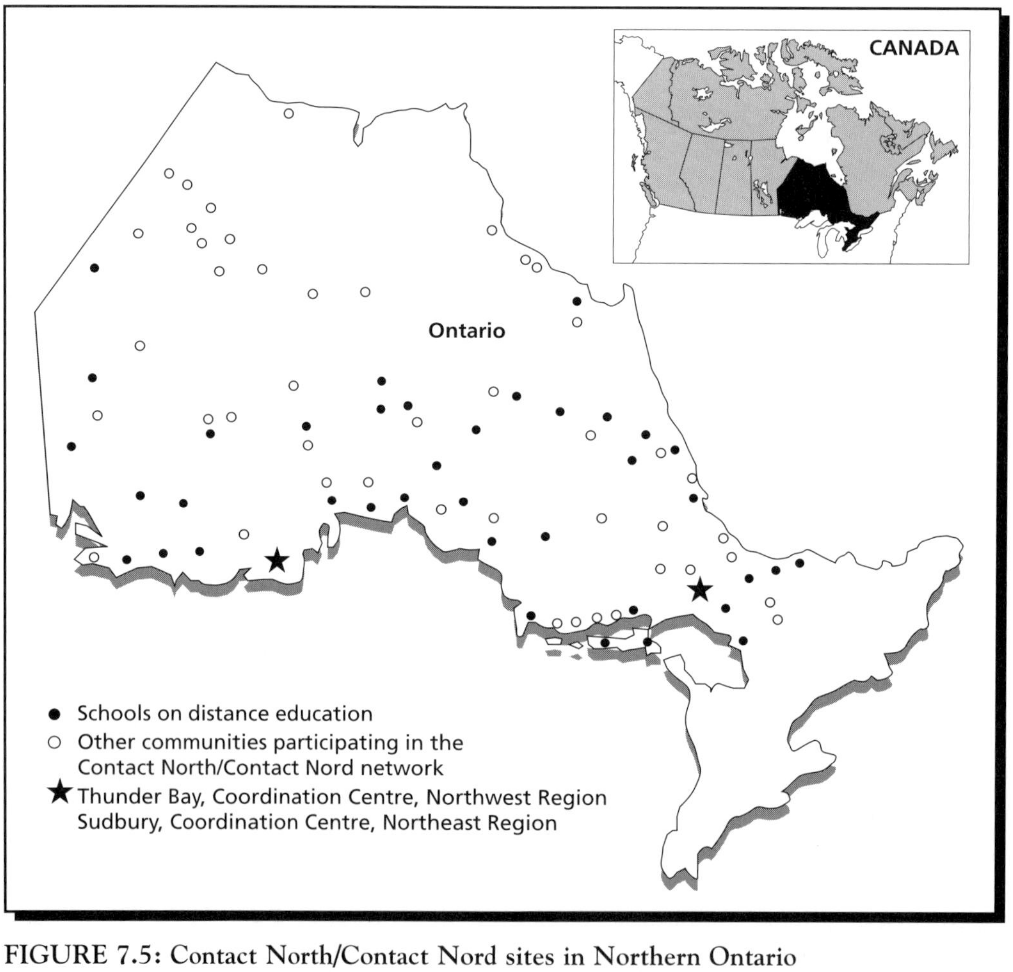


FIGURE 7.5: Contact North/Contact Nord sites in Northern Ontario

than me. Lecturing does not work." The second relates to learning how to teach in AL: " … it helps when people sit in on another teleconference [AL session] with an instructor. I had a lot of instructors sit in on my courses and it is so helpful for them to do that because they hear *what* you say and *how* you say it." Her third piece of advice relates to using the equipment: "Practice with the equipment. It is important to know what to do if you have a problem: e.g., the telephone number to call for help."

### Cost-Effective Learning in Developing Countries

*Distance Education Centre, University of the West Indies (UWI)*

Started in 1982, the University's AL and AGL network links 26 sites throughout the English-speaking Caribbean countries of the Commonwealth. Technical, program and administrative support comes through offices located on the three main UWI campuses. First-year university courses in arts, social science and education were the first programs available on the network. Approximately 2,000 students per year enroll in these courses, earning certificates in public administration, business administration and education. Program expansion is now under way, with second- and third-level courses being added to support specialties such as management studies, agribusiness management and construction engineering.

Typically, courses are taught by means of a two-hour-per-week AL or AGL session for each week in the semester, supported by at least one two-hour tutorial convened by a locally hired tutor approved by UWI faculty. Instructors are encouraged to prepare print supplementary materials and to use the audiographics device as they would a chalkboard in a classroom.

Michael Anyadike-Danes is a professor of economics at the UWI Barbados campus who has been using AL for the past six years. His classroom strategy relies heavily on question-and-answer techniques: "They completely inform my approach to instruction." After experiencing a number of problems because of the large numbers of students in his classes, the lack of a visual channel of communication and the burden of trying to use the graphics device, he has come to rely exclusively on AL and has developed two key strategies: he uses a course manual and prepares a carefully structured agenda.

The manual is written so that it can be easily referred to (each paragraph is numbered and units within the manual coincide with the weekly AL schedule). The most recent version includes learning activities that are designed to test retention of the material, focus on key discussion issues and guide the local tutorial sessions. A key feature of the agenda is a roll call of all sites: "I know what sites are on-line and it sends an important message to students right at the start." The previous week's work is then reviewed, off-line discussions may be held and group responses are solicited. "Knowing when and how to pose questions that will trigger a response is what I find the key to an effective session. … What I have learned from AL sessions is to wait and not worry about lengthy pauses on air." Sessions typically conclude with Michael reviewing key points and then setting up a case study for discussion in a tutorial session that occurs at each site and is facilitated by an on-site tutor.

## Competency-based Workplace Training

*United States Postal Service*

Over 950 audiographic devices have been installed in 460 cities throughout the United States in Post Office facilities where personnel repair and maintain vehicles and equipment. Although up to 48 concurrent AGL sessions can be held through the Post Office's bridge, there are typically only nine courses running during an average day. A course usually runs about four hours a day over a 9-to-12-day training cycle and has up to four participants at between 20 to 50 sites at a time. The network carries about 40,000 hours of instruction in any given year. A typical course combines AGL, access to on-site subject matter experts, print self-paced study "packets" and periodic proficiency assessment tasks. Courses are occasionally supplemented with live or prerecorded video. Instructors are drawn from the workplace, given training in the principles of adult learning and course development with on-the-job training using the audiographic equipment and awarded a certificate in adult vocational training. Says Network Director Zeke Osborn: "The technology itself is irrelevant ... it's what happens to the learner that counts" (MacDonald, 1998).

Initial reaction to the technology several years ago was that everyone wanted the traditional classroom-based method or, if that wasn't possible, television. "We have found, however, that our audiographic process is resulting in greater retention rates, shorter learning times and much better content and training materials. Instead of listening to someone else's interpretation of the content (as in face-to-face instruction), the approach [AGL] gets participants more focused on their own learning" (MacDonald, 1998). In 1997, the Network's tenth anniversay year, instructor and learner resistance to this approach has virtually disappeared. And the United States Post Office estimates that the program saves $6 to $7 million per year in avoided travel and other costs.

## Reducing Technical Costs through Partnership

*Contact North/Contact Nord, Sudbury and Thunder Bay, Ontario*

Established in 1986, Contact North/Contact Nord has a two-pronged mandate: (1) to improve access to formal and informal secondary and postsecondary education and training for residents of Northern Ontario, including the special needs of Francophones and aboriginal peoples and (2) to support innovation in learning through exploration and evaluation of new modes of delivery using technology. It shares information across Northern Ontario, nationally and internationally. Headquartered in Sudbury and Thunder Bay, Contact North/Contact Nord serves Northern Ontario communities through a combination of 150 community access and participating sites. Contact

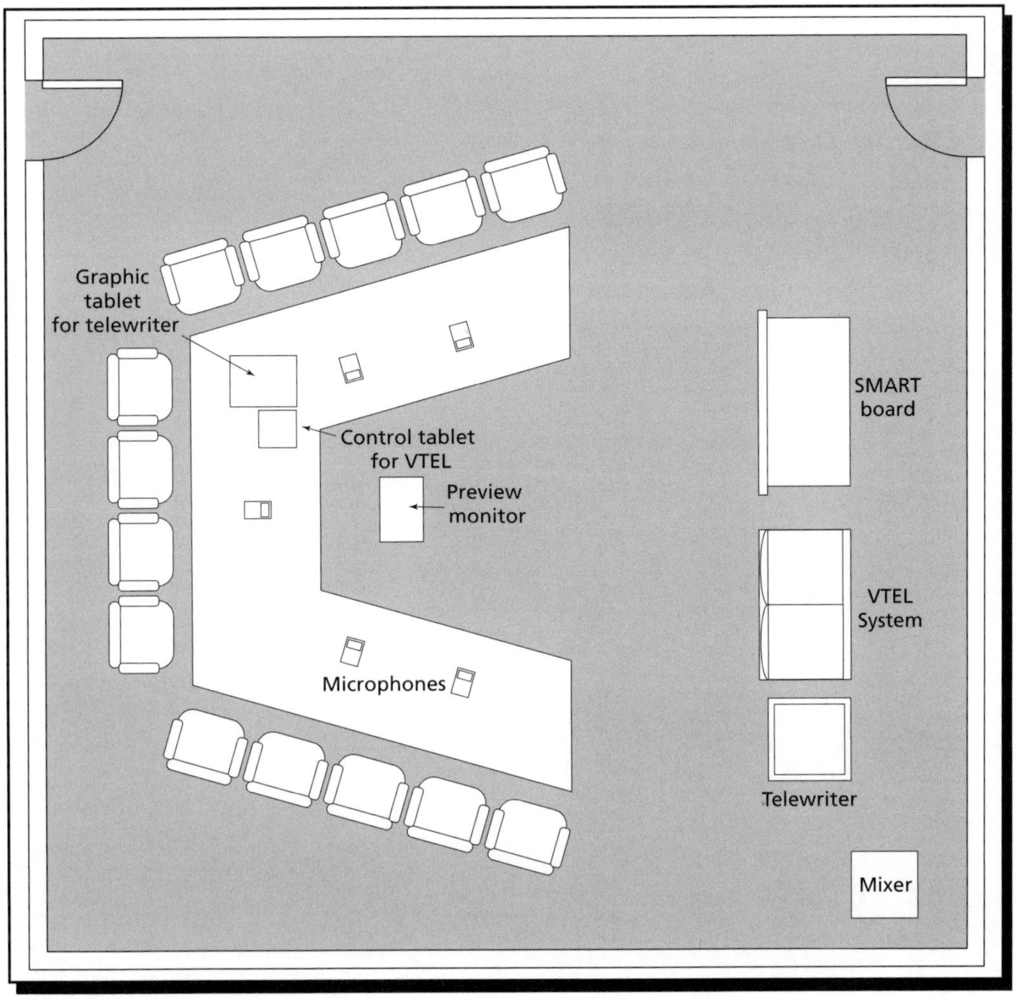


FIGURE 7.6: Example of a Contact North/Contact Nord site

North/Contact Nord's extensive communications network is used by educational institutions and non-profit and private sector organizations.

Sites are equipped with audio and audiographic conferencing systems, as well as with computers, printers, facsimile machines and audio and video recorders (see Figure 7.6). An increasing number of sites have compressed video learning equipment and Internet connectivity. Contact North/Contact Nord provides instructor training sessions on how to use its learning technologies.

## CONCLUSION

Through reading this chapter, you now know the basics of how AL and AGL technologies work and how they support learning. You have considered their opportunities, strengths and limitations. Preparation, delivery techniques and evaluation have been reviewed. Finally, you have read selected success stories that colleagues have shared.

We believe you will see how these techniques and technologies are the foundation for many issues we will now review concerning Networked Learning.

# References

Cookson, P. S. (1995). Audioconferencing: Instructor and participant responses to critical conditions. *Techtrends, 40*(4), 23-25.

———. (1989). Research on learners and learning in distance education: A review. *The American Journal of Distance Education, 2*(2), 22-34.

MacDonald, D. (1998). *Audio and audiographic learning: The cornerstone of the Information Highway*. Montréal, QC: Chenelière/McGraw-Hill.

Rowntree, D. (1994). *Teaching with audio in open and distance learning: An audio-print package for teachers and trainers*. London, UK: Kogan Page.

# Chapter 8

# Networked Learning: How Do We Facilitate Learning on the Internet?

*... [this paper describes] the joyful serendipitous discoveries that I'm eager to share with anyone who may be contemplating teaching by computer.*

MARY DERESHIWSKY,
NORTHERN ARIZONA UNIVERSITY, PHOENIX, ARIZONA

## INTRODUCTION

After reading this chapter, you will have explored how Networked Learning technologies offer key opportunities, strengths and limitations for learning. You will have more ideas about how to prepare for and deliver Networked Learning and how to evaluate the results.

## HOW DOES NETWORKED LEARNING WORK?

Networked Learning (NL) happens when learners and instructor use computers to exchange messages, engage in dialogue and access resources as part of a learning process. The interaction can occur in real-time, when learners and instructor are communicating at the same time from different places, or in delayed-time, when they are not linked simultaneously. Chat lines are examples of communication that occurs when all users are linked at the same time. E-mail is an example of communication that occurs in delayed-time, somewhat like writing and receiving a letter through the postal service. One person can compose and send a message at a totally different time from when the other person receives it.

Networked Learning has three technical elements (see Figure 8.1).

1. Individual computer terminals with relevant software and modems, or workstations, which look like computers but don't have modems.
2. Lines that modems use to dial other modems. These can be regular telephone lines or special, higher-speed computer lines, either of which can be provided by satellite, cable or telephone networks as shown in Figure 8.1, or they can be lines that permanently link the workstations.
3. Client servers that manage the linkages among the individual computers and permit activities such as e-mail, bulletin board systems and LISTSERV, as well as delayed or simultaneous discussions and resource searching.

When workstations exchange messages, they are almost always functioning in a proprietary organizational network called an Intranet, or a local area network

(LAN), or a wide-area network (WAN), depending on the geographic area, data speed and other technical features of the network. Figure 8.1 could be considered an Intranet.

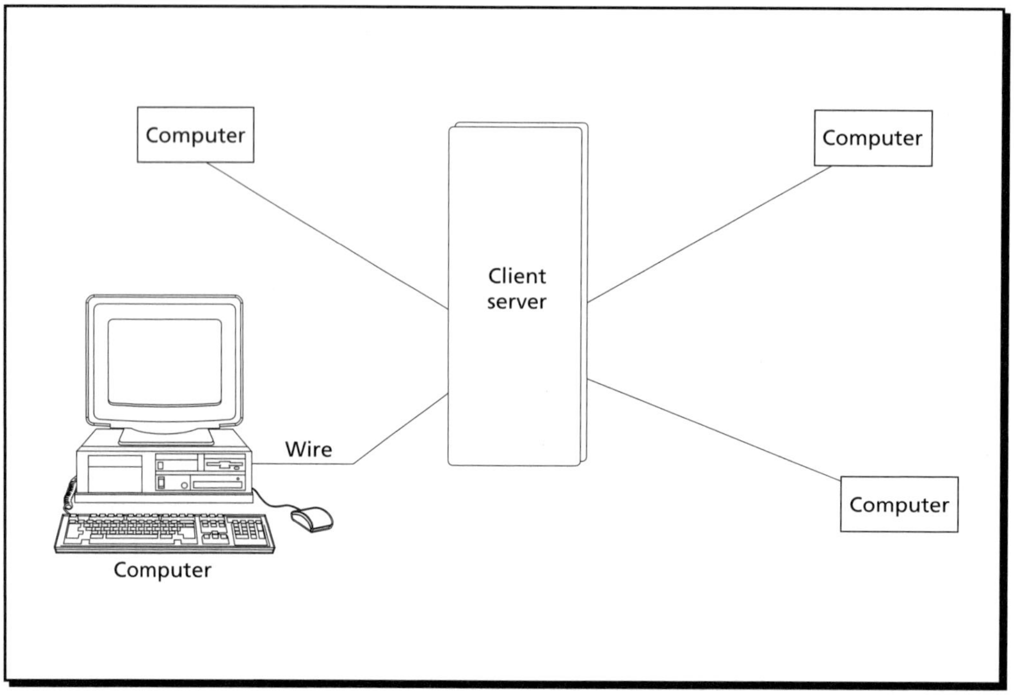


**FIGURE 8.1: Three technical components of an Intranet**

Increasingly, Intranets are acquiring access to, and joining, the Internet, in which case users have a choice of functioning within the proprietary environment or going beyond it to a wider context.

When individual computers with modems connect with one another, they are almost always using the vast "network of networks" called the Internet (see Figure 8.2). Colleges, universities and a growing number of schools tend to have direct access to the Internet, while home and workplace users generally have to purchase access through an Internet Service Provider (ISP).

Historically, the first types of NL to be developed were electronic mail (e-mail), which was sent to named individuals, bulletin board systems (BBS), where messages could easily be posted to a group, and list servs, another method of posting group messages. The latter two are sometimes referred to as computer conferencing. Such activities occur in delayed, or asynchronous, time (learners and instructors do not have to be linked at the same time as they do in Audio or Audiographic Learning). These types of NL are quite cost-effective and are the most frequently used. Recently, however, NL can occur simultaneously in real-time through specialized text-based computer conferencing software systems such as Multiuser Object Oriented (MOO) systems, which may be more expensive and require learners and instructors to coordinate their schedules. The World Wide Web (WWW) is a communications protocol of the Internet through which these types of activities may take place.

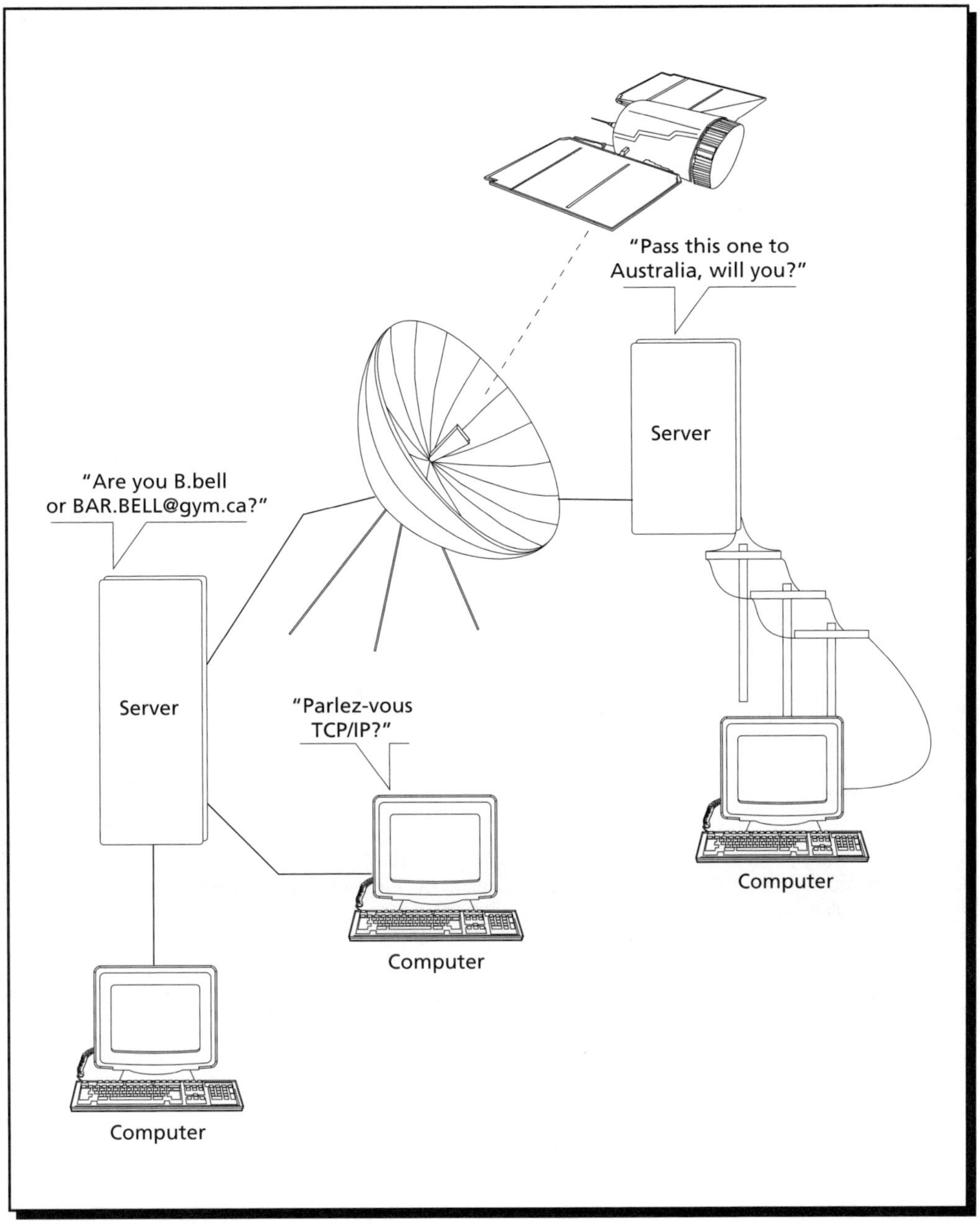


FIGURE 8.2: Technical components of the Internet

Technical support is needed for NL systems. Some support relates purely to the technology and does not need to be understood by users. Other support is important for users as it consists of the training and troubleshooting services available to them. Technical support can be available on-line, in tools stored in the software or through e-mail, in print guides or by telephone. You may have occasion to use all three at various times throughout a learning event.

We believe that there are a few terms that you, as an instructor, need to understand to ensure that your technical support person addresses them for you. They are screen wrap, virus and accent enabler.

INCLUDE A TECHNICAL SUPPORT PERSON IN YOUR PLANNING TEAM TO DETERMINE THE BEST ONGOING MODE OF SUPPORT FOR YOUR NEEDS. FOR EXAMPLE, IMMEDIATE TELEPHONE HELP COULD BE VITAL IN A SHORT SESSION WHEN ADVANCE TRAINING IS NOT POSSIBLE, WHEREAS ON-LINE TOOLS AND E-MAIL MESSAGES MAY BE ADEQUATE FOR AN EVENT SUCH AS A SEMESTER-LONG COURSE.

SCREEN WRAP Screen wrap means that text will be broken at the boundaries of your screen so that you can read screens easily. You will need to scroll up and down, but you should not have to move sideways to read comments. Screen wrap is essential for anything other than the exchange of very brief e-mail messages.

VIRUS A computer virus is a "rogue" computer program that is designed to replicate itself in the memory or storage devices of other computers. It is spread through computer networks and through the exchange of floppy disks. Virus protection is essential.

ACCENTS If you plan to work in a language other than English, special software may be needed so that the accents appear as they are supposed to. Figure 8.3 shows how a message may look if accent protection was not available.

Offre d'emploi
**************

Le Centre de conception et d'appui p=E9dagogique
Gestionnaire de projets
Contrat de 6 mois, renouvelable

Le Coll=E8ge est =E0 la recherche d'une personne pour combler le poste de gestionnaire du Centre de conception et d'appui p=E9dagogique externe. =

Le Coll=E8ge est un =E9tablissement de formation postsecondaire d=E9di=E9 =E0 l'excellence en =E9ducation et sp=E9cialis=E9= en formation =E0 distance.

R=F4le et responsabilit=E9s :

Sous la direction de la Vice Pr=E9sidence Innovation et D=E9veloppement, =
le ou la titulaire du poste devra entres autres offrir des services de
consultation en formation =E0 distance, en conception p=E9dagogique pour =
la formation =E0 distance et en apprentissage ouvert aux autres secteurs du
Coll=E8ge et =E0 des partenaires et clients =E0 l'ext=E9rieur du Coll=E8g=
e. Il, elle sera =E9galement responsable d'identifier et de g=E9rer en =E9troite=
collaboration avec les secteurs concern=E9s, des projets innovateurs en
formation et gestion =E0 distance et en apprentissage ouvert. Le, la titulaire devra trouver du
financement pour les divers projets du centre et repr=E9senter le Coll=E8ge aupr=E8s des
divers clien=ts.*

**FIGURE 8.3: Example of a message with faulty accent protection**

## WHAT ARE NETWORKED LEARNING'S STRENGTHS? WHAT ARE SOME KEY ISSUES?

Networked Learning has a number of strengths. But we need to pay attention to several key issues if we are to realize its benefits. Table 8.1 summarizes nine strengths and eight key issues related to the effective use of NL.

Let's now briefly consider each of these points.

CONVENIENCE Learning can occur at a desktop, study center, home or anywhere that is equipped with a computer. Learners with tight or unusual time schedules like the flexibility offered by asynchronous learning and find it to be

**TABLE 8.1:** NETWORKED LEARNING: STRENGTHS AND KEY ISSUES

| STRENGTHS | KEY ISSUES |
|---|---|
| • Convenience<br>• Potential quality of learning<br>• Affordability<br>• Equitableness<br>• Variety<br>• Creativity<br>• Reliability<br>• Expandability<br>• Convergence | • Clarity of needs<br>• Feedback<br>• Learner support<br>• Organization<br>• Comfort with technical skills<br>• Standardization<br>• Costs<br>• Health risks |

a significant advantage. Learners in different time zones can participate in classes because of the time delay. People can learn when they are ready to do so, not when they are coerced by an external schedule. Personal convenience may enhance learning effectiveness.

Typically, NL suits learners with well-developed independent study skills who have the organizational skills to search out and integrate Internet resources, which are far beyond what any one instructor could make available. These learners do not feel the need to see, hear or interact with colleagues in real-time and have the capacity for delayed-time interdependence and interactivity. Some might see this as a limitation, especially if learners are expected to have interaction skills as a prerequisite. What do you think?

POTENTIAL QUALITY OF LEARNING A. Freeman at Greenwich, England, has just completed a pilot project on teaching economics. He believes that the principal gains of NL for education are the improved quality of the student learning experience, not cost savings. "Computers make it possible to construct student-centered elements of the course, which gives them the confidence to explore the subject on their own, provided the subject specialist is there to catch them when they need a proper critical discussion of what they have done" (1996). This feature is not inherent to the technology but depends on how the technology is used.

AFFORDABILITY NL has a low delivery cost per unit of information compared with other technologies. Some institutions feel that, aside from some technical support, it does not require the extensive staffing, production or technical facilities that technologies such as broadcast television do. If students pay for printing course materials off the Internet, institutional printing costs are reduced. On the other hand, some may feel it inappropriate to transfer these costs to the learners.

EQUITABLENESS Some learners report that they do not feel intimidated by the instructor or their peers the way they do in the classroom or when using other types of learning technologies, because they do not have to deal with the visual or verbal indicators of power that discourage them from "speaking up."

Learners who are physically or socially restricted find NL an empowering technology. Some people are "just plain shy." This user perspective is, we believe, a common reason why people like NL: "I suffer terribly from 'stage fright' so I dread face-to-face or public speaking contact" (Burge & Roberts, 1993, p. 51). Learning activities such as role playing require learners to engage in decision making. Some instructors believe that decisions are reached more readily in networked environments because physical characteristics such as another person's size do not influence behavior.

VARIETY Interaction can occur with people (other learners, outside experts, colleagues) or learning resources (libraries, art galleries) in different formats (text, graphics, audio or video clips). These can be blended in a variety of learning activities (seminars, small-group discussions, independent study, debates, assignments) in ways that suit learner needs and styles. There is little pressure to respond "on the spot" to questions, so reflective learning is enhanced. This kind of learning is critical to some types of learners and some course content.

CREATIVITY Some learners and instructors feel that creativity is enhanced because they are not distracted by visual cues and are free to concentrate on ideas. "The self-consciousness monitor is turned off," is how Nicola Carter, former Technical Analyst, Computing Services Department at the University of New Brunswick in Fredericton, puts it. Real-time software should be used to support this type of NL so that the flow of innovative ideas is maximized.

RELIABILITY Established tools are available that enable instructors and learners to use well-tested approaches and retreat from the dangers of the "bleeding edge," which is to say, using "cutting edge" technologies in ways that damage the learning context, or using technologies that are so new they are prone to unknown problems.

EXPANDABILITY NL can start within a small, well-defined institutional environment and grow to be global in coverage as instructors gain confidence with the pedagogy and technology. Applications can also grow in scope because the hardware and software that support learning can also support the management and evaluation of learning. This increases the possibility that institutions may find it practical to offer services such as continuous registration and pre- and post-testing services the way organizations such as IBM's Desktop University do. Liz Sauter, manager of Technology Based Training at IBM Canada's Toronto office, notes: "We find that the learning and learning management software are highly interdependent. This software configuration enables learners to assess their own learning needs and access the content they require without being dependent on an instructor or a classroom schedule."

CONVERGENCE The computer's digital technology is the tool that is changing television, telephones and a wide range of devices that are, at present, physically separate pieces of equipment, but are rapidly becoming integrated. Learning how to use computer technology while it is still simple and separate could be a foundation skill for the future when it is complex and integrated.

The following eight key issues need to be addressed so that they do not limit the strengths that we have just discussed.

CLARITY OF NEEDS Appreciating the core learning objectives, strategies and activities will enable you and your technical support colleagues to select software that will fit your needs. Don't be afraid to give up the glitz if it is not functional given the learning plan and characteristics of your learners. In this, NL resembles all technologies—glitz can be distracting.

BE SURE TO TELL LEARNERS HOW OFTEN YOU PLAN TO GO ON-LINE PER WEEK AND HOW QUICKLY THEY CAN EXPECT A RESPONSE FROM YOU. DEPENDING ON THE SIZE OF THE CLASS, YOU MAY WANT TO SET LIMITS ON THE NUMBER OR LENGTH OF MESSAGES YOU CAN REACT TO. TRY ENCOURAGING LEARNERS TO RESPOND TO ONE ANOTHER AS MUCH AS POSSIBLE, SO THAT THE BURDEN DOES NOT REST SOLELY ON YOUR SHOULDERS.

FEEDBACK Margaret Baltkalns, a part-time student in the University of Calgary's Masters of Continuing Education Program, reports that she and others in the program find that giving and receiving feedback in a NL course is very difficult. "Indeed, that is the biggest challenge which I have identified to date," she notes. First of all, the feedback is not immediate, as it is in real-time environments, and a week, or even a few days, is a long time to "suspend your thinking" until others react.

Secondly, the written word can be much more cutting than a verbal comment that can be quickly clarified: "Once something is in print, it is hard to explain and hard to take back," she cautions. This drawback only appeared with time; in the first semester, "we were very 'polite' to one another and were almost afraid to challenge one another's opinions."

LEARNER SUPPORT A. Freeman, in Greenwich, England, reports that "for me, the main problem is not that the computers displace the humans so much as [that] the administrators have a chronic tendency to systematically underestimate the level of human support actually needed" (1996). A web of support systems is required involving technicians, administrators and librarians. Without appropriate support, learners may procrastinate or use time ineffectively. These risks are inherent in any form of self-paced learning, unless specific and "enforceable" targets are set that create group pacing. Freeman notes, for example, that students saw classroom-based activities as an essential complement to NL; Baltkalns reports that her cohort has a spring workshop each year, and that the University brochure mentions that video and audio conferences are planned as learner support activities.

MARGARET BALTKALNS BECAME AWARE OF A TIME CONSTRAINT. SCHEDULING USE OF THE TELEPHONE LINE AND/OR COMPUTER AMONG FAMILY MEMBERS CAN BE CHALLENGING IN A HOME-BASED NL SETTING.

ORGANIZATION There are two major ways to organize materials contributed during computer conferencing: by subject matter (threading), and by time and date (in either chronological or reverse chronological order). Each has advantages; the critical issue for you as an instructor is to pick the method most appropriate to your learners and content.

It is important to formulate a framework regarding the length, frequency and style of messages that support the learning objectives and learners, and to model those guidelines in your own behavior as an instructor. Messages in a philosophy course taken by students with a lot of time for reading may be longer than those in a business seminar attended by time-constrained executives.

IF YOU THINK YOU NEED TO PREPARE A LOT OF WRITTEN MATERIAL, SEND IT IN PRINT FORM, OR ASK STUDENTS TO DOWNLOAD AND PRINT OFF AS LONG AS IMPORTANT FORMATTING CAN BE KEPT. REGARDLESS OF THE OBJECTIVES OR THE LEARNERS, NL IS BEST USED FOR TWO-WAY INTERACTION, NOT ONE-WAY DELIVERY, AS SCREEN READING IS TIRING FOR THE EYES.

For example, you may want to ask learners to spell-check messages that are part of a formal assignment, but give them permission not to reread and correct messages in more informal types of learning activities. As a general rule, "write as you talk" facilitates group development.

COMFORT WITH TECHNICAL SKILLS Reduce any anxiety you feel about the hardware and software you will be using by getting as much training and experience as you need before you start the course or workshop.

Simulate features that are particularly new to you; don't rely on "reading the instruction manual." For example, find colleagues willing to stimulate learner discussion groups so you can see how to edit assignments on-line if you plan to use that function.

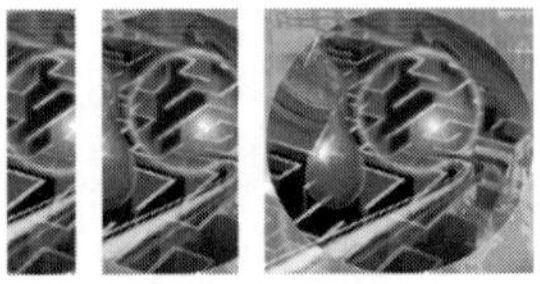

REMEMBER TO CREATE AN EQUALLY GENEROUS TIME FRAME FOR YOUR LEARNERS TO BECOME COMFORTABLE WITH THE TECHNOLOGY.

Keyboarding skills are essential to feeling that NL is "easy." Plan to acquire these skills before starting any type of NL. If you are going to share learning materials worldwide through the Web or within your organization through an Intranet, either you or a colleague need to know a specialized type of computer programming called HTML (Hypertext Markup Language).

STANDARDIZATION Many institutions find that the most efficient way to facilitate NL is to provide learners with software or to set a very specific software requirement that they must acquire. The time needed to troubleshoot 15 different software packages among 15 people is excessive, and the process is distracting to the learning. With consistency, there is no reason for a this-technology-never-works mentality to set in.

COSTS NL can be very inexpensive for learners if everyone composes messages off-line, keeps them short and uses the highest-speed modem possible. When learning in an Intranet environment where usage is "free," more work can be done on-line, but remember to respect colleagues' time by not writing more than is necessary. While the cost picture is changing so rapidly that most advice becomes immediately dated, we think it is important to note that NL time is probably "freer" to instructors than it may be to some or all learners. For example, an instructor working from an institutional environment will probably not be charged for computer time or access to the Internet, whereas learners who have to make a long-distance call in order to access the institutional computer or the Internet will be incurring charges. These can be minimized with off-hours, discount phoning, but as an instructor, you should be aware of your learners' cost environment when planning the frequency and length of NL activities.

HEALTH RISKS Excessive keyboarding with poor ergonomics or improper tools can lead to back or neck strain and various wrist injuries, including Repetitive Stress Injury (RSI). Techniques have been developed to avoid this problem. Ensure that elbows operate at 90° and that hands fall onto the keyboard, not stretch up to it. Eyes should look downwards. Practice proper techniques and share them with learners. Tools such as wrist rests and wrist guards are available. (See Figure 8.4 for correct posture.)

Chapter 2 also provides more information on this important topic. Using voice-driven software may allow you to avoid RSI, but it seems to create a new set of vocal health problems. Bodies under physical stresses and strains cannot work as well as they need to for effective learning.

Figure 8.4 and material in the Resource Kit give additional information on this often underestimated point.

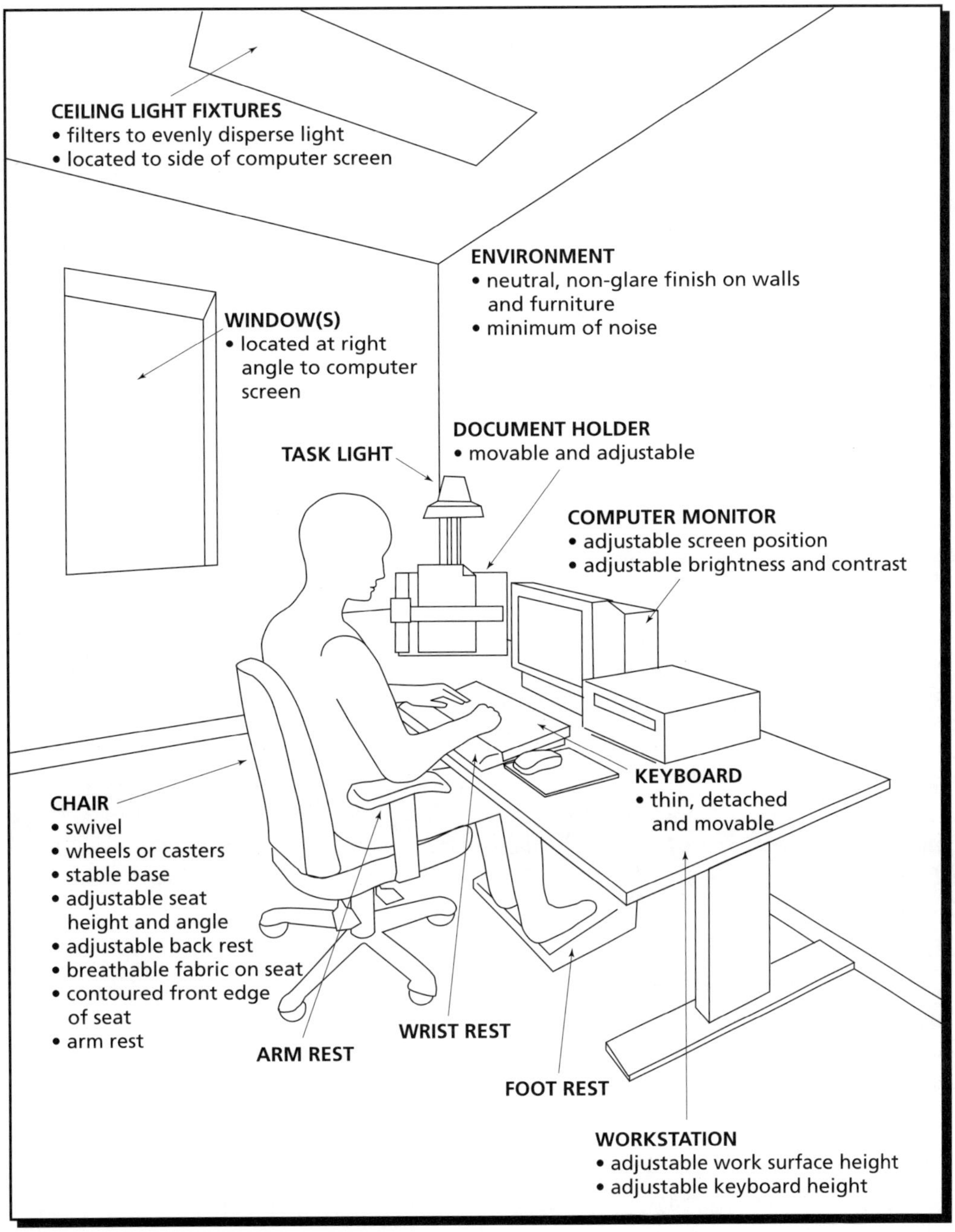


FIGURE 8.4: Effective ergonomics
Reprinted with the permission of the Canadian Centre for Occupational Health and Safety.

## HOW DO I USE NETWORKED LEARNING APPROPRIATELY?

### Preparation

When applying the CARE learning principles and strategies outlined in Chapters 3 and 4 to NL, we try to create classrooms that build on the interactive strengths of the medium. Our preparation framework in Table 8.2 features nine points. Let's consider each briefly.

**TABLE 8.2:** PREPARATION FRAMEWORK FOR NETWORKED LEARNING

| | |
|---|---|
| • Introductory document<br>• Visuals<br>• Lead time<br>• Learner characteristics<br>• Learning strategies | • Ergonomics<br>• Comfort with software<br>• Distraction<br>• Contingency planning |

THE LENGTH OF THE DOCUMENT WILL VARY DEPENDING ON FACTORS SUCH AS HOW EXPERIENCED THE LEARNERS ARE WITH COMPUTERS AND THE LENGTH OF THE LEARNING EVENT. MORE SOPHISTICATED LEARNERS NEED FEWER TECHNICAL INSTRUCTIONS. SHORTER EVENTS GENERATE LESS INFORMATION.

INTRODUCTORY DOCUMENT Prepared in print and then circulated, this document, which is a scaled-down Learner's Manual, is critical for both instructor and learners, particularly in longer learning events such as semester-long courses. However, it is a necessary tool even in a short training event. It should (1) contain clear directions for entering the NL environment(s), which learners will use to access the session, (2) outline the structure of the learning event and provide "module-by-module" expectations, so that learners are clear about what will happen and (3) present any off-line activities and materials required. Differences in learning styles may mean that some learners will not feel entirely comfortable relying heavily on NL. Long materials should be sent in print in any event (see Resource Kit).

VISUALS SHOULD ENHANCE PERCEPTION, NOT DISTRACT FROM IT. FOR EXAMPLE, THE HOME PAGE SCREEN SHOULD BE FREE FROM CLUTTER AND CLEARLY SIGNAL STRUCTURE AND MOVEMENT. AVOID CREATING FRIVOLOUS EXTRAS THAT CREATE INFORMATION OR TIME OVERLOAD.

VISUALS Build in variety and ensure that non-print materials are available. Most of what learners will create and share with one another will be text-based. To accommodate other learning needs, plan to direct learners to resources on the Internet that contain sound, color, still pictures and so on. To access these materials, learners need a graphical interface such as Netscape or Mosaic, and as powerful a modem as possible. The more sophisticated the graphic materials, the higher the modem speed that is required. Without a powerful modem, the time taken to download materials from the Internet can be lengthy. Not only will you and the learners be inconvenienced by the time, you will also pay more if you are using an Internet Service Provider.

If resources are not available on the Internet or your learners do not have high-speed modems, adopt other techniques. You could, for example, provide a videotape or a richly illustrated introductory document, or refer learners to a local library that may have accessible high-speed modems.

LEAD TIME Allow plenty of time, especially in a pilot project environment, for choosing the best software, pretesting technical configurations, and becoming comfortable with the software. As the instructor, you will inevitably be asked technical questions, and you will save a lot of time if you have already discovered the answer to one or two of the most obvious ones. Time is also needed to prepare, produce, copy and distribute the introductory document.

LEARNER CHARACTERISTICS In addition to thinking about whether your learners are self-motivated and independent learners who will find NL congenial, ask yourself a number of other questions. Are they likely to have a home or workplace computer? If there is a home computer, who gets priority access? Will it be an economic hardship to acquire one? Is there a computer at an institutional or community learning center that they could use? Will they need help in acquiring keyboarding or study skills? Will they have cost-effective access to the Internet or are long-distance charges an issue? Finding the answers to these practical questions will shape your learning design.

LEARNING STRATEGIES In addition to the generic learning strategies presented in Chapter 3, facilitators may develop approaches specific to a particular medium. Following the practice of our colleagues Margaret Haughey and Terry Anderson (1998), we chose these four categories to summarize NL learning strategies:

- strategies that capitalize on the distributed nature of NL
- strategies that stress critical thinking such as analysis, evaluation and argument
- strategies that focus on extending ideas and developing and considering alternatives
- strategies that enhance the sharing of ideas, learning with others and working together

ERGONOMICS Include tips on avoiding RSI and voice and other problems in the introductory document (see Resource Kit). Will learners need tips on lighting, font size and other screen writing and reading skills?

COMFORT WITH SOFTWARE Help learners learn how to use the software you've chosen and verify that they have a minimum level of comfort before starting intensive content-related learning. Be prepared for this technical learning process to take up to 30 percent of the time you allocated for the course or seminar.

DISTRACTION The Internet is such a rich environment that learners can get "lost" in it, particularly if they have a learning style that tends to seek more and more information. Plan ways to help them gain control. For example, suggest that they limit their time searching the Internet to a maximum of 20 minutes per topic, or recommend that they scan as many relevant references as possible before pursuing anything in depth.

CONTINGENCY PLANNING Don't be surprised if the occasional glitch occurs. It shouldn't, but it probably will and is not a cause for panic, especially if you have built adequate technical support into your overall learning plan. Chapter 10 provides examples and illustrates the sense of humor that is critical to success.

## Delivery

Once NL begins, learning can be enhanced if a number of task and social behavior protocols are observed throughout the learning process. Table 8.3 lists some task-related actions that the instructor, who should function largely as a moderator, can adopt to improve the learning process. In NL, the role of moderator is critical to keeping discussions on topic or to intervening with feedback when discussions among learners is inappropriate. If you are the moderator,

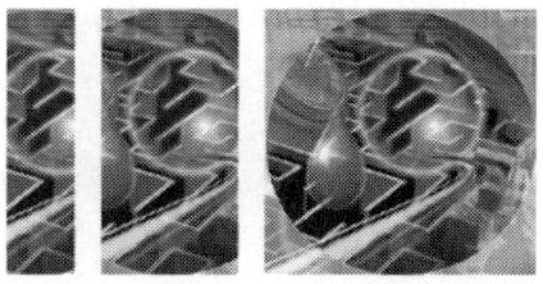

SHARI BALDWIN, EXECUTIVE DIRECTOR OF CANADIAN CABLE IN THE CLASSROOM, NOTES THAT "THE CABLE INDUSTRY IS ON THE LEADING EDGE OF HIGH-SPEED MODEM TECHNOLOGY USING THEIR FIBER COAXIAL BROADBAND NETWORK. THIS TECHNOLOGY PROVIDES TEACHERS AND STUDENTS WITH HIGH-SPEED ACCESS TO THE INTERNET ... [AND] ALLOWS THE INTEGRATION OF INTERNET RESOURCES INTO REAL-TIME TEACHING AND PRESENTATIONS. [IN CANADA] ROGERS' WAVE, SHAW'S QUEST AND COGECO'S LE RÉSEAU MULTIMÉDIA ARE JUST A FEW EXAMPLES OF THIS CABLE INDUSTRY INITIATIVE."

INCLUDE ONLY STABLE WWW ADDRESSES IN YOUR PLANNING. THEY CHANGE OFTEN SO CHECK THEM WHEN DESIGNING YOUR SESSION AND ON THE DAY YOU PLAN TO ASK LEARNERS TO USE THEM. BE CAUTIOUS ABOUT SHARING THEM IN PRINT.

you will need to be particularly alert to both task and social behavior given the lack of visual contact and, with some software, the time delay. When you have students sharing moderator duties, they may need initial guidance in how to manage the information flow and ensure equitable contributions.

**TABLE 8.3:** NETWORKED LEARNING TASK CHECKLIST

- ☑ Have clear objectives for the interactions. Learners should feel that their time on-line is well spent.
- ☑ Plan a structure of subconferences that focuses on specific topics and keeps messages linked. The "threading" software is an invaluable tool here.
- ☑ Don't create too many subheadings; two or three is generally a good maximum number.
- ☑ Keep all messages concise, on-topic and preferably no longer than one screen or 10 lines; one key idea per paragraph is recommended for easy tracking of ideas.
- ☑ Negotiate an acceptable grammatical style and rate of errors at the outset of the learning activity.

CREATE AN ELECTRONIC LOUNGE OR COFFEE SHOP, A PLACE WHERE LEARNERS CAN SOCIALIZE, AS EMOTIONAL BONDS ARE HELPFUL TO LEARNING. SUCH A PLACE HELPS KEEP SOCIAL MESSAGES WHERE THEY BELONG INSTEAD OF BEING DISTRACTIONS TO SUBSTANTIAL CONTENT-RELATED DISCUSSION.

A critical choice that you as learning facilitator and moderator of NL must make concerns the instructor style you will use. We offer three for your consideration:

- a directive style, in which you are fairly assertive and keep control of the session
- a facilitative style, where you stimulate peer learning through techniques such as learning circles and shared moderator duties
- a creative style, in which you are highly creative through techniques such as role playing and encourage learners to use their imagination to overcome the lack of visual and verbal cues

Which of these would you choose, when and why?

Next, we consider social behaviors. Table 8.4 lists nine social behaviors that, as moderators, instructors can use to encourage interactivity.

In spite of your best efforts, problems can occur. It is important to recognize them early so that the process is not distorted. Here are four of the more common pitfalls in NL to watch for and avoid:

- long messages
- brilliant off-topic messages
- lurkers
- frequent requests for technical help

Here are some steps you can take to address each of these situations.

STAY ON THE TIP OF AN ICEBERG BEFORE EXAMINING ITS MASSIVE HIDDEN BULK.

LONG MESSAGES Learners who send long, rambling messages that violate the protocols established by you and the group are the computer equivalent of microphone hogs in an audioconference. This behavior may be readily changed if you send a private e-mail message, or it may require voice communication to explore why this person is having problems participating appropriately.

**TABLE 8.4:** NETWORKED LEARNING SOCIAL BEHAVIORS CHECKLIST

- ☑ Use informal and courteous responses, directions and questions; they read better than a staccato, formal style.
- ☑ Introduce yourself and the conference rationale.
- ☑ Have learners introduce themselves to one another; use real names.
- ☑ Encourage people to stay current in reading and responding to their messages. A sudden enormous reply can create information overload and is discourteous to colleagues who are trying to maintain a learning schedule, albeit an elastic one.
- ☑ Use learners' responses constructively. Learners will feel respected and included.
- ☑ Model the writing style appropriate to your application of NL. In some subconferences, the style can be informal if you have created a "coffee break" subconference. In others, the style may have to be more formal and well argued if the agenda is a substantive discussion about content.
- ☑ Encourage learners to bypass you to talk to one another; ensure that you are not the message traffic cop.
- ☑ Encourage learners to follow the goals, objectives and protocols of the NL activities. Colleagues will not readily tolerate digressions from important topics or other dysfunctional social or intellectual behaviors.
- ☑ Use humor when you know the group very well.

MANY SOFTWARE PROGRAMS ENABLE YOU TO SET UP SUBCONFERENCES TO HELP ORGANIZE DISCUSSIONS. SOMETIMES CALLED "THREADING," THIS CAPACITY IS ESSENTIAL BECAUSE OF THE HIGH NUMBER OF MESSAGES EXPECTED; IF THEY ARE DISORGANIZED, THE LEARNERS' THINKING IS LIMITED.

BRILLIANT OFF-TOPIC MESSAGES These distract other learners and should be dealt with by private e-mail or telephone. Learners who consistently place messages in the wrong subconference need attention. They may not understand how the software works or appreciate how inconvenienced time-constrained colleagues are by having to read and discard inappropriate messages instead of being able to read and reflect on pertinent comments.

LURKERS Learners who never participate are called lurkers, or Read Only Members (ROMs). At the very least, they are violating the ethics of NL by not contributing while benefiting from the work of others. They may also be negatively affecting their own outcome, since passive participation is not as conducive to learning as active, engaged behavior. As moderator, you need to take corrective action. One or two lurkers may be normal, but if you have several, there is a critical problem that needs to be addressed by you and the group as a whole.

FREQUENT REQUESTS FOR TECHNICAL HELP This indicates either a serious technical flaw or insufficient learner training. If the latter, time should be found for learners to acquire competency. If the former, technical support staff should be urged to find a solution. Such requests may also be an indicator that your own behavior is at fault; consider whether the "technical" questions really indicate uncertainty about your instructions or a lack of perceived openness on your part to questions.

INTERNET PROTOCOLS CALLED EMOTICONS HAVE DEVELOPED TO INDICATE HUMOR, EMPHASIS AND OTHER VOICE INTONATION CUES.

## Evaluation

We suggest that you focus on three aspects of evaluation as a framework for your thinking about NL:

- evaluating participants' learning experience and outcomes
- designing appropriate evaluations
- finding examples of NL evaluations

First, participants' learning experience can be evaluated according to a number of process issues, including quality of interactions, ability to work with peers and instructor, evidence of participation and level of small-group skills. Learning outcomes can be assessed using specific measures such as individual written assignments, structured examinations, group projects, presentations or a portfolio of work.

The Resource Kit contains two examples of NL evaluations that meet very different goals. Could either be adapted to your needs?

Designing appropriate evaluations depends on many factors. You may be interested in effectiveness, ease of use, time, transfer of skills and cost. In general, results to date indicate that NL is easy to use, very cost-effective and, when used skillfully, facilitates both conceptual and skill-based learning.

## WHO IS USING NETWORKED LEARNING SUCCESSFULLY?

Schools, colleges, universities and employers are all successful users of Networked Learning. We cite one example from each sector and refer you to Margaret Haughey and Terry Anderson's book in this Series, *Networked Learning: The Pedagogy of the Internet* (1998), for more details.

### Expanding Options in High Schools

*Garden Valley Collegiate, Winkler, Manitoba*

Larry Danielson and Lawrence Peters, both teachers at Garden Valley Collegiate in Winkler, Manitoba, recently developed secondary school courses that they presently offer through the school's Intranet using computer conferencing software called FirstClass. The courses, one focused on technical communication skills and the other using business writing and non-fiction sources to help students develop communication skills for the workplace, are available on-site, on-line from any computer in the school able to access the server and on a dial-up basis from students' homes.

Larry Danielson, the initiator of the project, says that the courses provide many tangible benefits to students. "Given that we are a rural school, these courses give students the opportunity to meet students from elsewhere and to bring in guests from around the world whom we couldn't afford to meet in person." He shares three additional lessons related to preparation time, learner characteristics and team members.

PREPARATION TIME The decision to move to Networked Learning was taken after a lot of discussion with experts and users, visits to sites where Networked Learning was in operation and a careful examination of competing technologies. After the initial decision to proceed in principle, the team took over a year to select the software system. Larry advises others: "Both in terms of pedagogy and technology, get as much information as you can before you start. Once you are under way, there are thousands of decisions to make."

LEARNER CHARACTERISTICS Larry also notes that it is important to know your learner and course characteristics. He wishes he had had another year to offer the course in a regular classroom before converting it to Networked Learning, so that he could have had more experience in knowing how students would react to assignments and topics.

THE TEAM Larry recommends having an instructional design specialist as part of the team, even if you are able to keep up to date with your own professional reading. The school now works with an instructional designer from the local community college. At the instructional design level, for example, it is important to monitor students' reading skills and not assume that they read everything on their screens even though they complete assignments. Questions that require students to do critical reading, not computer-text scanning, will reduce this problem. He also notes that it is essential to involve technical people from the beginning in all decisions. "While they had different questions, it was a strong alliance and helped prevent us making mistakes on many occasions," he added.

The school plans to move its course materials to the WWW and to include hyperlinks to additional resources "to provide a layered rather than a linear course."

## Developing a Virtual University

*University College of the Cariboo, Kamloops, British Columbia*

Multiple Academic User Domains (MAUDs) are an advanced type of computer-based "virtual university" environment. A MAUD enables students and instructors to pursue academic studies even though they are at different locations and interact with one another at different times. Jeff McLaughlin, a philosophy instructor in bioethics at the University College of the Cariboo, and Stephen Downes, a new instructional media design specialist at Assiniboine Community College in Brandon, Manitoba, have collaborated in developing the concept.

In a MAUD, courses, seminar groups, tutorials and a host of other resources are available seven days a week, 24 hours a day, with access simply "a modem away." Students who cannot attend a university campus for whatever reason log on to the MAUD. Instructors teach classes and hold office hours in the MAUD; they leave notes about assignments, give quizzes and tests, develop self-directed tutorials and attend professional conferences without leaving their offices. These, and other types of formal and informal activities, can take place in real-time or delayed-time.

In Jeff's philosophy course, class sizes range from 20 to 30 students. Sometimes everyone is on at once for a virtual meeting or professional development session. At other times students sign on at a time of their own choosing. A significant challenge experienced to date is the inability of persons unfamiliar with the MAUD environment to follow the directions and to spend time familiarizing themselves with it. He resolved this problem by creating an electronic tutorial that all new users must complete before they are allowed into the main area. Jeff offers these suggestions for overcoming learner unfamiliarity: (1) recognize that different learners have different abilities regarding the technology, (2) instead of expecting learners to start working on their projects immediately, give them some time to play and get comfortable with the system and (3) recognize that some learners may find informal "play" elements annoying, while others may become addicted.

### Graduate Business Degrees through Networked Learning

*Athabasca University, Athabasca, Alberta*

Athabasca's Centre for Innovative Management (CIM) offers Canada's first electronic Executive MBA program. The highly interactive, asynchronous format provides students with the flexibility of studying while continuing in their careers and the convenience of being able to study wherever and whenever they wish as long as they have access to an appropriate computer, modem and telephone line. CIM provides each student with Microsoft Office and Lotus Notes; the latter's software is used to link student computers and the Centre's server. Backup services are available through access to a group of graduate student advisors (GSAs) who can be reached by telephone and fax and who provide linkages with CIM's administrative and academic services.

CIM guarantees a minimum turnaround time of less than a week on all student assignments and expects all tutors to be in daily contact with their course to respond to student e-mail messages.

All content mastery and dialogue take place through the text, graphics, spreadsheet, e-mail and computer conferencing functions resident in Microsoft Office and Lotus Notes. CIM is currently developing other Internet-related delivery methodologies. The only other "technology" used is in-person contact tailored to meet the University's residency requirements. Over the three-year period, students are required to attend a one-week summer school and two weekend-long "schools."

Since the first intake of students in September 1994, over 287 people in Canada and Europe have enrolled in the Advanced Graduate Diploma and MBA programs. As a consequence, CIM now houses the largest and fastest-growing Executive MBA program in Canada (CIM, 1995).

Stephen Murgatroyd, executive director of University Development, notes that two key design features are: (1) a focus on the learning process and customer service and (2) a commitment to developing new course materials as the most cost-effective way to meet students' needs.

### Providing Internet-based Resources from the Workplace

*National Aeronautics and Space Administration (NASA), Moffett Field, CA*

NASA staff, parents and others interested in working on-line with students design and offer a series of interactive classroom activities through the Quest program. Designed to allow students to share in the excitement and results of some of NASA's work in science and engineering, such as Antarctic biology and robotics, the projects combine on-line interaction on the Internet with television broadcasts, videotapes and printed workbooks. In a 1994 report, the Quest group documented their experience, from which our colleagues Margaret Haughey and Terry Anderson (1998) have extracted four "lessons learned": (1) teachers are best able to use projects that respect the constraints of the classroom; (2) not all content experts are created equal, in other words, experts must have the personality, commitment, time and communication skills to ensure successful dialogue with remote students; (3) simplicity is the catchword for a successful project; and (4) "catch them while you can," which is a reminder that gathering evaluation data after a series ends is much more difficult in Networked Learning than in a classroom because no one is standing at the door collecting forms as the students leave the room.

Sharing resources and experts from your workplace through Networked Learning is highly rewarding, judging from NASA's enthusiasm, but it requires adaptation and planning.

## CONCLUSION

You have explored the opportunities, strengths and limitations offered by this technology. We hope you feel more secure about how to think about Networked Learning.

We will now explore Compressed Video Learning.

# References

Burge, E. J., & Roberts, J. M. (1993). *Classrooms with a difference: A practical guide to the use of conferencing technologies*. Toronto, ON: The Ontario Institute for Studies in Education—Distance Learning Office.

Centre for Innovative Management. (1995). *CIM in numbers*. St. Albert, AB: Athabasca University, Centre for Innovative Management.

Dereshiwsky, M. I. (1996). Murphy's Law (Mega)Bytes the dust: Debunking the myths of teaching by computer. *ED Journal, 10*(2), J-10-J-14.

Freeman, A. (1996). ALT-J (alt@vax.ox.ac.uk) Vol. 4, No. 1. Paper presented at the Association for Learning Technology.

Haughey, M., & Anderson, T. (1998). *Networked learning: The pedagogy of the Internet.* Montréal, QC: Chenelière/McGraw-Hill.

# Chapter 9

## Compressed Video Learning: How Do We Create Active Learners?

*The videoconference technology lends itself to the lecture mode, which I felt had to be avoided if I were to facilitate learning.*

SANDRA HODDER,
SHERIDAN COLLEGE, OAKVILLE, ONTARIO

### INTRODUCTION

By the end of this chapter, you will be able to identify the key opportunities, strengths and limitations of Compressed Video Learning (CVL) and how all these factors influence learning and teaching. You'll have more ideas about how to prepare, deliver and evaluate the results. The chapter concludes with some success stories.

### HOW DOES COMPRESSED VIDEO LEARNING WORK?

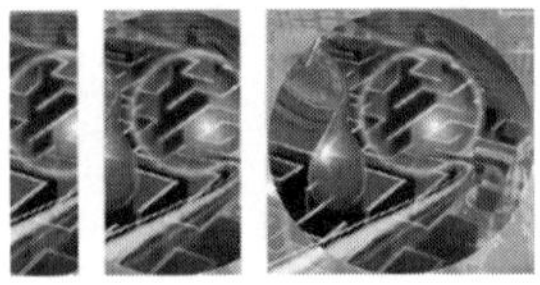

THINK ABOUT THE VISUAL FEATURE: WHEN AND WHY IS IT NECESSARY IN LEARNING?

Compressed Video Learning occurs when instructor and learners use microphones, cameras and other television equipment to exchange verbal and moving color images to engage in discussions, exchange messages and access experts as part of a formal or informal learning process. All such interactions occur in real-time, which means the learners and instructor are present at the same time and must coordinate their schedules.

Other terms for this activity include interactive television and interactive videoconferencing. The term *videoconferencing* can also be used to describe different equipment configurations from those treated in this chapter (one-way television with two-way audio). Because of these variations in terminology and equipment, it is important to know enough about the technology to ensure that the learning event is appropriate to your technical environment and your learning requirements.

Compressed Video Learning can occur in rooms or at the desktop. Our discussion applies to both locations.

As Figure 9.1 shows, CVL consists of three technical elements:

- a room environment with a minimum of one camera, a television monitor, a codec (video encoder and decoder), a microphone and a control pad for changing camera angles (Most vendors sell all these elements in a cart that can be wheeled from room to room.)

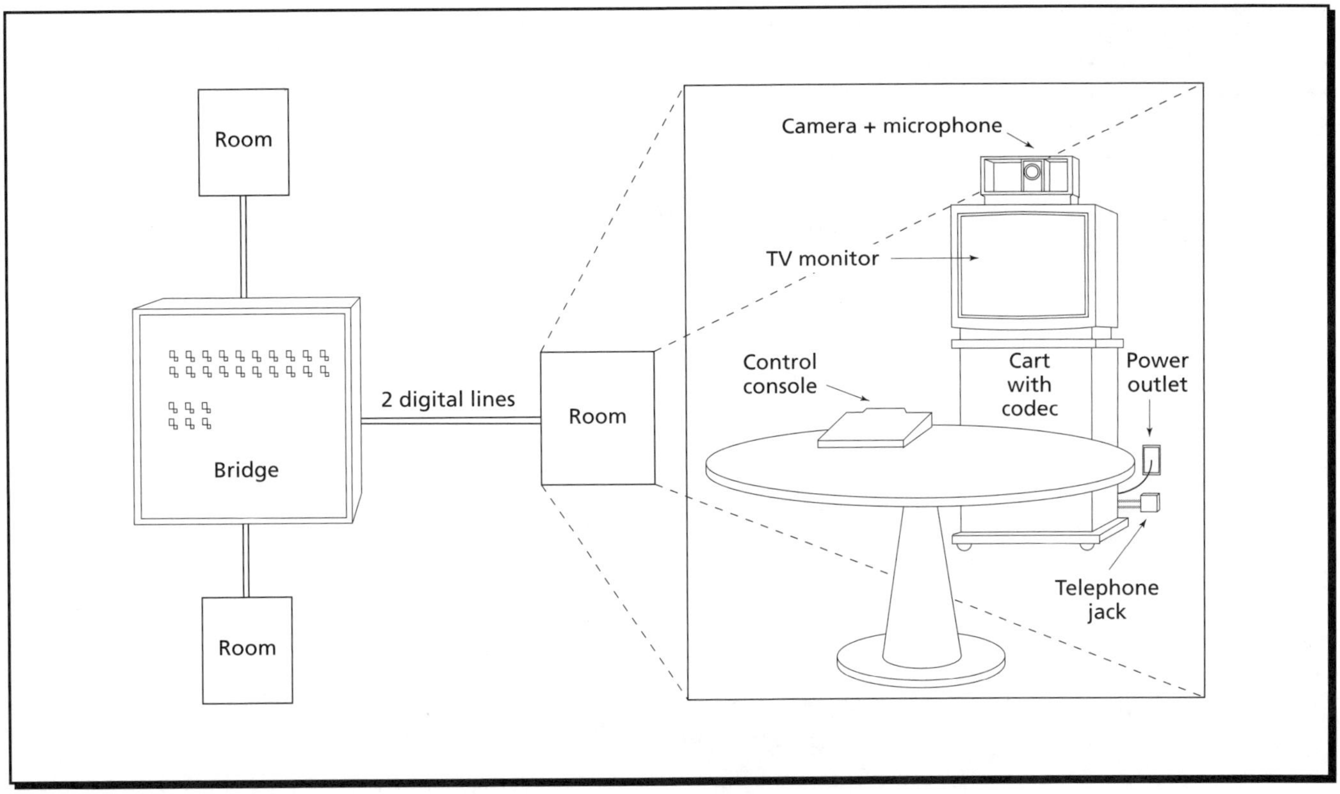


**FIGURE 9.1: Three technical components of Compressed Video Learning**

- the equivalent of two digital telephone lines (minimum)
- a mechanism for linking three or more sites called a bridge

Compressed video conference is the term used to describe this technical configuration.

A word about compression. Why are we using this term and what does it mean? Historically, "full motion" video such as we see on commercial television or a videotape required the equivalent of 1,200 non-digital telephone lines for each site to transmit a video signal. This capacity gives the illusion of full or natural motion. Compressed video equipment "squeezes" a picture down into a signal that can be sent on as few as two digital telephone lines or as many as 24. The equipment that does this compression (encoding) at the transmitting end and the decompression (decoding) at the receiving end is called a codec. The greater the compression, the less similar the CVL picture quality may be to that of full-motion video; you will see jerky motions instead of smooth ones.

Not all sites have the correct type of digital service. Either you or a technical support person should verify the kind of digital service available at each participating site before committing to a project.

Once you acquire an appropriate level of communications services, you may want to design your room different from the basic layout shown in Figure 9.1. Figures 9.2 and 9.3 show different room layouts for you to consider as starting points.

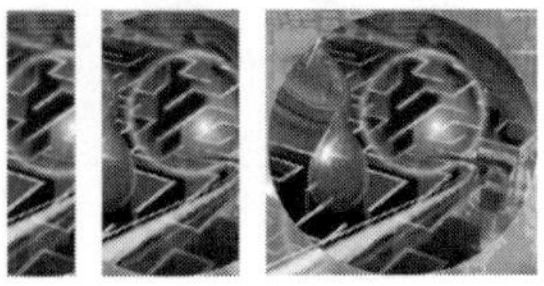

For convenience, we refer to the "telephone" lines involved, because telephone companies are major providers of the required service, and the concept of "number of lines" is easy to understand. However, cable companies and other types of vendors can also provide the communications service you need. Institutions can choose different technological solutions to provide the same level of technical service in their classrooms.

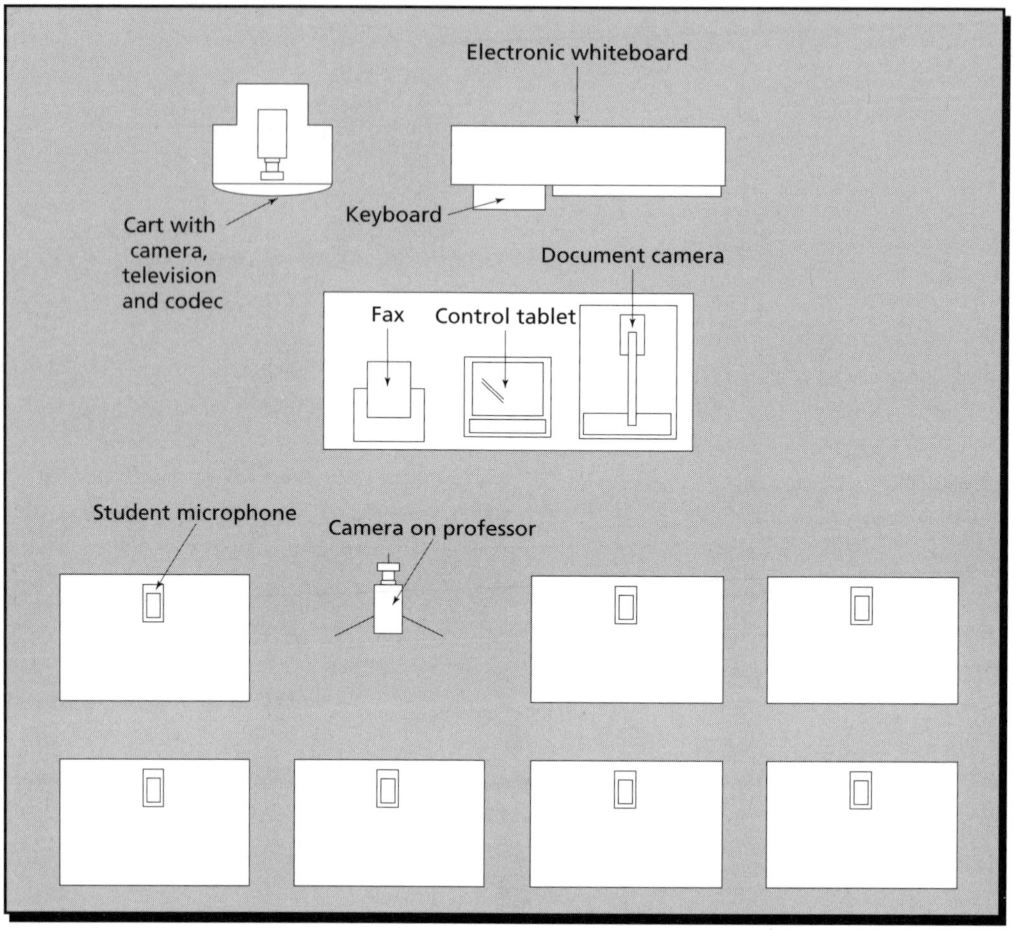


**FIGURE 9.2: Typical room in the Franco-Ontarian Distance Education Network**

Room layout is only one element that varies depending on user needs and preferences. Another is the design of the control pad. Figures 9.4 and 9.5 illustrate two different types of control pads. In general, the control pads provide the same functionality but look quite different. Typically, instructor comfort with the design of a control pad is a critical element when an institution is evaluating different brands of compressed video equipment.

As with Audiographic Learning, an instructor wanting to use Compressed Video Learning needs to know how to manipulate some of the equipment controls in order to plan a learning session. When you deliver the session, it is a good idea to have a second person operate the control pad, leaving you free to concentrate on learning issues. A learner can readily perform that function at each site. A technician is needed to service the equipment. Many organizations have a technician on call during learning events. As everyone gains experience, they tend to call the technician less and less frequently.

One specific challenge to orderly interaction occurs when switching between various sites in compressed video conferencing. The switching is typically sound-driven, which means the bridge connecting the sites shows a picture of the site that has requested the floor. However, the bridge cannot distinguish between

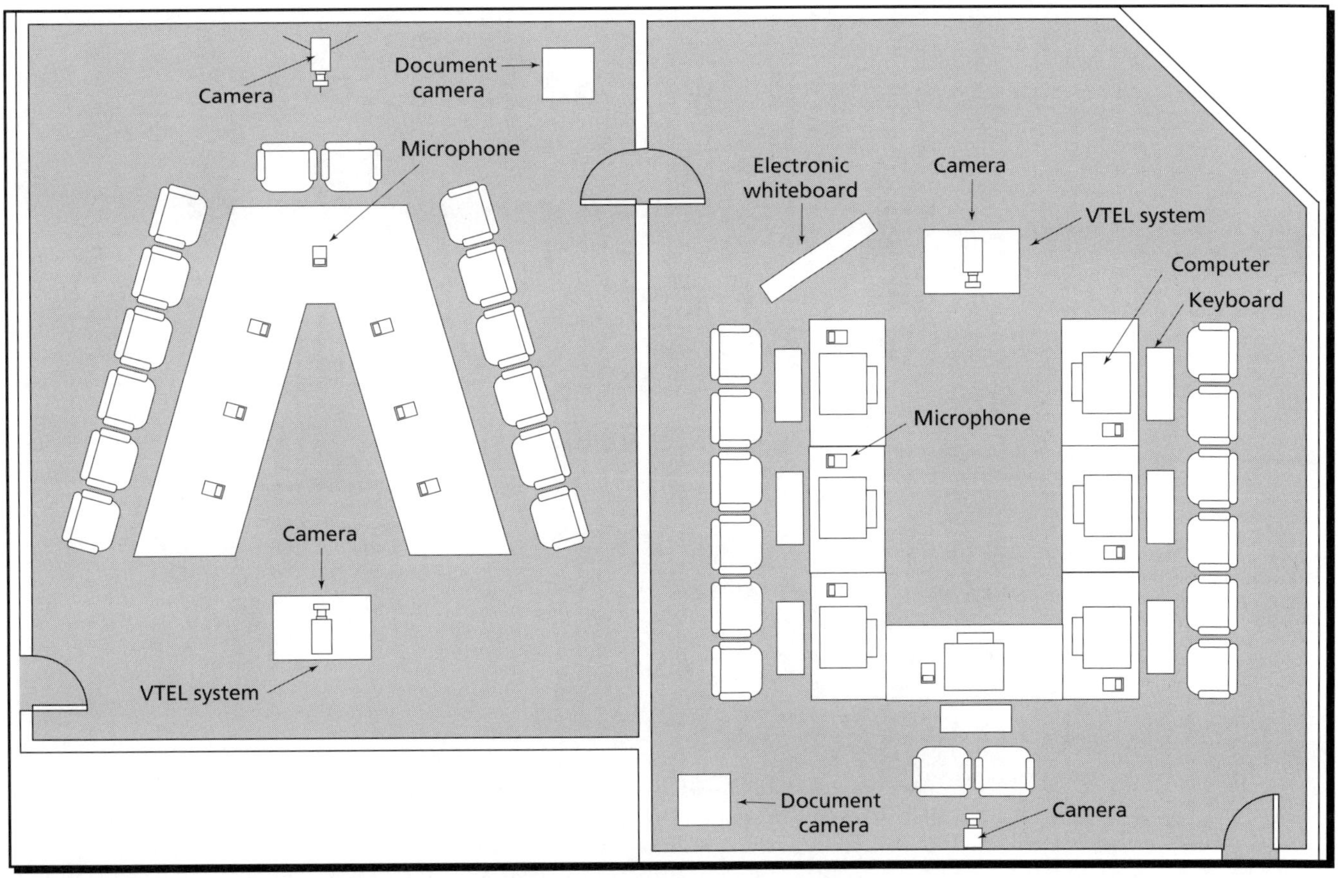


FIGURE 9.3: Le Collège des Grands Lacs room layouts

"approved noise" generated by a participant's comment and unintended noise generated by shuffling papers or side conversations. In her book on Compressed Video Learning in this Series, Judy quotes Jef Van den Branden of EuroPACE 2000 in Belgium, who reports that "it is therefore a good idea to have at each site a tutor or animator who is previously briefed about these issues and the seminar's agenda. This tutor can assist the seminar moderator by, for example, monitoring the local site for unintended noise, by facilitating discussion when questions are called for and by managing on-site activity when a technical problem occurs—which of course will happen now and then!" (1998, p. 47).

## WHAT ARE COMPRESSED VIDEO LEARNING'S STRENGTHS? WHAT ARE SOME KEY ISSUES?

CVL has a number of strengths but requires that we pay attention to several key issues. Table 9.1 shows our summary of 10 strengths and five issues.

Let us elaborate a little.

VISUAL PRESENCE Some instructors and learners have high social needs or a strong interpersonal learning style. Seeing a person adds an important extra dimension to learning dynamics for some people.

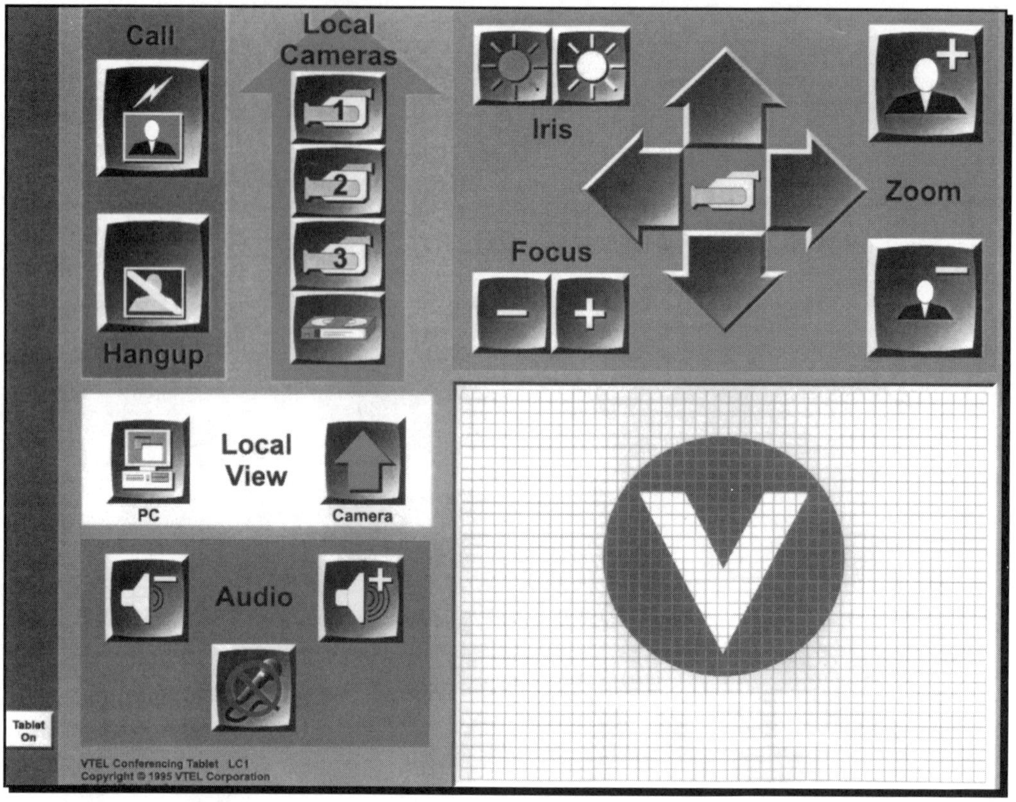


FIGURE 9.4: VTEL control tablet used by Laurentian University in the Franco-Ontarian Distance Education Network
Reprinted with permission of VTEL Corporation.

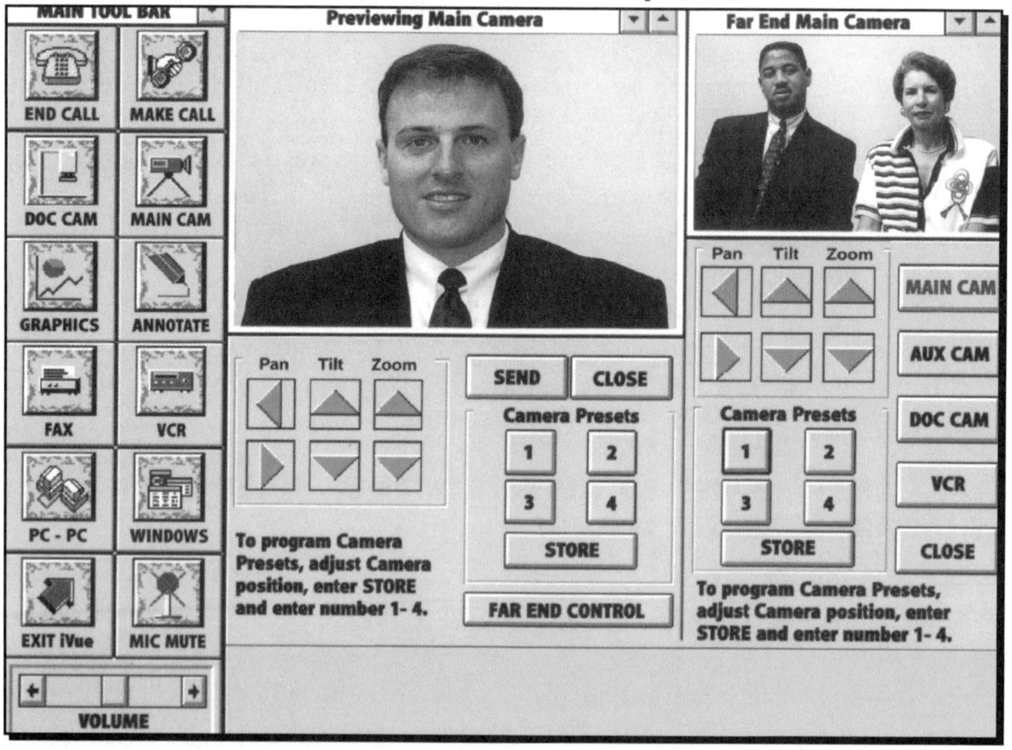


FIGURE 9.5: PictureTel control tablet used in the OLTEC Project at the University of Toronto. Reprinted with permission of ADCOM Inc.

**TABLE 9.1:** STRENGTHS AND KEY ISSUES OF COMPRESSED VIDEO LEARNING

| STRENGTHS | KEY ISSUES |
|---|---|
| • Visual presence<br>• Color and movement<br>• Interactivity<br>• Symmetry<br>• Flexibility<br>• Convenience<br>• Cost<br>• New revenue<br>• New partnerships<br>• Interconnectability | • Active learners<br>• Visual presence<br>— Using the camera<br>— Picture clarity<br>— Motion and pattern<br>• Ergonomics<br>• Sound quality<br>• Preparation |

Visual presence is important when attitude and learning with an emotional component are involved. It is less important when studying highly theoretical conceptual topics. Videoconferencing equipment would therefore be an advantage in teaching intercultural communication skills but would not add much to a course in philosophy.

COLOR AND MOVEMENT Being able to present colored moving visuals can be essential for some learning goals. For example, a simulated interview would benefit greatly from CVL, as body language is very important in such a situation. Learning activities such as role plays cited in Chapter 3 also lend themselves well to CVL.

INTERACTIVITY In both the human and technical sense, compressed video is a highly interactive medium that permits learners to be active participants in the process, not passive viewers of a screen. Figure 9.6 describes two techniques to stimulate the interaction and active engagement discussed in Chapter 3.

SYMMETRY The videoconference equipment shown in Figures 9.1 to 9.3 enables each site, and each group of learners, to originate learning activities. It is not like other types of television, where only one site, or studio, can originate programs, while the others are primarily recipients, with their interaction limited to voice or data. From a learning design perspective, therefore, all learners can be expected to contribute equally.

FLEXIBILITY Compressed Video Learning can be used for a wide variety of learning applications such as (1) showing case-study material, (2) conducting role plays, (3) demonstrating interview techniques and (4) presenting information requiring high-quality graphics or movement. Réal Samson, president of Le Collège de l'Acadie in Nova Scotia, cites an instructor who reports that "the technology allows me to be innovative and creative in presenting my material."

1. What is a project?
2. Which of the following could be classified as projects suitable for management by project management tools?
   a) Planning and holding a wedding reception
   b) Filling up at the local gas station
   c) Implementing a new Accounts Receivable System
   d) Billing clients for outstanding legal fees
   e) Building a wind-driven generator
   f) Fabricating a communication tower
3. What is a deliverable?
4. When planning a project, cost is one important aspect. Identify two other important aspects.
5. Before beginning your project, what factors should be considered?
   T F Purpose and objectives
   T F Detailed reporting format
   T F Obstacles
   T F Constraints
   T F Holidays
   T F Evaluation methodology
   T F Detailed time schedule

*This is a built-in quiz on a section of material that has just been presented in a session. Note that the questions are rather simple, but they permit the presenter to encourage participation.*

*He or she might assign some questions to each site to answer as a group or might ask specific persons to answer specific questions.*

*The quality of the answers will allow the presenter to know whether the learners have had any difficulties with any of the material and if so, he or she can conduct a quick review of a particular topic.*

*Learners like these quizzes as it allows them to discover whether they truly understood the content while they have the presenter available to help with any problems.*

*It stimulates discussion in a natural way.*

*This is an example of a fill-in type of exercise where teams at all sites complete the 5-minute assignment and then share their results using the document camera.*

**Connect the tasks to show predecessors and successors**

Draft proposal

Write proposal

Cost proposal

Submit proposal to management for approval

Submit proposal to client

*Note how the boxes have been sized for easy viewing on the document camera and how the page is oriented for that media also.*

FIGURE 9.6: Techniques to stimulate interaction
Source: Sandra Hodder, Sheridan College, Oakville, Ontario.

CONVENIENCE The equipment often sits on a cart, which can be rolled in and out of any classroom equipped with the right telephone jack (see Figure 9.1). The equipment can also be permanently installed in one room shared by many users. The choice is yours, depending on your needs.

COST Compared with the cost of many other types of educational television, or with the cost of travel, compressed video is cost-effective. For example, Transport Canada estimates that it recovered the cost of purchasing its equipment within 12 months because of the direct and indirect travel expenses that were saved (Roberts, 1998).

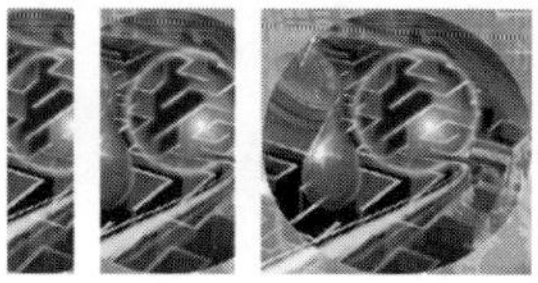

THERE ARE MANY PUBLICLY AVAILABLE ROOMS YOU CAN RENT IN ORDER TO EXPERIMENT BEFORE HAVING TO COMMIT MONEY TO PURCHASING EQUIPMENT. ADCOM INC. IN CANADA AND VTEL IN THE UNITED STATES ARE TWO EXAMPLES.

NEW REVENUE Users such as the Huron County Board of Education in Ontario plan to recover some of their costs by selling unused time to other education and business users in their community. Elizabeth Katz (1995) and her colleagues at the Bridgewater Research Group conducted an analysis of trends in the use of technology in the United States and reported that many institutions, especially schools, are adopting that same strategy in order to make videoconferencing affordable.

NEW PARTNERSHIPS Sharing equipment, whether yours or theirs, may lead to new partnerships among education and training stakeholders in a community.

INTERCONNECTABILITY Vendors have agreed to some common standards so that several different brands of equipment can be linked up. As a result, you do not have to be unduly concerned about what brand of equipment a colleague might have, as long as it has international standards-based software.

Five key issues need to be addressed so as not to limit these strengths or hinder the effective application of Chapter 2's CARE learning principles to Compressed Video Learning.

ACTIVE LEARNERS First, let's revisit the need to create an active learning environment. We know how essential that is and repeat it here for one reason—everyone's familiarity with broadcast television. The CVL screen is a television monitor, and that fact often encourages the same sort of audience passivity that watching TV does. So, when we are offered the opportunity to use what looks like a normal television set for learning, we have to change our habits and focus on the people at the other end to engage ourselves actively with the minds on the screen. The television set, camera and microphone are our channel to learners. If learners are not encouraged to take responsibility for some of the learning activities, then you may have a difficult task generating productive learning.

VISUAL PRESENCE A second set of issues clusters around three features involved in creating a visual presence: (1) the camera, (2) picture quality and (3) motion and pattern. First, it is critical to use the camera in such a way that gives you a good picture of a person without making him or her feel too self-conscious about being in a "close-up." If the camera angle is so wide that a face appears as a small dot, we haven't created much of a sense of visual presence. Later on, we make some more specific suggestions on how to use the camera appropriately. Second, compressed video equipment produces different levels

**DOCUMENT 1**
**for Overhead Projector**

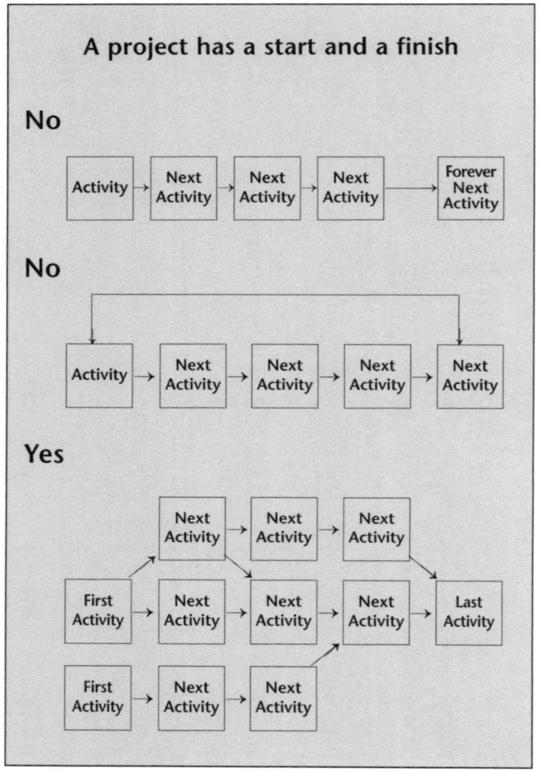


**DOCUMENT 2**
**for Document Camera**

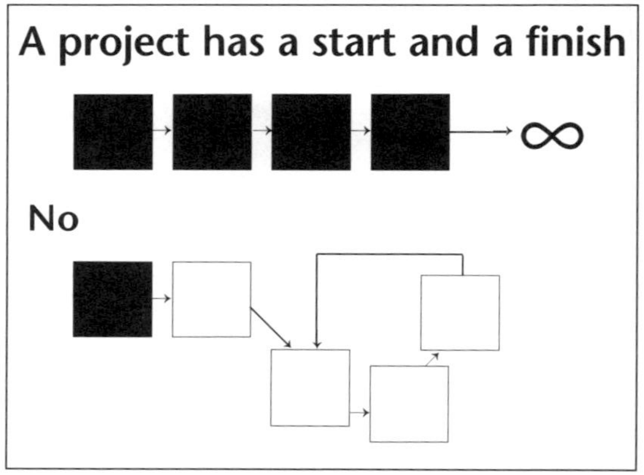


**DOCUMENT 3**
**for Print Handout**

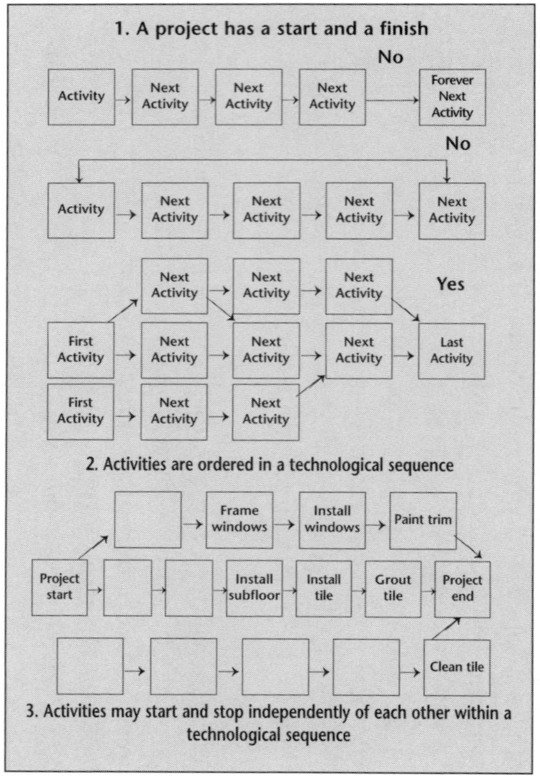

| | DOCUMENT 1 for Overhead Projector | DOCUMENT 2 for Document Camera | DOCUMENT 3 for Print Handout |
|---|---|---|---|
| Method of display | Overhead projector | Document camera — either slide show or paper or overhead | Print — handout for participants |
| Orientation | Portrait — progressive disclosure of segments would be used. | Landscape — all the content is seen at one time. | Portrait — all the content is seen at one time. |
| Font size | Can be 12 or 14 points as the projector increases the image. | Must be much larger — 24 to 30 points. | Is much smaller — normal print fonts 10 to 12 points. |
| Number of needed visuals to contain the content | One | Two needed to permit the font size increases and diagram shape size increases. | One print page contains the material from 2 overheads or 3 document camera pages [slides]. Here the objective is to save material production costs by using less paper. |
| Words and labels | Normal labeling guidelines would be used. | Small words are removed altogether. Color is used more effectively to contain content and direct the eye. | Small words for labels are present. Here the purpose is to provide as much detail as necessary so the learner has accurate notes. |
| Use of symbols and pictures | It is always a good idea to find a symbol to replace a phrase as it is a memory aid. | Using symbols and pictures is even more important here as one would strive for less complexity. Note how the infinity symbol has replaced the words «Forever Next Activity.» | Here, the highest level of detail can be used. Pictures and symbols make the handout more interesting for the learner and more inviting to use afterwards to review the content. |

FIGURE 9.7: Example of a visual adapted to CVL from print
Source: Sandra Hodder, Sheridan College, Oakville, Ontario.

ALTHOUGH STANDARDS-BASED SOFTWARE IS RELIABLE, WE RECOMMEND THAT A TECHNICAL TEST TAKE PLACE BEFORE THE LEARNING SESSION AS UNEXPECTED PROBLEMS DO OCCUR.

of picture quality depending on the number of telephone lines used. The most cost-effective option uses the equivalent of two telephone lines. Many users find that they need as many as six lines to produce the clarity needed for their application. Factors that affect the degree of clarity needed include the subject matter being taught, the teaching model used and learner characteristics such as special sight needs. As for the third feature, compressed video is different from full-motion, broadcast-quality television and cannot, especially when only two lines are used, accommodate quick-motion and highly patterned material. Figure 9.7 shows an example of a still visual that was adapted to CVL so that too much pattern was avoided; the complex still visual was included in the print learner's manual, not transmitted by the camera.

ERGONOMICS Color, lighting, acoustics and other features of the room you use need special attention. Factors such as where to put the television monitors to avoid glare from the windows need to be added to the baseline ergonomic issues we described in Chapter 2.

SOUND QUALITY Most compressed video vendors provide a standard type of microphone setup. Many users interviewed for Judy's book on Compressed Video Learning, such as Memorial University of Newfoundland, indicated that achieving good sound quality was a greater challenge than creating picture quality. They found it necessary to upgrade the standard package provided by vendors.

PREPARATION The richness of the video learning environment comes with a price—additional preparation. Each component of the information delivery and communication processes must be planned for: print materials must be pre-circulated, graphics must be created for the document camera and verbal and visual presentation skills to be used during the session must be practiced. We will touch on each of these in a later section.

If this seems complicated, don't panic. Lots of people agree with Sandra Hodder that "the second day was much easier than the first, and, by the third day, I don't think that I would have noticed that the classroom was 'electronic'" (Roberts, 1998, p. 9).

KEEP YOUR FOCUS ON THE LEARNERS. HOW WILL THEY GET THE INFORMATION THEY NEED BEFORE THE CLASS? HOW CAN THEY BEST TALK ABOUT THEIR ANALYSES OF THE MATERIAL DURING THE CLASS? CONCENTRATING ON THESE TWO QUESTIONS MAY HELP YOU SET PRIORITIES AS YOU PREPARE FOR YOUR CVL SESSION.

## HOW DO I USE COMPRESSED VIDEO LEARNING APPROPRIATELY?

### Preparation

When applying the CARE learning principles and strategies outlined in Chapters 3 and 4 to CVL, we try to create classrooms that build on the interactive and visual strengths of the medium. Our preparation framework in Table 9.2 features four points.

**TABLE 9.2:** PREPARATION FRAMEWORK FOR COMPRESSED VIDEO LEARNING

| | |
|---|---|
| • Technical | • Verbal presentation |
| • Visual materials | • Integration |

TECHNICAL We recommend three essential technical preparations. First, familiarize yourself with the equipment at an early stage in the course planning process. You need to assess its strengths and weaknesses regarding teaching and learning strategies. Second, meet with technical members of the team to brainstorm ideas; they may be able to make wonderful things happen! Third, do a dry run of a session while you still have time to modify your approach, and while the technicians still have time to change the lighting, get better microphones or whatever. Irene Blayer, coordinator of an international conference involving Canada, the United States and Mexico held at the 1996 Learned Societies Congress at Brock University in St. Catharines, Ontario, noted: "The one thing I would have done differently was to budget the time and money for a technical rehearsal of our session. Without such a test, you run a significant risk of problems, especially in an international event."

VISUAL MATERIALS A print manual for learners is needed, for the same reasons as we discussed in Chapters 7 and 8. In addition, you can use visual learning resources such as maps, diagrams, illustrations, models and printed text. Prepare them ahead of time and tailor them to the aspect ratio and color described in Table 9.3.

VERBAL PREPARATION How you and your learners use your voices in the session will affect how actively everyone engages in the process. Review Chapter 7 and apply those points to Video Learning. Include those points in the learner's manual: we find that most people are unaware of their speaking styles.

COMBINING VISUAL AND VERBAL MATERIALS To retain learners' involvement, it is critical that both the visual and verbal elements conform to the guidelines discussed in previous sections; e.g., prepare documents and visuals ahead of time, use different types of media during a session, and limit the lecture (formal presentation) segments given by you, invited experts or learners. Equally important, however, is how and why the visual and verbal elements are combined. We recommend that you focus on duration, synchronization,

**TABLE 9.3:** VISUAL MATERIALS CHECKLIST FOR COMPRESSED VIDEO LEARNING

- ☑ Use pastel-colored paper, not white, to minimize glare.
- ☑ Design your graphics to conform to television's three-by-four aspect ratio; e.g., respect the proportion or shape of a television screen. As Figure 9.8 illustrates, videoconference graphics should be extended on the horizontal axis.
- ☑ Use large, well-spaced characters. We recommend a minimum font size of 24 points.
- ☑ Don't put information near the edges; stay within the "safe area" shown in Figure 9.9 (the safe area is 10 percent smaller than the camera scan area). In addition, a square border should be drawn around the scanning area to allow visuals to be framed more easily.
- ☑ Keep written text to five lines and a maximum of 20 words per screen image.
- ☑ Make a number of "message slides" such as 15 MINUTE BREAK or READ PLEASE. Put them under the document camera at appropriate points in the session.

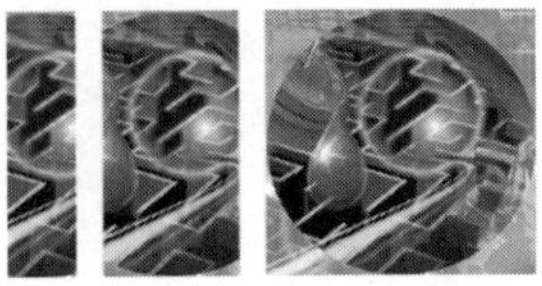

CHECK THAT YOUR FONT SIZE IS LARGE ENOUGH. THROW THE PAPER DOWN ON THE FLOOR— YOU SHOULD BE ABLE TO READ THE PRINT EASILY WITHOUT STOOPING OVER! (ADCOM INC., 1995).

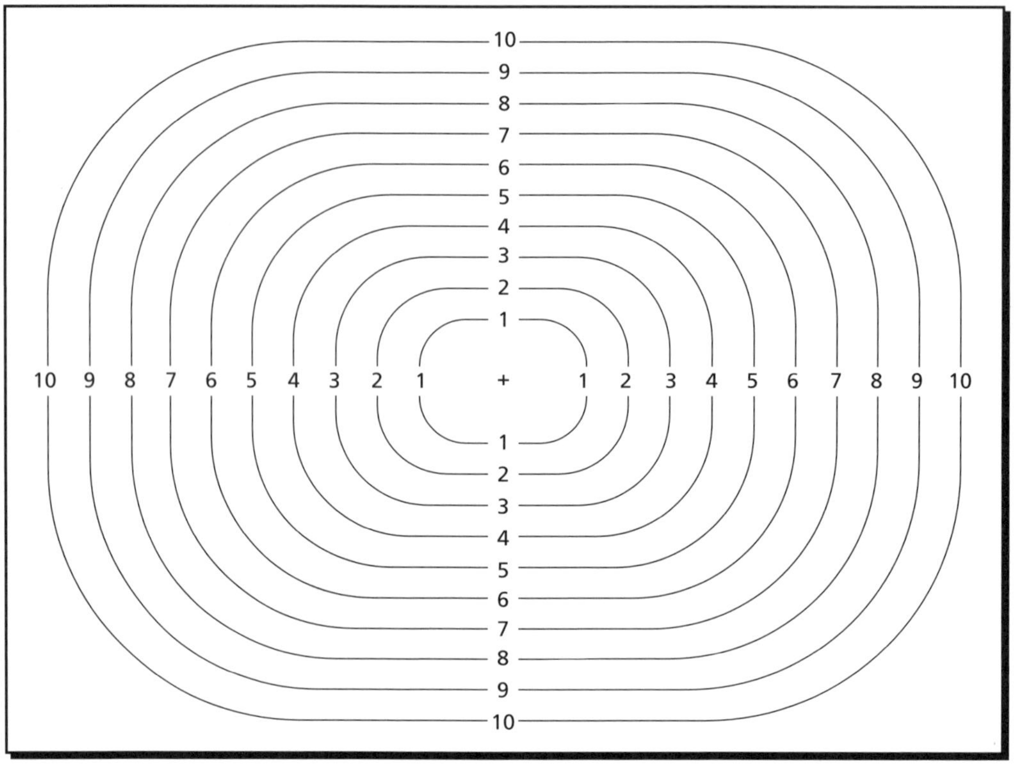


FIGURE 9.8: Aspect ratio for visual materials
Source: Adapted from Hakes et al., 1993.

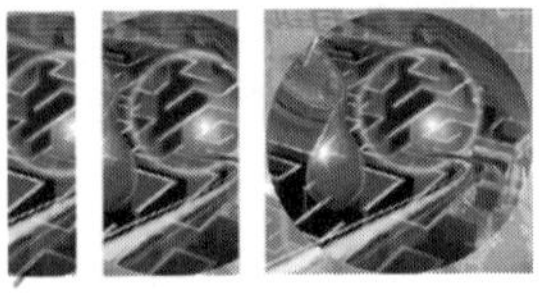

USE THE GRAPHIC IN FIGURE 9.9 AS A TRANSPARENCY TO VERIFY "WHETHER YOUR SAFE AREA IS SAFE!" (HAKES ET AL., 1993).

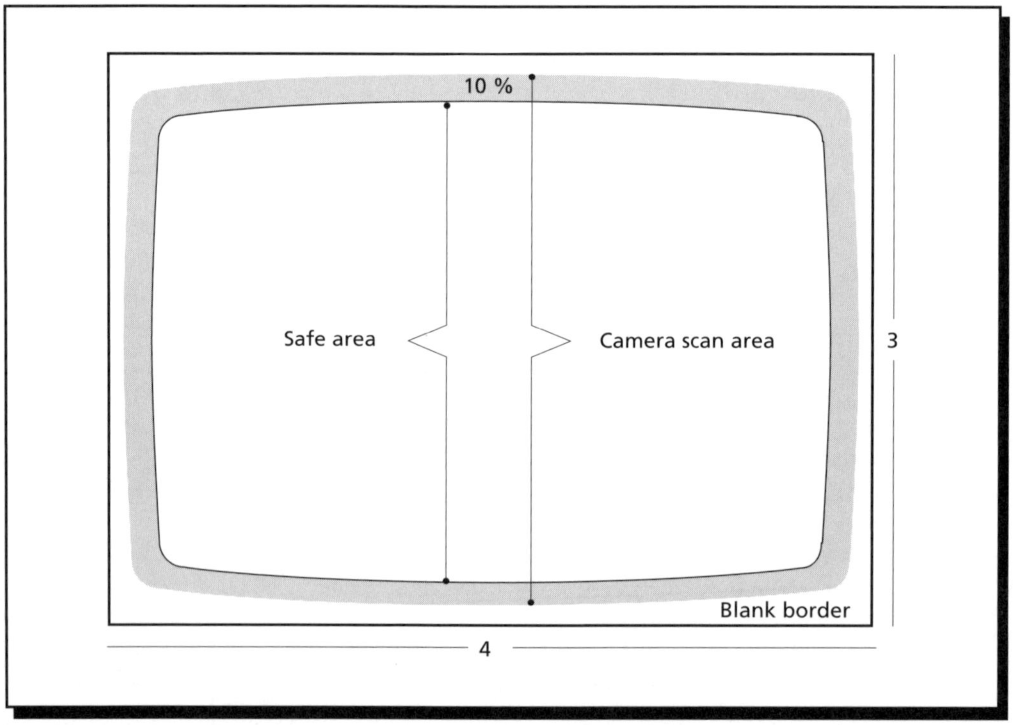


FIGURE 9.9: Template to guide preparation of visual materials
Source: Adapted from Hakes et al., 1993.

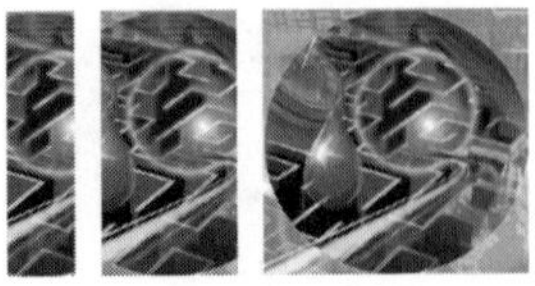

MAKE A TAPE OF THE AUDIO PORTION OF THE SESSION AND LISTEN TO HOW YOU SOUND. THE TAPE COULD ALSO HELP YOU EVALUATE THE VIDEO SYSTEM'S AUDIO QUALITY.

coherence and pertinence when deciding how best to combine the various elements of your presentation, both in individual sessions and throughout a sequence of sessions.

- Duration: No verbal presentation segment should be more than 10 minutes. There is abundant evidence that interactive technologies such as compressed videoconferencing are poor conveyers of factual information, and that print is the more appropriate delivery technology to use for information transmission. Whether you are leading an individual session or an entire series, resist the temptation to give a lecture.
- Synchronization: Visual aids and documents should be inserted where appropriate within the content and flow of the verbal presentation. Displaying graphic materials in advance or after you have already talked about them interferes with learning. What people see should be congruent with what they hear. Media research indicates that when visuals do not match or enhance the information given verbally, the viewer gets conflicting information and is much less likely to process and retain information effectively.
- Coherence: The session should not give the impression that various materials were pulled together at random just to have a variety of documents.
- Pertinence: Any document that is used should make a unique, not redundant, contribution to the information to be processed by learners.

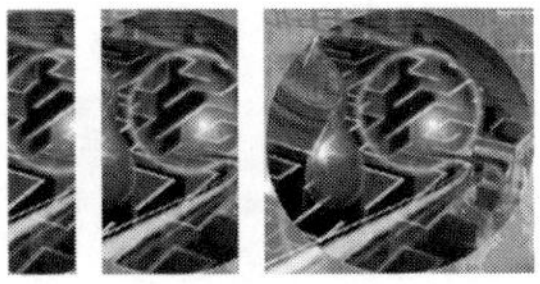

KEEP YOUR MATERIALS ORGANIZED IN THE SEQUENCE IN WHICH YOU WILL USE THEM, SO THAT THE MICROPHONES DO NOT TRANSMIT THE SOUND OF PARTICIPANTS FLIPPING BACK AND FORTH FROM DIFFERENT SECTIONS IN THEIR LEARNER'S MANUAL.

## Delivery

Once you are prepared and the session begins, pay attention to task and social protocols.

Task protocols relate to camera technique (Table 9.4 ) and clothing (Table 9.5).

Social behaviors are also important; they create the sense of presence at a distance. Welcome the participants at the outset and give them some clear guidelines describing how you plan to facilitate the session. Table 9.6 suggests helpful social behaviors.

Our third topic in this section on delivery relates to avoiding the common pitfalls discussed in Table 9.7. Maintain a vigilant eye for these types of dysfunctional behaviors and engage everyone in trying to produce helpful behavior and shared responsibility.

PICTURE BREAKUP There is too much motion. Urge people not to move so rapidly.

CONFUSING GRAPHICS If the graphics are hard to read, the material has been poorly designed. Revisit the preparation and task checklists and revise the graphics.

UNRECOGNIZABLE PEOPLE The camera is physically too far away from the participants, or the camera close-up feature is not being used appropriately.

You may need to remind learners of these two points so that everyone feels a part of the group. This camera fixation may feel strange at first, but you will rapidly get used to it.

**TABLE 9.4:** CAMERA TECHNIQUES CHECKLIST

- ☑ If no one is with you at your site, look straight into the camera, not at the television monitor, when you speak. Otherwise, the learners at the other sites will feel that you are not looking at them and therefore not "with" them.
- ☑ If learners are with you at your site, try to look straight into the camera as much as possible. This is not a typical behavior, of course, so you may find it challenging, but it is vital to make the effort so that a sense of shared presence is established.
- ☑ Avoid waving your hands as you speak. They are distracting.
- ☑ Don't move too quickly. When only two lines are used, the movement will appear jerky.
- ☑ Don't move too far away from the camera (into the corners of the room). The camera may not automatically follow you, and it will be distracting for others not to see you.
- ☑ Try to vary the camera shots. Medium-angle shots that are concentrated on one person, and group shots, are appropriate. Very wide-angle shots can be helpful, but don't use them too often. You don't want people feeling sea sick as the camera scans around the room.
- ☑ Compose the picture on the screen as well as you can, avoiding expanses of blank tabletops, tiny people or cluttered backgrounds.
- ☑ Ensure that backgrounds such as walls are pastel in color, not white. Otherwise the camera will automatically focus on the white and not transmit clear pictures of people.

**TABLE 9.5:** CLOTHING CHECKLIST

- ☑ Avoid bright, glittery jewelry and striped or bulky clothes.
- ☑ Wear pastel colors, not bold ones, as they are easier to look at. Avoid solid colors such as white, black and red, as they are distracting.
- ☑ If you wear glasses, avoid tinted lenses because they tend to create a raccoon look!

**TABLE 9.6:** SOCIAL BEHAVIORS CHECKLIST

- ☑ Refer to, and reinforce, the session's structure by underlining meaning, summarizing and emphasizing.
- ☑ Recognize and use emotional reactions.
- ☑ Call upon learners to speak either individually by name or as a group by site.
- ☑ Encourage and support interaction from all the sites. Don't let one or two individuals or sites monopolize the discussion. Learners should share the responsibility for making everyone feel competent and connected.
- ☑ Ask, and insist, that learners speak directly to each other. Don't become a traffic cop.

**TABLE 9.7:** FIVE COMMON PITFALLS IN CVL

| | |
|---|---|
| • Picture breakup<br>• Confusing graphics<br>• Unrecognizable people | • Long lectures<br>• Disinterested instructor |

Using the pre-set functions of the equipment can save confusion during the class.

LONG LECTURES "Talking head" television is never effective for learning. Presentation segments should not exceed 10 minutes.

DISINTERESTED INSTRUCTOR Learners feel "the instructor never looks at me." It takes a while to learn to talk into a camera and not gaze off to the side, and it takes attention to respond constructively to participants' contributions.

IN LARGE GROUPS, PEOPLE MAY NEED TO "WAVE," AS IT WILL BE DIFFICULT TO TELL WHO IS TALKING.

## Evaluation

One of the functions of evaluation is to share lessons you have learned with colleagues. "Learning from those who have gone before us is critical to our getting started," Linda Krakow, Railway Transportation Institute in Montréal. In addition to journals, newsletters and print sources of evaluation results, electronic sites are being organized. For example, Pacific Bell has established a moderated computer conference on videoconferencing designed to help teachers and librarians share lessons learned. To subscribe, use the form at <http://www.kn.pacbell.com/wired/vidconf/ed1vidconf.html>.

Evaluation can occur at several levels, as we read in Chapter 4. Here we present an approach rooted in the work of Donald Kirkpatrick (1994), a former president of the American Society for Training and Development, who is now professor emeritus at the University of Wisconsin. Using jargon-free language to adapt his four-level evaluation model, Transport Canada (1993) recommends that its instructors assess four areas: participant reaction, learning, application and impact (p. 28).

- Participant reaction refers to assessing whether or not instructors, learners, administrators and other stakeholders were satisfied with their Video Learning experience.
- Learning assessment relates to the measurement of whether learners acquired and retained the content the instruction was designed to convey.
- Application refers to whether learners can apply the knowledge, skills or new attitudes they acquired in the Video Learning session to a practical setting such as their work environment.
- Impact looks at whether applying their acquired knowledge, skills or attitudes makes any difference in their personal or professional lives.

To date, most CVL evaluations have focused on participant reactions. They indicate that participants, both instructors and students, are satisfied and would use it again. A Nova Scotia student's comment in 1993 is typical of those made in most evaluations: "The technology is interesting for the first couple of classes. After that, I don't even realize the teacher is not in my classroom and I'm focused on learning and making the best marks I can" (Burge & Roberts, 1993, p. 59).

It has been well established that anyone can learn effectively this way and that there is no longer any need for studies to compare the scores obtained by students taking a course through Video Learning with those achieved by students taking the same course in a classroom. There is no significant difference. (Lamy, 1995)

As issues such as return on investment and performance improvement continue to assume a strategic importance in training and education, we all need evaluation studies that give priority to application and impact.

The Resource Kit contains examples of participant evaluation forms. Each served its purpose and was useful to its creator. Select, and adapt as necessary, the tool most appropriate to your needs.

The issue of when to evaluate participant reaction is so critical that it bears emphasis. Many learners who were interviewed for this chapter felt that continuous evaluation was important to success, particularly over a series of learning sessions. Small but ongoing adjustments to your videocommunication process can make all the difference between success and failure. Learners often have good ideas for improvement once they've become accustomed to the medium. Both the participant reaction research and the learning assessment literature agree that how one designs CVL is critical and that a continuous adjustment may be necessary if instructional strategies are to be as effective as possible.

## WHO IS USING COMPRESSED VIDEO LEARNING EFFECTIVELY?

Schools, colleges, universities and private sector organizations are all successful users of Compressed Video Learning. We cite one example from each sector.

### Changing the Mind Set: A Pilot Project

*Huron County Board of Education, Clinton, Ontario*

The Huron County Board of Education in Clinton, Ontario, participated in a pilot project to explore the ways in which Video Learning could be used in elementary and secondary schools. Its experience in 1994-95 illustrates one way in which organizations can cost-effectively assess the relevance of Video Learning (collaboration with a vendor). Stephen Oliver, a classroom teacher and technology consultant, was seconded half-time by the Board to facilitate applications. Activities included:

- several one-hour meetings with Ministry of Education officials in Toronto
- a drama club session with an author at the Massachusetts Institute of Technology regarding a play of his that the club planned to produce
- a one-time friendship link with elementary students at a school in the United Kingdom
- professional development sessions with teachers in the Perth/Huron-Perth Separate Board of Education using equipment supplied by another vendor, CBCI
- teaching a high school English course between two schools in Goderich and Clinton

The schools continue to use the equipment, which they have since purchased. Stephen Oliver reports that one of the valuable lessons from the pilot project was room setup. He shared three recommendations (Roberts, 1998, pp. 47-49):

- The power and telephone outlets should be close together so wires do not snake in different directions.
- In a tiered classroom, light from windows can reflect off the television monitors if they are not positioned appropriately.
- A readily accessible backup telephone line for telephone and voice communication is needed in the event of problems with the digital lines.

Stephen illustrates one type of technical support available to instructors—a teacher with a technical bent who is seconded to a pilot project.

## Remediation Training in the Financial Sector

*Canadian Imperial Bank of Commerce (CIBC), Toronto, Ontario*

CIBC is an international bank that serves over a dozen countries, with headquarters in Toronto, Ontario. This pilot project shows the feasibility of starting with a very low-key trial within a large organization.

In the spring of 1994, CIBC's Learning Systems Group mounted a pilot project in which the CVL format was used to teach three modules on financial statements, financial accounting and taxation. These modules are part of a series of remediation training sessions being offered by the Group in response to a general test of credit knowledge and skills taken by personnel in the Bank's lending and risk management populations. The project involved a partnership between Credit Risk Management (the client), the Learning Systems Group (instructional design and project management) and internal and external subject matter experts.

CVL was chosen because:

- the organizers hoped it would appeal to those who were chosen to participate in the session
- it provided a means of offering somewhat smaller "chunks" of content than had been previously offered in the classroom method
- it enhanced dialogue across the country
- it enabled the Bank to take national advantage of local expertise
- it was estimated that CVL would reduce delivery costs compared with classroom delivery

The purposes of the pilot were (1) to assess participant reaction to the medium, (2) to experiment with pacing and with the structuring requirements of the medium and (3) to evaluate a particular course offering.

The content chosen for the pilot was an existing six-hour "Quality of Financial Statements" course from an external expert. Subsequent modules are being adjusted to reflect learner feedback. The primary design change being made, based on participant feedback, is to give participants more opportunity for interaction and reduce the proportion of time spent in delivering content.

## Minimizing Costs in a Consortium for Graduate Education

*EuroPACE 2000, Heverlee, Belgium*

Founded in 1993, EuroPACE 2000 is a trans-European consortium of universities and their partners in education and training whose goal is to demonstrate the potential of information and communications technologies for the European universities of the future. EuroPACE 2000's membership currently consists of over 45 universities, more than seven enterprises and research institutions and eight regional, national or international organizations.

EuroPACE 2000 works on a partnership model with its members; it provides several technical platforms and instructional models while its members develop all the programs. "We want to improve the science and technology literacy of those in educational institutions, the workplace and the general public," notes Jef Van den Branden, educational director at EuroPACE 2000 (Roberts, 1998, p. 45).

Compressed videoconferencing, alone or in combination with technologies ranging from print to satellite television, is a significant feature of the technical infrastructure supporting these programs. Thirty of the 250 sites managed by EuroPACE 2000 are equipped with this technology; the aim is that at the end of 1997 at least 100 sites will be using this technology. While organizations with appropriate equipment are welcome to join a given program, the EuroPACE 2000 centers are established to serve those who do not have their own equipment. "Although costs are coming down, we and our members still feel that there is a role for a consortium such as ours because it minimizes the costs," reports Van den Branden (Roberts, 1998, pp. 45-46).

Jef Van den Branden reports that Video Learning is particularly suited to Ph.D. programs and other live programs for three reasons:

- Seeing the other participants creates a greater access to them. EuroPACE finds that videoconferencing technology avoids the rituals that are connected to other ways (formats) of communication; seeing yourself as well as the other learners minimizes the differences.
- The equipment has become affordable for institutions and even for individuals; the technology is stable as long as standards are respected, and it is as easy to use as making a normal telephone call.
- Obtaining digital telephone lines from providers is no longer difficult in most European countries, and because videoconferencing in its lower level (two-line mode) costs only twice the amount of a normal call, communication costs are very reasonable.

One particularly good example of the use of CVL in combination with other technologies is a recent transnational course in advanced computer science designed for an audience of graduate and postgraduate students at university research centers and researchers in corporate environments. After an interactive satellite broadcast that linked 14 sites, a series of six multipoint compressed videoconference seminars was held linking the six universities involved in the Ph.D. course. Each of these seminars followed a similar format. After an expert reviewed the subject in lecture format, using graphics and illustrative demonstrations where appropriate (about 45 minutes), an interactive discussion occurred between the lecturer and participants for another 45 minutes. A computer conferencing facility facilitated discussion between the seminars and delivered handouts to the participants. A total of 32 Ph.D. students attended the full series of "broadcast plus seminars"; approximately 30 other people participated in the broadcast but not the seminars.

### Knowledge Transfer in Science and Engineering

*The Ontario Learning and Technology Exchange Pilot Project (OLTEC), Toronto, Ontario*

Founded as a small working group in December 1992, OLTEC became a pilot project sponsored by a number of public and private sector stakeholders in southern Ontario. Its primary aim was to help improve the competence, knowledge and skills of engineers, scientists and technologists throughout their careers by facilitating continuous knowledge transfer through distance learning networks and technology-based approaches to learning.

OLTEC brought together organizations from three key sectors: engineering and technology-based industries and agencies, postsecondary educational institutions and providers of communications and information technologies. To achieve its objectives, OLTEC conducted a feasibility and business planning process. It also mounted a Video Learning demonstration project consisting of three one-to-two-day workshops on three different topics.

Sandra Hodder, program coordinator in the School of Computing and Information Management at Sheridan College in Oakville, Ontario, taught the course, entitled Project Management Tools and Techniques. She has taught this subject as a one-day, face-to-face workshop, in which the effective teaching time was approximately six hours. She and a team of graphics specialists, technicians and other specialists adapted it to two three-hour CVL sessions.

Sandra's "tips from a novice videoconference instructor" focus on preparation. She developed an 80-page course manual based on the one normally used in the classroom. It provided one page for every point made in the course, with lots of white space so that students could make notes on each page. There were three differences in preparing the material for the videoconference, rather than for the classroom: (1) there were more pages in the videoconference version, so that everything would be clear for the learners; (2) any page to be transmitted by the document camera had to be redesigned (Figure 9.6); and (3) any pages that could not be easily transmitted by the document camera *had* to be in the manual. Once something like a detailed computer printout was in the manual, Sandra could easily explain it. A sample of the visuals was tested in a point-to-point session at a rehearsal organized by the University of Toronto Media Centre. Factors tested included background color and size and type of font.

Participation in OLTEC helped members identify their Video Learning needs. Many are continuing to use this approach to better serve learners.

## CONCLUSION

You now know the basics of how CVL technologies work and how they support learning. Their opportunities, strengths and limitations shape how you prepare, deliver and evaluate your sessions, sometimes in ways that are not as intuitive as we would have expected.

# References

ADCOM Telecom Systems Group. (1995, February). Conferencing tips. *The inside Edge, 2*(2), 2.

Burge, E. J., & Roberts, J. M. (1993). *Classrooms with a difference: A practical guide to the use of conferencing technologies*. Toronto, ON: The Ontario Institute for Studies in Education—Distance Learning Office.

Hakes, B. T., Sachs, S. G., Box, J., & Couchenour, J. (1993). *Compressed video: Operations and applications*. Washington, DC: The Association for Educational Communications and Technology.

Katz, E. J., Tate, R. G., & Weimer, W. A. (1995). *Survey of telematics for education and training. Vol.II: United States*. Heerlen, The Netherlands: European Association of Distance Teaching Universities.

Kirkpatrick, D. L. (1994). *Evaluating training programs: The four levels* (1st ed.). San Francisco, CA: Berrett-Koehler.

Lamy, T. (1995). *Videocommunication: A faculty guide to learning and communicating by compressed videoconferencing*. (J. Roberts, Trans.). Sudbury, ON: Laurentian University, Centre for Continuing Education.

Roberts, J. M. (1998). *Compressed Video Learning: Creating active learners*. Montréal, QC: Chenelière/McGraw-Hill.

Transport Canada, Training Directorate. (1993, October). *Videoconferencing technology as a medium for distance learning*. Ottawa, ON: Transport Canada.

# Chapter 10

# What Does It Look Like When We Bring It All Together?

*The ability of instructors to exploit the learning opportunities offered by the Information Highway is a function of their creativeness, the amount of time they have to prepare the course, their motivation to go beyond the simple "talking head" or lecture mode, and their understanding of the learning process.*

DON MCDONELL,
CENTRE FOR DISTANCE EDUCATION,
UNIVERSITY OF OTTAWA, OTTAWA, ONTARIO

## INTRODUCTION

At this point, we offer three sections that are designed to interlink the earlier chapters. This chapter introduces (1) a framework for integrating elements in the learning environment, (2) a sense of our "Top Ten" learnings from the experience of writing this book and (3) a smile as you read what can happen when Murphy and his extended family come for a visit.

## HOW CAN I INTEGRATE ALL THE ELEMENTS?

Historically, instructors tended to have access to one learning technology within their institution. For example, Memorial University of Newfoundland's Telemedicine Centre had only audioconferencing facilities when it was founded in the mid-1970s. Now, some institutions are able to install multiple types of technologies in learning centers such as those administered by Contact North/Contact Nord, or in classrooms at institutions such as Le Collège des Grands Lacs. Don McDonell (1995), a colleague at the University of Ottawa, describes the full range of technologies available at that institution in some detail in his article. Computers offer the capability of having all the media described in Part 2 available on one machine, thus eliminating the need for separate pieces of equipment. This convergence of hardware has presented educators and trainers with a complex challenge: how to converge, or integrate, the learning and human elements with an appropriate mix of technologies.

We believe that the best integration results from analyzing the dynamics of learning and then the strengths of each learning technology. Throughout the book, we have sign-posted the key issues that we think you should consider; we now highlight the most salient ones as a summary framework.

1. The principles and general strategies for stimulating interaction in Audio Learning are relevant to all other learning modalities, with relatively minor adaptations according to the features of each technology.

2. The principles of effective screen design for Compressed Video Learning apply to the design of screens for Audiographic Learning and some types of Networked Learning.
3. Learners may want access to CVL to establish a sense of presence at the outset of a course but will not likely benefit from the continuing use of video conferencing equipment unless colored moving visuals are required for the content.
4. Instructors should make choices about learning technologies within a team context, drawing upon the knowledge of learning designers, graphic artists, technicians and others. They should not feel that the entire decision-making responsibility rests on their shoulders.
5. While the inherent capacities of each technology are important factors governing the integration of technologies, first priority has to be given to the course content, learning outcomes, learner characteristics, time resources, availability of appropriate technical support and cost (see Tables 6.2 and 6.3).
6. Cost varies so much from jurisdiction to jurisdiction and changes so rapidly that we have not hazarded actual numbers in this book. Instead, we have talked about the essential categories of expenditure related to the proper use of learning technologies and rely on your ability to determine the costs specific to your own situation. References at the end of this chapter direct you to people such as Tony Bates (1995) and Judith Cukier (1996) who are researching cost-benefit frameworks in more detail as part of the work of the Telelearning Network of Centres of Excellence. Other References and Further Readings have been cited specific to the cost of each technology in the appropriate chapter.
7. All of the learning principles, strategies and activities described in Part 1 are essential foundations for the application of the learning technologies described in Part 2. No learning strategy or class activity is unique to a particular technology.
8. All learning technologies are well accepted by instructors and learners. However, you will inevitably encounter users who, for reasons often associated with their learning styles and communication skills levels, may experience difficulties, especially initially.
9. There is no significant difference in learning outcomes when traditional, face-to-face learning is compared with any of the conferencing technology-mediated learning approaches described in this book.

Table 10.1 presents our summary of key points about each learning technology. Note our focus on the human elements of learning and teaching. What would you add, based on your experience and knowledge?

**TABLE 10.1:** INFORMATION HIGHWAY TECHNOLOGY SUMMARY

| TYPE OF TECHNOLOGY | DESCRIPTION | SPECIAL FEATURES | | APPROPRIATE USE | |
|---|---|---|---|---|---|
| | | STRENGTHS | KEY ISSUES | PREPARATION | DELIVERY |
| Audio | Telephone or group terminal<br>Telephone network<br>Bridge | Availability<br>Affordability | Equipment quality<br>No visual contact | Print guide<br>Lead time<br>Ergonomics | Vary the voice in tone, rhythm, etc.<br>Use pauses |
| Audiographic | Telephone or group terminal<br>Graphics device<br>Telephone network<br>Bridge | Affordability<br>Visuals | Connectability<br>Data with or without voice | Good visuals<br>Comfort with equipment | Integrate voice and visuals |
| Networked | Computer<br>Communications lines<br>Modems<br>Client servers | Convenience<br>Expandability<br>Convergence<br>No distraction | Comfort with software<br>Learner support | Introductory document<br>Learner charac-teristics<br>Use of print materials | Message style<br>Organization of messages<br>Lurkers |
| Compressed Video | Video equip-ment<br>Digital lines<br>Bridge | Visual presence<br>Color and motion<br>Interconnectivity<br>Symmetry | Active learners<br>Sound quality<br>Preparation | Visual<br>Verbal<br>Integration | Looking at camera<br>Simple visuals |

## WHAT ARE OUR TOP TEN LEARNINGS?

You have read a lot of detail so far and may be looking for a short list of ideas that are both reassuring and helpful to guide you through the hype and the hope. Here are our "Top Ten" lessons from many years of practice.

1. Make no assumptions about what learners need and want; give them space and time and they will tell you.
2. Think in terms of what is "necessary and sufficient"—nothing more.
3. Anything more will lead to overload, distractions and other vexations.
4. Integration of course or workshop components can save learning time and effort.
5. The biggest shift for many instructors learning the communications technologies is the change from being "the sage on the stage" to the "guide on the side."

6. There is always a trade-off in how you use any technology; each one brings promises and pitfalls, intended and unintended effects.
7. Ask not what learners can do for the technology, but what the technology can do for learners. Any technology will move data, but it will not of itself move minds.
8. Don't fret about asking which technology is best for which learning activity; it's the wrong question.
9. Do fret about asking why and when technology is really necessary; it's the right question.
10. Be fearless in your scrutiny of anything new; newness is no guarantee of effectiveness.

## WHAT SHOULD I DO WHEN MURPHY'S LAW HITS?

"If something can go wrong, it will." Murphy does not wait for an invitation, nor does he care about the effects of his visit. Despite your best efforts, you too can play host to this mischief-maker.

After you have made all the big decisions about content, learning strategies, activities and choice of technologies, be compulsive about the small details of how it will work on the ground. If you are not a detail person, find someone who will happily accept the task of keeping Murphy (and his family) at bay.

If Murphy does arrive, then keep your sense of humor, offer an aspirin or three to those under stress, and remember how it all happened. That's why the list below has such a special title. Malachy Mandeville, during the 1980s at Memorial University of Newfoundland, once walked into a scene of panic and pandemonium caused by malfunctioning technology. He sized up the situation right away and laconically asked: "Aspirin, anyone?" The question made everyone laugh, and things got better. Malachy, who is a witty fellow, later compiled a list of actual aspirin situations; here it is.

Aspirin, anyone? Twenty-seven things that can go wrong with a distance education course.

1. Manuals are late.
2. Textbooks are late.
3. Readings are late.
4. Tapes are in the [local study] center but the VCR has been moved.
5. There is sound but no video on tapes.
6. Tape gets stuck in VCR.
7. Microphones and speaker were moved to another room.
8. Teachers are on strike and all materials are locked in the school.
9. Wrong exam is sent in the envelope.
10. Exam supervisor forgets about exam schedule.
11. VCR is stolen.

12. VCR is shipped to St. John's for repair but is shipped back to center without having been repaired. Start all over again.
13. Manuals are placed in mailbox to speed delivery; phone call is received from resident to say that manuals are all over the street.
14. Coordinator allows students to register without prerequisite for course.
15. Regional Office enforces prerequisite, only to find out that instructor is waiving same.
16. Wrong edition of book is sent to center because new edition is being kept for on-campus students.
17. Bookstore reduces copies in stock; students decide to buy books.
18. Taxi driver fails to deliver books and tapes.
19. Number of students is misjudged.
20. Students decide course is too difficult; no one registers.
21. Wrong tapes are delivered to center.
22. Instructor changes date of mid-term exam and does not inform staff.
23. Canada Post decides to discontinue mail pickup on weekends.
24. Professor refuses to sign contract.
25. Insufficient number of reference books was ordered.
26. Mail truck that contained final exams burns.
27. Instructor has heart attack and dies.

And here are three more from another part of Canada.

28. Power to center is cut off half an hour before class begins.
29. Audio bridge operator knows nothing about class.
30. Absolutely essential connector wire has been removed from equipment.

## CONCLUSION

That's it for our book. We hope you've enjoyed it. We'd like your feedback.

# References

Bates, A. W. (Tony) (1995). *Technology, open learning and distance education.* London, U.K.: Routledge.

Cukier, J. (1996). Cost-benefit analysis of telelearning: Developing a methodology framework. Presented at First Annual Meeting & Conference, TeleLearning-NCE. Constructing a vision for the Knowledge Society. November 5-7, Sheraton Centre Hotel, Montréal, Québec.

Mandeville, M. (1995). Aspirin anyone? *Open Praxis, 2,* 13.

McDonell, D. J. (1995). Audio, audio graphics, compressed video, computer conferencing and the Internet: Distance education at the University of Ottawa. In H. Maurer (Ed.), *Proceedings of ED-MEDIA 95 World Conference on Educational Multimedia and Hypermedia* (pp. 454-459). Charlottesville, VA: Association for the Advancement of Computing in Education.

# Further Readings


## Chapter 1
### How Do We See Classrooms Changing?

Barker, J. A. (1993). *Paradigms: The business of discovering the future.* New York, NY: Harper Business.

Bates, A. W. (Tony) (1995). *Technology, open learning and distance education.* London, UK: Routledge.

Bloom, M. R. (1994). *Enhancing employability skills: Innovative partnerships, projects and programs.* Ottawa, ON: The Conference Board of Canada.

Burge, E. J. (1996). Inside-out thinking about distance teaching: Making sense of reflective practice. *Journal of the American Society for Information Science, 47*(11), 843-848.

Carter, V. (1996). Do media influence learning? *Open Learning, 11*(1), 31-40.

*Communiqué* (1997): Special issue on technology policy (v. 12 (3 & 4). Ottawa, ON: Canadian Association for Distance Education/Association canadienne de l'éducation à distance.

Dertouzos, M. (1997). *What will be: How the new world of information will change our lives.* New York, NY: Harper Collins.

Franklin, U. (1997). *Every tool shapes the task: Communities and the Information Highway.* Vancouver, BC: Lazara Press.

Gibson, C. C. (Ed.). (In press). *Distance learners in higher education: Institutional responses for quality outcomes.* Madison, WI: Atwood Publishing.

Henderson, C. (1995/1996). Of power and partnerships. *College Canada, 1*(4), 7-9.

Menzies, H. (1996). *Whose brave new world?: The Information Highway and the new economy.* Toronto, ON: University of Toronto Press.

Roberts, J. M. (1996). The story of distance education: A practitioner's perspective. *Journal of the American Society for Information Science, 47*(11), 811-816.

———. & Keough, E. M. (Eds.) (1995). *Why the Information Highway? Lessons from open and distance learning.* Toronto, ON: Trifolium Books Inc.

Roth, G. L., & Niemi, J. (1996). Information technology systems and the learning organization. *International Journal of Lifelong Education, 15*(3), 202-215.

Stahmer, A. E. (1995). Learners in the workplace. In J.M. Roberts & E.M. Keough (Eds.), *Why the Information Highway? Lessons from open and distance learning* (pp. 41-59). Toronto, ON: Trifolium Books Inc.

Tenner, E. (1996). *Why things bite back: Technology and the revenge of unintended consequences.* New York, NY: Knopf.

Tiffin, J., & Rajasingham, L. (1995). *In search of the virtual class: Education in an information society.* London, UK: Routledge.

Watkins, K., & Marsick, V. (1993). *Sculpting the learning organization.* San Francisco, CA: Jossey-Bass.

## Chapter 2
### What Do Learners Bring to Learning?

Belenky, M. F., Clinchy, B.M., Goldberger, N.R., & Tarule, J.M. (1986). *Women's ways of knowing: The development of self, voice, and mind.* New York, NY: Basic Books.

Collier, L. (1993). Teaching native students at the college level. *Canadian Journal of Native Education, 20*(1), 109-117.

Gruber, S., & Coldevin, G. (1995). Distance education for aboriginal communities in Canada: Past experience and future potential. *American Journal of Distance Education, 9*(3), 48-61.

Hiemstra, R. (Ed.). (1991). Creating effective environments for effective adult learning. *New Directions for Adult and Continuing Education.* #50(Summer), 5-32. San Francisco, CA: Jossey-Bass.

———. & Sisco, B. (1990). *Individualizing instruction: Making learning personal, empowering and successful.* San Francisco, CA: Jossey-Bass.

Kirkup, G., & von Prümmer, C. (1997). Distance education for European women. *The European Journal of Women's Studies, 4*(1), 39-62.

Knirk, F. G. (1992). Facility requirements for integrated learning systems. *Educational Technology, 32*(9), 26-32.

Learning Disabilities Association of Canada (1997). *Learning disabilities in the classroom: Handbook for instructors.* Ottawa, ON: The Association.

Lüscher, M. (1969). *The 4-color person.* New York, NY: Random House Pocket Books.

MacKeracher, D. (1993). Women as learners. In T. Barer-Stein & J. Draper (Eds.), *The Craft of teaching adults* (2nd ed., pp. 69-86). Toronto, ON: Culture Concepts.

Miller, C., & Swift, K. (1988). *The handbook of nonsexist writing* (2nd ed.). New York, NY: Harper & Row.

Office of Learning Technologies, Human Resources Development Canada. http://olt-bta.hrdc-drhc.gc.ca

Sawyer, D. (1991). Native learning styles: Shorthand for instructional adaptations? *Canadian Journal of Native Education, 18*(1), 99-105.

Smith, P., & Kearny, L. (1994). *Creating workplaces where people can think.* San Francisco, CA: Jossey-Bass.

Zemke, R., & Zemke, S. (1995). Adult learners: What do we know for sure? *Training, 32*(6), 31-40.

## Chapter 3
## What Is Adult Learning All About?

Belenky, M. F., Clinchy, B. M., Goldberger, N. R., & Tarule, J. M. (1986). *Women's ways of knowing: The development of self, voice, and mind.* New York, NY: Basic Books.

Boud, D., & Griffin, V. (Eds.) (1987). *Appreciating adults' learning: From the learners' perspective.* London, UK: Kogan Page.

Brookfield, S. (1987). *Developing critical thinkers: Challenging adults to explore alternative ways of thinking and acting.* San Francisco, CA: Jossey-Bass.

Cranton, P. (1992). *Working with adult learners.* Toronto, ON: Wall & Emerson.

Garland, M. (1994). The adult need for 'personal control' provides a cogent guiding concept for distance education. *Journal of Distance Education, 9*(1), 45-60.

Knowles, M. S. (1985). *Andragogy in action: Applying modern principles of adult learning.* San Francisco, CA: Jossey-Bass.

Kolb, D. A. (1984). *Experiential learning: Experience as the source of learning and development.* Englewood Cliffs, NJ: Prentice-Hall.

MacKeracher, D. (1996). *Making sense of adult learning.* Toronto, ON: Culture Concepts.

Merriam, S. B., (Ed.) (1993). *An update on adult learning theory. New directions for adult and continuing education, #57.* San Francisco, CA: Jossey-Bass.

———. & Caffarella, R. S. (1991). *Learning in adulthood: A comprehensive guide.* San Francisco, CA: Jossey-Bass.

Olgren, C. (1992). *Strategies for directing your learning: A resource guide for distance learners.* Madison, WI: University of Wisconsin—Madison, Department of Continuing and Vocational Education.

Stairs, A. (1991). Learning processes and teaching roles in native education: Cultural base and cultural brokerage. *The Canadian Modern Language Review, 47*(2), 280-294.

Turkle, S. (1996). *Life on the screen: Identity in the age of the Internet.* New York, NY: Simon & Schuster.

von Oech, R. (1986). *A kick in the seat of the pants: Using your explorer, artist, judge, and warrior to be more creative.* New York, NY: Harper Perennial.

## Chapter 4
## How May Instructors Best Respond?

Burge, L. (1995). Electronic highway or weaving loom? Thinking about conferencing technologies for learning. In F. Lockwood (Ed.), *Open and distance learning today* (pp. 151-163). London, UK: Routledge.

Caffarella, R. S. (1994). *Planning programs for adult learners.* San Francisco, CA: Jossey-Bass.

Carter, V. (1996). Do media influence learning? *Open Learning, 11*(1), 31-40.

Craig, R. L. (1996). *Training and development handbook: A guide to human resource development* (4th ed.). New York, NY: McGraw-Hill.

Davis, B. G. (1993). *Tools for teaching.* San Francisco, CA: Jossey-Bass.

Dick, W., & Carey, L. (1995). *The systematic design of instruction* (4th ed.). Glenview, IL: Scott, Foresman & Co.

Gagné, R. M., Briggs, L. J., & Wager, W. W. (1992). *Principles of instructional design* (4th ed.). Fort Worth, IN: Harcourt Brace Jovanovich.

Henerson, M. E., Morris, L. L., & Fitzgibbon, C. T. (1987). *How to measure attitudes.* Newbury Park, CA: Sage.

Jones, T., & Schieman, E. (1995). Learner involvement: A review of the elements of more effective distance education. *Canadian Journal of Educational Communication, 24*(2), 97-104.

Joyce, B., Showers, B., & Rolheiser-Bennett, C. (1987). Staff development and student learning: A synthesis of research on models of teaching. *Educational Leadership, 45*(2), 11-23.

Kirkpatrick, D. L. (1994). *Evaluating training models: The four levels.* San Francisco, CA: Berrett-Koehler.

Lyons, P. (1992). *Thirty-five lesson formats: A sourcebook of instructional alternatives.* Englewood Cliffs, NJ: Educational Technology Publications.

Ory, J. C., & Ryan K. E. (1993). *Tips for improved testing and grading.* Newbury Park, CA: Sage.

Robinson, D. G., & Robinson, J. C. (1989). *Training for impact: How to link training to business needs and measure the results.* San Francisco, CA: Jossey-Bass.

Vella, J., Berardinelli, P., & Burrow, J. (1997). *How do they know they know? Evaluating adult learning.* San Francisco, CA: Jossey-Bass.

Wilson, B. G. (Ed.) (1996). *Constructivist learning environments: Case studies in instructional design.* Englewood Cliffs, NJ: Educational Technology Publications.

Wlodkowski, R. J., & Ginsberg, M. B. (1995). *Diversity and motivation: Culturally responsive teaching.* San Francisco, CA: Jossey-Bass.

## Chapter 5
## What Does the Real Action Look Like?

Burge, E. J. & O'Rourke, J. (In press). The dynamics of distance teaching: Voices from the field. In C. Latchem, & F. Lockwood (Eds.), *Staff development in open and distance learning.* London, UK: Routledge.

Hartley, J. (1994). *Designing instructional text* (3rd ed.). London, UK: Kogan Page.

Jacques, R., Preece, J., & Carey, T. (1995). Engagement as a design concept for multimedia. *Canadian Journal of Educational Communication, 24*(1), 49-59.

Lockwood, F. (1992). *Activities in self-instructional texts.* London, UK: Kogan Page, in association with the Institute of Educational Technology, Open University.

———. (Ed.) (1995). *Open and distance learning today (Part VIII: Evaluation).* London, UK: Routledge.

Marsh, P. O. (1983). *Messages that work: A guide to communication design.* Englewood Cliffs, NJ: Educational Technology Publications.

Mills, R., & Tait, A. (1996). *Supporting the learner in open and distance learning.* London, UK: Pitman Publishing.

Misanchuk, E. R. (1992). *Preparing instructional text: Document design using desktop publishing.* Englewood Cliffs, NJ: Educational Technology Publications.

Rothwell, W. J., & Kazanas, H. C. (1997). *Mastering the instructional design process* (2nd ed.). San Francisco, CA: Jossey-Bass.

Rylatt, A., & Lohan, K. (1997). *Creating training miracles.* San Francisco, CA: Jossey-Bass.

Schwier, R. A., & Misanchuk, E. R. (1993). *Interactive multimedia instruction.* Englewood Cliffs, NJ: Educational Technology Publications.

Wileman, R. E. (1993). *Visual communicating.* Englewood Cliffs, NJ: Educational Technology Publications.

Zubot, M. (1993). *Writing your course: a short guide for writers of distance education materials.* Saskatoon, SA: University Extension Press.

## Chapter 6
## How Do We See the Information Highway?

Angus, E., & McKie, D. (1994, May). *Canada's Information Highway: Services, access and affordability.* Ottawa, ON: Industry Canada, New Media Branch & Information Technologies Industry Branch.

Bates, A. W. (Tony) (1995). *Technology, open learning and distance education.* London, UK: Routledge.

Burge, E. J. (1996). Technology and learning: Finding the balance. In Taylor, G. (Ed.), *Learning for the workplace: Nordic and Canadian perspectives* (pp. 48-56). Helsinki, FI: KVS Institute.

Canadian Studies Directorate. (1995). *Media and distance education in Canada.* Ottawa, ON: Canadian Studies Directorate. [Published in print and videotape format in collaboration with La Télé-université].

Council of Ministers of Education, Canada (CMEC). (1995, December). A guide to successful partnerships in distance education in Canada. Toronto, ON: CMEC. (Aussi disponible en français.)

Evans, T., Nation, D., Renner, W., & Tregenza, K. (1996). *Educational reform and converging technologies in Australian higher education: Preliminary findings from two case-studies.* Presented to the 12th Annual Canadian Association for Distance Education Conference, Université de Moncton, New Brunswick. May 22-25.

March, T. (1995). Nonprofit prophets: A telecommunications-based community action project. *The Distance Educator, 1*(3), 24-28.

Mason, R. (1995). *Using communications media in open and flexible learning.* London, UK: Kogan Page.

Ministry of Education, Skills and Training of British Columbia. (1996). *Postsecondary education, Student services, Directory of Innovation Fund Projects.* http://www.stl.gov.bc.ca

Moore, M. G., & Thompson, M. M. (1997). *The effects of distance learning: A summary of literature* (rev. ed.). ACSDE Research Monograph, No. 15. University Park, PA: The Pennsylvania State University, American Center for the Study of Distance Education.

Moran, L., & Mugridge, I. (Eds.). (1993). *Collaboration in distance education: International case studies.* London, UK: Routledge.

Open Learning Technology Corporation Ltd. (1996). *Open learning case studies.* http://www.oltc.edu.au/

Organisation for Economic Co-operation and Development. *Adult learning and technology in OECD countries.* Paris, FR: Author.

Organisation for Economic Co-operation and Development (OECD). (1996). *OECD Proceedings: Adult learning in a new technological era.* Prepared by S. Ehrmann. Paris, FR: Author.

———. (1996). *OECD Documents: Information technology and the future of post-secondary education.* Paris, FR: Author.

RMI Media Productions Inc. (1996). *Distance learning today video series.* Olathe, KS: The Cochran Communication Center.

Roberts, J. M., & Keough, E. M. (Eds.). (1995). *Why the Information Highway? Lessons from open and distance learning.* Toronto, ON: Trifolium Books Inc.

Schatz, L. (1996). Michigan takes major steps toward developing a statewide telecommunications network. *ED, Education at a Distance, 10*(5) 6-7.

Schultz, D. W., & Wiljanen, J. (1996). Telecommunications as a catalyst for education reform. *EDJournal, 10*(5), J-1-J-2.

Twigg, C. (1995). The need for a national learning infrastructure. *Educom Review, 29*(4), 22-25; *29*(5), 16-20; *29*(6), 20-24.

Zirkin, B. B., & Sumler, D. E. (1995). Interactive or non-interactive? That is the question!!! An annotated bibliography. *Journal of Distance Education/Revue de l'éducation à distance, 10*(1), 95-112.

## Chapter 7
### Audio and Audiographic Learning: Why Are They the Cornerstone of the Information Highway?

Boone, W., & Keough, E. M. (1994). The challenge of providing equality of education opportunities for secondary students in small schools in rural Newfoundland and coastal Labrador. In *Distance! Quelle Distance?* Résumé des communications/Abstracts (p. 16). Ottawa, ON: Canadian Association for Distance Education.

Burge, E. J., Norquay, M., & Roberts, J. M. (1987). *Listening to learn: The use of the voice in distance education.* Toronto, ON: The Ontario Institute for Studies in Education, Instructional Resources Development Unit.

Contact North/Contact Nord. (1994). *User's guide.* Sudbury, ON: Author.

Hill, G., Skene, J., Walls, H., & Parker, L. (1994). Audio teleconferencing. In P. S. Portway & C. Lane (Eds.), *Guide to teleconferencing and distance learning.* (2nd ed., pp. 15-39). Livermore, CA: Applied Business teleCommunications.

Kirkpatrick, D. L. (1994). *Evaluating training programs: The four levels.* First edition. San Francisco, CA: Berrett-Koehler.

Laurillard, D. (1993). *Rethinking university teaching: A framework for the effective use of educational technology.* New York, NY: Routledge.

MacKeracher, D. (1995). *Course manual notes on audio-conferencing for learning.* Fredericton, NB: University of New Brunswick, Department of Adult and Vocational Education.

Monson, M. (n.d.). *Instructional design for teleconferencing: A handbook.* Madison, WI: University of Wisconsin-Extension, Instructional Communications Systems.

Open Learning Technology Corporation Ltd. (1996). *Models for evaluating audio, audiographics and teleconferencing.* http://www.oltc.edu.au/reports/models/modelsft.htm

Parker, L. (1996). Making the most of teleconferencing. *Training & Development, 50*(2), 28-29.

TéléÉducation NB TeleEducation. (1996). *Guide to audio-graphic conferencing.* Fredericton, NB: Author.

Wilis, B. (n.d.). Instructor student interaction. In *Instructional audio communications at a glance* (pp. 77-81). Anchorage, AK: University of Alaska System, Statewide Distance Education.

## Chapter 8
### Networked Learning: How Do We Facilitate Learning on the Internet?

Allen, B. S. (1995). Customizing mass distributions of e-mail. *The Distance Educator, 1*(3), 18-19.

Berge, Z. L., & Collins, M. (1996). *Wired together: The online classroom in K-12. Volume II: Case studies.* Cresskill, NJ: Hampton Press.

———. (1996). *Wired together: The online classroom in K-12. Volume III: Teacher education and professional development.* Cresskill, NJ: Hampton Press.

Burge, E. J. (1994). Learning in computer conferenced contexts: The learners' perspective. *Journal of Distance Education/Revue de l'éducation à distance, 9*(1), 19-43.

Canadian Home and School Federation. (1996). *The electronic classroom: A parents' guide.* Ottawa, ON: Author.

Carroll, J., & Broadhead, R. (1997). *The Canadian Internet Handbook: 1998 Edition.* Scarborough, ON: Prentice-Hall Canada Inc.

Frankel, D., & Sniderman, R. (1996). Michigan meets the Internet challenge. *EDJournal, 10*(5), J-14-J-16.

Garrison, D. R. (1997). Computer conferencing: The post-industrial age of distance education. *Open Learning, 12*(2), 3-11.

Gillis, L. (1996, May). *Innovations in course delivery for a distributed university: The evaluation of the Interactive Learning Connection-University Space Network Pilot Project.* Toronto, ON: Knowledge Connection Corporation.

Hackbarth, S. (Ed.). (1997). Web-based learning [Special issue]. *Educational Technology, 37*(3).

Harasim, L., Hiltz, S. R., Teles, L., & Turoff, M. (1995). *Learning networks: A field guide to teaching and learning online.* Cambridge, MA: MIT Press.

Heide, A., & Stilborne, L. (1996). *The teacher's complete and easy guide to the Internet.* Toronto, ON: Trifolium Books Inc.

Horton, W. (1995). *Illustrating computer documentation: The art of presenting information graphically on paper and online.* New York, NY: Wiley.

Kahn, B. H. (Ed.) (1997). *Web-based instruction.* Englewood Cliffs, NJ: Educational Technology Publications.

Kouki, R., & Wright, D. (1996). Internet distance education applications: Classification and case examples. *ED, Education at a Distance, 10*(7), 9-14.

Mesher, D. (1996). 'Mission: Critical' thinking critically about Web-based instruction. *EDJournal, 10*(10), J-1 to J-3.

Office of Learning Technologies, Human Resources Development Canada. http://olt-bta.hrdc-drhc.gc.ca

Open Learning Technology Corporation Ltd. (1996). *Models for evaluating computer-based learning technologies.* http://www.oltc.edu.au/reports/models/modelsft.htm

Owen, T., Owston, R., & Dickie, C. (1995). *The learning highway: A student's guide to using the Internet.* Toronto, ON: Key Porter.

Pisik, G. B., (1997). Is this course instructionally sound? A guide to evaluating online training courses. *Educational Technology, 37*(4), 50-59.

Ross, J. A., Crane, C. A., & Robertson, D. (1995). Equity of access to computer-mediated distance education. *Journal of Distance Education/Revue de l'éducation à distance, 10*(2), 17-32.

Tagg, A. C., & Dickinson, J. A. Tutor messaging and its effectiveness in encouraging student participation on computer conferences. *Journal of Distance Education/Revue de l'éducation à distance, 10*(2), 33-56.

Wilson, W. (1996). *Connecting: A student's guide to researching on the Information Highway.* Scarborough, ON: Prentice-Hall Canada Inc.

Wulf, K. (1996). Training via the Internet: Where are we? *Training & Development, 50*(5), 50-55.

Yeomans, K. (1996). *Learners on the superhighway? Access to learning via electronic communications.* Leicester, UK: National Institute of Adult Continuing Education.

## Chapter 9
## Compressed Video Learning: How Do We Create Active Learners?

Aubé, S., Chilibeck, M., & Wright, D. (1996). *Cost analysis of video conferencing for distance education at the University of Ottawa.* Working Paper 96-45. Presented at First Annual Meeting & Conference, TeleLearning-NCE. *Constructing a vision for the Knowledge Society.* November 5-7, Sheraton Centre Hotel, Montréal, Québec.

Brooksby, R. (1994). Two-way interactive video. In P. S. Portway & C. Lane (Eds.), *Guide to teleconferencing and distance learning.* (2nd ed., pp. 55-68). Livermore, CA: Applied Business teleCommunications.

Bruce, M. A., & Shade, R. A. (1995, September). Effective teaching and learning strategies using compressed video. *Techtrends, 40*(4), 18-22.

Burge, E. J., & Carter, N. (1997). It's building, but is it designing? Paper for the 18th Conference of the International Council for Distance Education, Penn State University, June 2-6.

Corner, V. (1996). Management training: The age of video. *Impact, 2*(3), 1-4.

Dooley, L. M. (1997). Instructional use of compressed video teleconferencing: A report from faculty users. *EDJournal, II* (2), J-11 to J-13.

Hackley, P., & Webster, J., (n.d.). *Initial recommendations for courses taught through the compressed-video distance telelearning facility.* Unpublished paper, University of Waterloo.

Hakes, B., Couchenour, J., Rezabek, L., & Sachs, S. (1995). *Compressed video for instruction: Operations and applications.* Revised and enlarged. Washington, DC: The Association for Educational Communications and Technology.

Haughey, M., & Jacobson, B. (1996). *Instructional strategies for multi-site videoconferencing.* Presented to the 12th Annual Canadian Association for Distance Education Conference, Université de Moncton, New Brunswick. May 22-25.

———. (1996, April). *Flipping the channels: Multiple-site video-conferencing.* Presented to the Standing Committee on Educational Technology (SCOET)

Conference *Connections 96*, Vancouver, British Columbia.

Kirkpatrick, D. L. (1987). Evaluation. In R. L. Craig (Ed.), *Training and development handbook: A guide to human resource development* (3rd ed., pp. 301-319). New York, NY: McGraw-Hill.

Lakin, J. (1994). The digital video revolution. In P. S. Portway, & C. Lane (Eds.), *Guide to teleconferencing and distance learning.* (2nd ed., pp. 49-54). Livermore, CA: Applied Business teleCommunications.

Lawrence, B. H. (1995). Teaching and learning via videoconference: The benefits of cooperative learning. *Journal of Educational Technology Systems, 24*(2), 145-149.

MacKinnon, A., Walshe, B., Cummings, M., & Velonis, U. (1995). An inventory of pedagogical considerations for interactive television. *Journal of Distance Education/Revue de l'éducation à distance, 10*(1), 75-94.

McCaskill, B. J. (1996). *The perceived distance education telemedia needs of faculty.* Presented to the 12th Annual Canadian Association for Distance Education Conference, Université de Moncton, New Brunswick. May 22-25.

Moore, M. G., & Koble, M. A. (Eds.). (1995). *Video-based telecommunications in distance education.* Number 4 in the series Readings in Distance Education. University Park, PA: The Pennsylvania State University, American Center for the Study of Distance Education.

Niemi, J. A., & Owens, K. (1996). Evaluation research for the development of effective practice in the video-teleconferencing distance education human resource development classroom. In E. F. Holton III (Ed.), *1996 Conference Proceedings.* Austin, TX: Academy of Human Resource Development.

Office of Instructional Development. (1995). *Interactive video network: Faculty guide and technical training manual.* College Park, MD: University of Maryland University College.

Open Learning Technology Corporation Ltd. (1996). *Models for evaluating interactive video and videoconferencing.* http://www.oltc.edu.au/reports/models/modelsft.htm

Portway, P. S. (1994). Desktop. In P. S. Portway & C. Lane (Eds.), *Guide to teleconferencing and distance learning.* (2nd ed., pp. 69-87). Livermore, CA: Applied Business teleCommunications.

Reed, J., & Woodruff, M. (1995). Using compressed video for distance learning. *The Distance Educator, 1*(3), 2, 6-10.

Roberts, J. M., & Sowa, W. (1995, June). Knowledge exchange and distance education: Ontario Learning and Technology Exchange Consortium. In D. Sewart (Ed.), *One world, many voices: Quality in open and distance learning* (pp. 149-152, Vol. 1). Selected papers from the 17th World Conference of the International Council for Distance Education, Birmingham, United Kingdom.

Van der Perre, G., Van den Branden, J., Van Heddegem, J., & Ketels, M. (1995). EuroPACE 2000: Professional and academic channel for Europe 2000. In D. Sewart (Ed.), *One world, many voices: Quality in open and distance learning* (pp. 179-181, Vol. 1). Selected papers from the 17th World Conference of the International Council for Distance Education, Birmingham, United Kingdom.

Webster, J., & Hackley, P. (in press). Teaching effectiveness in distance telelearning. *Academy of Management Journal.*

## Chapter 10
### What Does It Look Like When We Bring It All Together?

We recommend that you think about what conditions you need to learn effectively—it's often a good guide.

# Glossary

ACTION RESEARCH A systematic and context-adaptive method of collecting and analyzing data to develop real-world, practical knowledge that could later lead to change in that context.

AFFECTIVE DOMAIN (see also COGNITIVE DOMAIN and PSYCHOMOTOR DOMAIN) One of three domains that form a hierarchy or taxonomy of educational objectives. This domain refers to the development of values, emotions and attitudes, and to the outlooks and behaviors that characterize each level of development.

ANALOG An electronic, non-digital signal that is in a continuous format, as opposed to a digital signal, which is discrete.

ASPECT RATIO The ratio of height to width in a visual image presented on paper or on a video or computer screen.

ASSOCIATION OF CANADIAN COMMUNITY COLLEGES (ACCC) A national organization of college-level educational institutions from provinces and territories across Canada.

ASYNCHRONOUS Communication that occurs when learners and instructors are not linked at the same time. The originators of messages create and send the messages at a time convenient to them; the messages are stored until the recipients find it convenient to retrieve them. Letters, voice-mail messages and e-mail are all examples of asynchronous communication.

AUDIOCONFERENCING A technical arrangement in which three or more telephones or speakerphones are connected by a central device called a bridge so that people in three or more places can talk to one another.

AUDIOGRAPHIC CONFERENCING A technical arrangement in which audioconferencing (telephones or speakerphones and a bridge) is supplemented by graphic devices that send text or still pictures.

AUDIOGRAPHIC LEARNING (AGL) Learning that occurs when learners and instructors use telephone and graphics technologies (audiographic conferencing) to facilitate dialogue, exchange messages and access experts as part of a learning process.

AUDIOGRAPHICS TECHNOLOGIES (see also GROUPWARE) Devices that work on analog or digital telephone lines and facilitate the real-time exchange of text and still, color graphics information. Historically, such devices have been separate pieces of equipment.

AUDIO LEARNING (AL) Learning that occurs when learners and instructors use audioconferencing technology to engage in discussions, exchange messages and access experts as part of a formal or informal learning endeavor. All such interactions occur in real-time; the learners and instructors are present at different sites at the same time and must coordinate their schedules.

BACK-UP Create a duplicate copy.

BRIDGE A telecommunications device that links three or more telephone, computer or video terminals so that all participants can communicate.

BROWSER (see also SEARCH ENGINE) A software program that enables users to access and navigate the Internet and the WWW to find the content they want.

BULLETIN BOARD SYSTEM (BBS) A small computer system that allows members to exchange messages, maintain discussion groups and download software.

CAMERA SCAN AREA The area framed by the television camera. Since detail at the edge of the scanning area is sometimes lost, it is advisable to design information to fit within the safe area (the area within the border that is 10 percent smaller than the scanning area).

CHAT LINES Also called chat groups, chat lines are created using software programs that allow several users to interact through text-based conversations in real-time.

CLIENT Client in computer-network terminology can have two meanings. Sometimes it is synonymous with user. Other times it denotes a relationship between two computers, in which one is a host that serves a client machine. In the latter case, the client computer becomes a guest on the host computer in order to use the host computer's resources.

CODEC (ENCODER AND DECODER) An electronic device that converts analog signals to digital ones, usually incorporating a compression protocol. The codec encodes, or compresses, the signal at the transmitting end and decodes, or decompresses it, at the receiving end.

COGNITIVE DOMAIN (see also AFFECTIVE DOMAIN and PSYCHOMOTOR DOMAIN) The second of three domains that form a hierarchy or taxonomy of educational objectives, this domain is the most widely used. It refers to knowledge outcomes and the thinking skills that characterize each category of outcome. The higher the level of required outcome, the more sophisticated the thinking skills. Each category includes behaviors needed in prior categories.

COLLABORATIVE LEARNING A proactive approach to learning in which the learner interacts with peers to hear new information, compare different and sometimes conflicting points of view and life experiences, and work cooperatively on instructor-directed or self-directed learning projects.

COMPACT DISC-READ ONLY MEMORY (CD-ROM) A disc that can store a large amount of text, audio, video and graphics information. Your computer needs a special device so these materials can be displayed on your screen, and it must meet certain minimal technical specifications for the device to work.

COMPRESSED VIDEO LEARNING (CVL) Learning that occurs when instructors and learners use microphones, cameras and other videoconferencing equipment to exchange verbal and moving color images to engage in discussions, exchange messages and talk to experts as part of a formal or informal learning process. All such interactions occur in real-time; that is, the learners and instructors are present at different sites at the same time and they must coordinate their schedules to do this.

COMPUSERVE One of many commercial Internet Service Providers.

COMPUTER CONFERENCING A central computer is used to receive, hold and distribute messages among participants' computers.

COMPUTER VIRUS A "rogue" computer program designed to replicate itself in the memory or storage devices of other computers.

(THE) CONFERENCE BOARD OF CANADA The Conference Board of Canada is an independent, not-for-profit research organization with affiliates in the United States and Europe. Its mission is to help its members anticipate and respond to the increasingly changing global economy.

CONSTRUCTIVIST LEARNING (CONSTRUCTION) A process of creating meaning in which learners are actively engaged in analyzing their own perspectives, organizing information and developing their own interpretations. Learners interact with each other and with actual, complex, real-world environments to construct a personal knowledge framework.

DAISY CHAIN The sequential linking of microphones in the AL or AGL context where the first is connected to the second, which is connected to the third, and so on, as opposed to all the microphones being linked to one central source.

DESKTOP SOLUTIONS Term used to describe information and communications technologies that can operate on the home or office "desktop" computer.

DIGITAL Information contained in the form of zeros (0) and ones (1) for transmission. Digital information formats may include video, audio, graphics and text.

DISTANCE EDUCATION (see also OPEN LEARNING) Educational opportunities that are made available to students who are separated by place and/or time from the institution offering the learning opportunities. Communication between learners and instructors and/or among learners occurs through technology such as print, computers, television or telephone. Some face-to-face contact may also occur.

DOCUMENT SCANNER Equipment that resembles a photocopier in that pictures or pieces of paper are put on a clear piece of glass or plastic and scanned by a light source. Photocopiers are designed to reproduce the material on a piece of paper; document scanners convert the material into a digital signal so that it can be entered into a computer and reproduced on a computer screen.

DOWNLOAD (see also UPLOAD) The process of copying a file from a remote computer to one's own computer. The process uses a protocol (usually File Transfer Protocol) to guarantee that the transfer is error-free and arrives in exactly the same format as it is stored on the remote computer.

E-MAIL (ELECTRONIC MAIL) The exchange of textual and nontextual messages from one computer to another using software packages designed to store and forward messages received or sent.

EMOTICONS Keyboard characters used to indicate humor, emphasis and other emotions and reactions that we usually obtain from voice or gestures.

ERGONOMICS The study of how humans interact physically with machines and environments.

GROUP AUDIO TERMINAL A telephone that can be used by an individual or a group of learners at home, in the workplace or in a seminar or classroom environment. Also known as a speakerphone.

GROUPWARE Computer software that creates audio and audiographic conferencing environments through a desktop computer, rather than through telephones, speakerphones or specialized graphics equipment.

HOLISTIC APPROACH An approach that acknowledges the interconnectedness of reality and the concept of wholeness, rather than fragmentation. In education, holistic methods recognize that we are physical, psychological, affiliative, spiritual and economic beings.

HYPERLINKS Words that are specially tagged by HTML in a WWW document to create links to other WWW resources.

HYPERTEXT MARKUP LANGUAGE (HTML) The protocol used to create documents for publication and distribution on the World Wide Web. HTML consists of tags added to text documents that format and create links to other WWW resources.

ICONS Drawings or symbols that appear on the screen and that allow you to perform various functions on the computer.

INFORMATION HIGHWAY The term used to describe once-separate telephone and television communications networks and computing systems that are converging into a single global network of networks.

INFORMATION LITERACY The ability to use print and multimedia indexing tools and resources to access relevant information efficiently in formal and informal settings such as the library or the home.

INTERNET A worldwide collection of computer networks. The networks use a common communications protocol and addressing scheme to share resources with one another. Owned by no one, it is maintained collectively by the individual national, regional, commercial and institutional networks that make up the Internet. It is a learning, information and business tool.

INTERNET SERVICE PROVIDER (ISP) A company or institution that provides Internet connection to any user willing to pay the stated fee. An ISP will provide you with an e-mail address and connectivity software, as well as access to the Internet through a bank of modems and telephone numbers you call.

INTRANET (see also LAN AND WAN) A network of servers and computers or workstations within a single company or organization that uses Internet protocols and programs.

LISTSERV The software that manages electronic discussion groups or computer conference distribution lists. These discussion groups are often called lists. Once a person's electronic address is on a list, he or she can send or receive a message. LISTSERV sends a message from one person directly to everyone else on the list.

LOCAL AREA NETWORK (LAN) (see also INTRANET and WAN) A network (usually high-speed) that connects computers and other communications devices inside a single building or throughout a group of buildings that are close to one another such as a campus.

LOG ON Computer jargon for accessing your e-mail or other services on your computer.

LURKER A person who reads or "listens to" a chat line or course discussion without actively participating in the discussion. Lurking for a short time is encouraged for newcomers to a group, but is discouraged in learning environments on the practical grounds that learning does not occur effectively without participation, and on the ethical grounds that "all take and no give" is not fair.

META-LEARNING STRATEGIES Self-reflective and self-managing strategies that enable us to assess the effectiveness of how we learn, as distinct from assessing whether we have learned what we intended to learn.

MODEL A generalized and structured way of seeing events and processes that helps us clarify our values and outlooks, see linkages between concepts and events, predict likely results, figure out alternative solutions to problems and compare what we can do with what we might do.

MODEM A piece of equipment that typically converts the digital signals internal to a computer into analog signals that can be transported over ordinary telephone lines. A modem can be inside the computer and so invisible to the user, or it can be a visible piece of equipment outside of the computer. Modems are often defined by the highest speed at which they can transmit and receive data. Common speed formats, measured in kilobits per second (Kbps), are 14.4 and 28.8.

MULTI-USER DOMAIN (MUD) A text-based virtual-reality program in which users interact in real-time as they move between different rooms in an environment.

MULTI-USER OBJECT ORIENTED (MOO) A newer version of the MUD, it allows users to create characters, objects and rooms for text-based virtual-reality sites.

NETWORKED LEARNING (NL) Learning that happens when learners and instructors use computers to exchange messages, engage in dialogue and access resources as part of a learning endeavor. Interaction can occur in real-time, when learners and instructors are all present at the same time, or in delayed-time, when they are not linked at the same time.

OFF-LINE Work that is done when the user is not connected to the Internet or an Intranet. The product of this work is often shared with others at a later time.

ON-LINE Work that is done when the user is connected to the Internet or an Intranet.

OPEN LEARNING An instructional system that places many aspects of the learning process under the direct control of the learner so that she or he can choose when and how to study.

PARADIGM A world view. The way in which an individual or society organizes and values its actions. A paradigm is based on beliefs and expectations.

PEDAGOGY The science, art and practice of teaching and learning. From the Greek, "to lead a child." Literally, it refers to the teaching of children; andragogy should be used to refer to helping adults learn. Pedagogy is often used loosely to refer to teaching both adults and children.

PLAIN OLD TELEPHONE SERVICE (POTS) The basic (analog) telephone set, linked by copper wires.

PROTOCOL An agreed-upon set of rules that govern the format, timing and error control of transmissions on a network so that networks can communicate with one another.

PSYCHOMOTOR DOMAIN (see also AFFECTIVE DOMAIN and COGNITIVE DOMAIN) The third of three domains that form a hierarchy or taxonomy of educational objectives. This domain refers to operational skills and the physical movements and controls that characterize each skill category. Objectives in this domain usually include related thinking (Cognitive Domain) and feeling (Affective Domain) aspects.

SCREEN-WRAP Software that ensures that text is displayed on a computer screen within the horizontal edges of the monitor. You may have to move down the screen to read a long message, but you do not have to continue to move sideways.

SEARCH ENGINE (see also BROWSER) A computer program that allows users to enter key words and be linked to materials on the Internet, an Intranet or a single computer system.

SERVER A software program that runs on a "central" computer connected to the Internet. It manages the linkages among remote computers and permits activities such as e-mail, BBS, LISTSERV, delayed or simultaneous discussions and resource searching.

STENTOR More properly called The Stentor Alliance, Stentor is a consortium of Canada's full-service telecommunications companies and their holding companies.

SYNCHRONOUS Taking place at the same time (in real-time). For example, talking with someone on the telephone could be described as "synchronous communication."

TAXONOMY An ordered classification system based on a hierarchy of levels that contains general and specific categories of learning objectives (or, in other disciplines, of plants and animals).

TRANSFER CONTROL PROTOCOL/INTERNET PROTOCOL (TCP/IP) The software protocol used to link computers on the Internet.

TWISTED COPPER PAIR A telephone line. Copper has been the standard for telephone lines since before the turn of the century, as it is a better conductor of electricity than other metals. A telephone line is comprised of two wires: a grounded wire that is twisted around another wire that carries the signal.

UPLOAD (see also DOWNLOAD) To send a file from one computer to a remote computer, which other users then access to retrieve the file.

VIDEOCONFERENCE A technical arrangement in which television monitors, cameras and microphones are linked together by a bridge so that people in three or more sites can see, hear and speak to one another.

VIDEO LEARNING See COMPRESSED VIDEO LEARNING.

VIRTUAL REALITY An environment that simulates on a computer screen a real-life context.

VIRUS A computer program designed to replicate itself in the memory or storage devices of other computers; it often has destructive or practical-joke components that can damage materials stored on the infected computer.

WHITEBOARD A white display device that is marked with a dry-erase marker. In the AGL context, a whiteboard is typically a three-by-four-foot electronic display device that can be activated by touch or by an electronic marker. It can be linked by telephone to other such devices so that whatever is written at one site is seen at all other sites.

WIDE AREA NETWORK (WAN) (see also LAN and INTRANET) A network of computers and other communications devices that are located over a large geographic area such as a city, province or state.

WORLD WIDE WEB (WWW) A communication protocol of the Internet that deals with text, audio, video and any other type of format.

# Contact Names for the Success Stories

## Chapter 7

**Enriching Senior High School Curriculum**
WILBERT BOONE
Department of Education
Government of Newfoundland & Labrador
St. John's, NF

**Serving Mature Learners**
DONNA MESE
Early Childhood Education Programme
Cambrian College of Applied Arts and Technology
Barrydowne Road
Sudbury, ON

**Cost-Effective Learning in Developing Countries**
MICHAEL ANYADIKE-DANES
Professor of Economics
University of the West Indies (UWI)
Barbados Campus
Barbados, WI

**Competency-based Workplace Training**
ZEKE OSBORN
Network Director
United States Postal Service

**Reducing Technical Costs through Partnership**
MAXIM JEAN-LOUIS
Executive Director
Contact North/Contact Nord
North-east Regional Coordinating Centre
634 Notre Dame Avenue
Sudbury, ON P3C 5L2
Tel: (705) 671-2713
Fax: (705) 671-9605
maxim@mail.cnorth.edu.on.ca
WWW: cnorth.edu.on.ca

## Chapter 8

**Expanding Options in High Schools**
LARRY DANIELSON
Garden Valley Collegiate
Winkler, MB R6W 4C8
ldaniels@MBnet.mb.ca

**Developing a Virtual University**
JEFF MCLAUGHLIN
Instruction and Learning Support Group
University College of the Cariboo
900 McGill Road, Box 3010
Kamloops, BC V2C 5N3
jmclaughlin@cariboo.bc.ca

STEPHEN DOWNES
Distance Education & New Instructional Media Design Specialist
Assiniboine Community College
1430 Victoria Avenue East
Brandon, MB R7A 2A9
downes@adminnet.assiniboinec.mb.ca

**Graduate Business Degrees through Networked Learning**
STEPHEN MURGATROYD, Ph. D.
Executive Director
University Development
Athabasca University
P.O. Box 10,000
Athabasca, AB T9S 1A1
stephenm@cs.athabascau.ca

**Providing Internet-based Resources from the Workplace**
MARC SIEGEL
Director
Quest Program
NASA Ames Research Center
Mailstop T-28H
Moffet Field, CA 94035
msiegel@nsipo.nasa.gov

## Chapter 9

**Changing the Mind Set: A Pilot Project**
STEPHEN OLIVER
Central Huron Secondary School
Huron County Board of Education
165 Princess Street East
Clinton, ON N0M 1L0
Tel: (519) 482-3471
Fax: (519) 482-9718
soliver@hookup.net

**Remediation Training in the Financial Sector**
TRACY HUTCHEON
Employee Development Centre
Canadian Imperial Bank of Commerce (CIBC)
750 Lawrence Avenue West, E2
Toronto, ON M6A 1B8
Tel: (416) 784-2333
Fax: (416) 784-8970

**Minimizing Costs in a Consortium for Graduate Education**
JEF VAN DEN BRANDEN
Educational Director
EuroPACE 2000
Celestijnenlaan 200A
3001 Heverlee, Belgium
Tel: + 32-16-32 75 73
Fax: +32-16-21 79 95
jef.vandenbranden@europace.be

**Knowledge Transfer in Science and Engineering**
MICHAEL E. CHARLES, Ph.D., P.Eng.
Dean
Faculty of Applied Science and Engineering
University of Toronto
35 St. George Street, Room 170
Toronto, ON M5S 1A4
Tel: (416) 978-3131
Fax: (416) 978-4859
charles@ecf.utoronto.ca